MINDING
AMERICA'S
BUSINESS

MINDING AMERICA'S BUSINESS

**The Decline and Rise
of the American Economy**

**IRA C. MAGAZINER
ROBERT B. REICH**

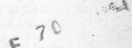

**Vintage Books
A Division of Random House
New York**

First Vintage Books Edition, February 1983
Copyright © 1982 by Law & Business, Inc.
All rights reserved under International and
Pan-American Copyright Conventions. Published in
the United States by Random House, Inc., New York,
and simultaneously in Canada by Random House of
Canada Limited, Toronto. Originally published by
Harcourt Brace Jovanovich, Inc. in 1982.

Library of Congress Cataloging in Publication Data
Magaziner, Ira C.
Minding America's business.
Includes index.
1. Industry and state—United States.
2. Industrial management—United States.
3. United States—Economic conditions—1971-
4. United States—Industries.
I. Reich, Robert B. II. Title.
HD3616.U47M286 1983   338.0973   82-49087
ISBN 0-394-71538-1 (pbk.)

Manufactured in the United States of America

338
M189

The authors are indebted to several people who contributed substantially to the preparation of this book; in particular, Bertrand Dechery, Jacques Feuillan, Suzanne M. McTigue, and Edward Morrison.

The authors also wish to thank Denise Petrillo, Susan Cowell, Robert Leibenluft, Mark Nordenson, Charles Benda, Mary Howard, Judith Gelman, Michel Bacchetta, Richard Feinberg, Debra Morris, Jane Houlton, and Chantelle Bizet for their assistance.

Contents

Table Of Exhibits

x

Introduction

Rampant inflation and high unemployment are symptoms of economic stagnation. Our standard of living is no longer rising. In 1980, our median family income declined 5.5 percent in real terms. In contrast with the 25 years following the Second World War, when the real goods and services we could purchase for every hour we worked steadily increased, the past decade has witnessed a decline in our productive growth.

To be sure, all other industrialized countries faced economic problems during the 1970s. But many were more successful than we in improving the living standards of their citizens. Some have now surpassed the United States in average living standard.

Our initial response to the economic crisis of the 1970s was to impose measures that had served us well in the preceding quarter century—aggregate fiscal and monetary policies. Broadly, these policies aim to moderate the ebbs and flows of the business cycle to prevent runaway inflation and massive unemployment.

But these policies have not worked. Inflation and unemployment both remain high and our living standards continue to stagnate. Why have these policies failed? What has changed in our economy?

The most obvious culprit has been the cost of energy. Sudden and significant rises in oil prices in 1974 and again in 1979 seriously affected our economy. And yet, rising energy prices constituted less than 15 percent of our total inflation during the 1970s. More importantly, other industrialized countries that were more dependent on foreign oil managed to confront the energy crisis more successfully than we, maintaining better productivity growth and more rapidly rising living standards.

A less obvious, but perhaps more important factor has been our increasing integration into the world economy and our failure to maintain international competitiveness.

The value of imports and exports together now equal almost 40 percent of the total value of all goods produced in the U.S. In 1969, they accounted for only 16 percent. During the past decade in the United States, nearly 2 million manufacturing jobs have been lost, a situation that is directly due to increased imports. Only costly protectionist measures, which have raised prices for American consumers, have prevented even further losses. Over the same period, the share of the world market claimed by U.S. manufactured goods has declined by 23 percent. Over 20 percent of our domestically sold autos are now made abroad, compared to 8 percent in 1970; 14 percent of our steel, compared to 9 percent in 1970; over 50 percent of our consumer electronics products, compared to 10 percent in 1970. The list goes on, growing longer year by year: hand calculators, cameras, metal-forming machine tools, textile machinery, tires, watches, footwear, electrical switching equipment, and motorcycles—a sizable percentage of all these manufactured goods are made abroad.

In too many industries, U.S. companies have not remained competitive with foreign rivals. In certain cases, this lack of competitiveness was inevitable; some countries can exploit indigenous raw materials that are inherently superior and more accessible than ours, others can depend on an abundance of low-wage labor. In most cases, however, our lack of competitiveness has stemmed from our inability to improve productivity and deliver higher-quality products for a lower price than competitors in other high-wage industrialized economies. This decline of relative productivity is the major *reversible* cause of our present economic woes.

Today there is an emerging consensus on this diagnosis, but sharp disagreement remains about what government and industry in the United States should do to remedy the problem.

Some argue for preserving economic relationships as they were. This means controlling price increases, erecting further tariffs and quotas against foreign imports, preventing factory closings and relocations, limiting direct investment abroad, and investing government funds into bankrupt companies. While a few of these measures might be of limited use as part of an overall industrial development program, in the aggregate they are counterproductive. Markets, unlike Brigadoon, cannot be frozen in time, however much we may yearn for years gone by. Indeed, restrictions such as these might have the perverse effect of stifling economic growth while imposing substantial costs on the economy.

Other people blame our declining competitiveness on government interference in the economy. They call for greater private capital investment, to be achieved by lowering taxes for individual savers and companies and at the same time reducing the rate of growth of public expenditures for social security, health, and welfare programs. Further, they seek curtailment of government regulations pertaining to environmental protection, occupational safety and health, and consumer protection—measures, they allege, that have diverted large amounts of resources to nonproductive uses.

At the very least, such adjustments in government intervention would have inequitable effects. Because the ability to save is greater for the rich than for the poor and middle classes, a tax cut for savers and investors would be likely to result in a regressive shift of the tax burden. Moreover, a decline in spending on social services might reduce the standard of living for a substantial number of our citizens who, because of age, ill health, or lack of job training, must rely to a significant extent on public assistance. Lower- and middle-class citizens are also more dependent on clean air, safe working conditions, and consumer protection. Our wealthier citizens can compensate by living in less polluted neighborhoods, drinking bottled water, vacationing in scenic environments, opting for safer jobs, and purchasing higher-quality products.

Proponents of these so-called "supply side" solutions argue that the sacrifices and inequities are short-term conditions that are necessary to stimulate overall economic growth, which will improve everyone's living standards in the long term. They also claim that many government services are now so inefficient that some cuts could be made without dire consequence.

Surely government can be more efficient. And perhaps some short-term sacrifice is warranted for the sake of long-term gains. But the fact is that increased competitiveness will *not* result from reduced government intervention in the economy. Our failure of competitive strategy, not government interference, has been responsible for our decline. For example, Japanese steel companies are far more productive than their American counterparts, yet they have spent far greater sums on pollution control, provided better working conditions, and paid higher taxes than our steel companies. Meanwhile, over the past 20 years, American steel companies have spent more than $60 billion (1978 dollars) in capital investment. If our steel companies had had more liberal tax deductions or fewer environmental mandates, would they have invested more heavily? If they had increased their investments by 10 or 20 percent, would their competitiveness have improved?

We doubt it. Their declining competitiveness has been due to poor investment strategies: an unwillingness to use new technologies or to undertake more fundamental investments, a lack of aggressiveness in managing their overheads, and a failure to push for exports.

In any event, the relationship between aggregate capital investment and increasing productivity is unclear. Between 1967 and 1973, our rate of productivity growth declined, although the rate of growth of capital formation was stronger than it has been at any time in the postwar period. In the last five years, a larger share of our national product has been devoted to business investment than at any other time since the Second World War. Our annual investment in manufacturing as a percentage of manufacturing output has increased steadily over the decade. Highly touted statistics about our low level of investment compared to that of other countries are misleading because they fail to take account of differences among economies. Our economy has a large service sector and a high proportion of knowledge-intensive industries that are not dependent primarily on capital investment. Moreover, our manufacturing companies lease a significant percentage of their equipment and invest a significant proportion of their total investments abroad; such expenditures are not counted in comparative investment statistics.

By contrast to economic policies that focused almost exclusively on the management of aggregate demand, supply-siders are now asking how investment can increase our standard of living. The question is appropriate. It is their answer that is wrong.

In this book, we offer an alternative view of how to increase national wealth. We focus on increasing the *competitive* productivity of our industry. We suggest that U.S. companies and the government develop a coherent and coordinated industrial policy whose aim is to raise the real income of our citizens by improving the pattern of our investments rather than by focusing only on aggregate investment levels. Our country's real income can rise only if (1) its labor and capital increasingly flow toward businesses that add greater value per employee and (2) we maintain a position in these businesses that is superior to that of our international competitors. Our companies must undertake appropriate strategies in line with these goals; our government must have explicit policies to promote this industrial restructuring and competitive productivity.

The guiding discipline for both business strategy and government industrial policy derives from the international competitive market-place. Success depends on gaining and sustaining a competitive advantage in specific business segments. The means to accomplish this vary from business to business, depending upon its cost structure, growth rate, and the evolution of technology and markets. Generalized solutions to the problem of our declining competitiveness are inappropriate.

Once dominant in most of the world's businesses, many U.S. companies have not kept pace in recent years with changes in the international competitive environment. Our systems for evaluating investment decisions have not sufficiently considered the competitive evolution of businesses. Our accounting systems have given managers incorrect signals about investments. Our systems for measuring total product costs have misallocated manufacturing and distribution overheads and have failed to provide accurate information on the total costs of improvements in process and quality control. Our pricing policies have allowed foreign competitors to gain strong footholds in U.S. markets. We have allowed foreign competitors to gain advantages in other national markets from which they can better penetrate the U.S. market. In managing our international businesses, we have overemphasized the importance of cheap labor in production at the expense of productivity improvements and long-term market penetration. We have failed to give workers a stake in productivity improvements. Finally, we have paid too much attention to rearranging our industrial assets and too little attention to building our industrial base.

The U.S. government has also failed to help our companies gain competitive productivity in world markets. Hundreds of government programs directly or indirectly affect both resource-allocation decisions across industries and competitive positions among firms. But no government program has been viewed as part of a coherent industrial policy.

The federal government affects the pattern of industrial investment through a wide variety of tariffs, quotas, orderly marketing agreements, special tax laws and rulings, loan guarantees, targeted subsidies, patents, and export promotion and financing programs. Usually developed *ad hoc*, often in response to political pressures, these programs have affected industrial development unevenly. In many cases, they have retarded the flow of capital and labor from more productive uses. In those cases where the programs have contributed significantly to advancing the competitive position of U.S. producers, this effect has often been accidental.

By contrast, Japan and many European countries have adopted explicit policies for promoting selected businesses. In some instances, these policies have resulted in misallocations of resources, but our trading partners are becoming more sophisticated about how they selectively assist industrial development. Increasingly, their industrial policies enhance the creation of wealth by improving the international competitiveness of a number of growing businesses and by easing the transition of declining businesses.

The debate over industrial policy in this country has been more ideological than pragmatic, framed in terms of the ideal relationship between governments and markets rather than in terms of the hard realities of international competition. Surely the market decisions of countless consumers and investors are generally preferable to government direction for determining which goods and services should be produced in the economy and how investment should be allocated. These transactions provide a rich source of information about the size and competitive potential of various businesses, and they spread the results of mistakes and poor decisions among all actors in the market instead of focusing them in one place.

But the practical choice is not between government intervention and nonintervention. To a significant degree, the governments of all industrialized countries, regardless of political ideology and rhetoric, inevitably affect the pattern of investment in their economies through procurement, tariffs and quotas, guarantees, and various selective tax breaks and subsidies. In the U.S., these measures are usually formulated by agencies and Congressional subcommittees in response to special pleadings from well-established and politically powerful industries. Other nations understand that the only real alternative to developing a rational industrial policy that seeks to improve the competitive performance of their economy in world markets is for the government to cede the formation of policy to the politically strongest or most active elements of industry.

Industrial policies are necessary to ease society's adjustment to structural changes in a growing economy. New products are discovered and others become outmoded; productivity improvements reduce employment in some factories and increase output and employment in others; some industries migrate to low-wage regions or to developing countries, while technological breakthroughs create new industries in high-wage countries; some skills become obsolete and new ones are needed. Harsh social dislocations can result when workers lose their jobs and communities lose their industrial base. The speed and incidence of new industrial developments may not automatically remedy these declines. Unless government affirmatively acts to ease the adjustment, affected groups may seek to resist economic change through political means.

An effective industrial policy ensures that no group is driven to oppose economic change because it fears being forced to bear an unfair share of the burden of that change. Through programs of retraining, relocation, and targeted public investment, hardships caused by industrial restructuring can be remedied in ways that do not hinder economic progress. Countries that have anticipated and planned for changes in industrial structure have avoided the industrial costs associated with massive layoffs and plant shutdowns, such as paying large subsidies to dying companies.

Government industrial policies are also appropriate when the public return on investment is likely to exceed the private return. For example, governments have long subsidized the creation of industrial infrastructures (transport, education, and communication) necessary for economic development. Similarly, the benefits to the public from discoveries in basic research often outweigh the benefits realized by an individual firm. Indeed, as the pace and scale of technological development have accelerated in recent years, many private companies cannot sustain on their own the costs of basic research and development. Lastly, the success or failure of key industries upon which many other industries are dependent may have serious consequences for the general health of the economy. Thus, the specific return-on-investment calculations of industry managers may be different from a public calculation that considers these vital linkages.

The course currently being pursued in U.S. economic policy will require great sacrifices from those in our society who can least afford them and will jeopardize many of the values we as a nation have come to hold dear. These sacrifices are justified as being necessary to regain economic prosperity. But these policies will not bring prosperity. Prosperity can be achieved only by means of an industrial policy carefully geared to international competition.

This book is a guide to such an industrial policy for business and government. It raises many questions—and answers only a few of them—in an attempt to provide a framework within which future questions and answers can be debated. Our intention has been to introduce the reader to issues that will be at the center of economic discussions over the next decade, and to challenges that will be faced by both business managers and government policymakers.

I

THE PROBLEM

1

The American Standard of Living

The primary goal of a nation's economic policy should be to improve the standard of living of its citizens. The concept of "standard of living" is, of course, vague and subjective. Basically, it is comprised of at least three elements: (1) the real goods and services that can be purchased by a nation's citizens; (2) the availability of certain goods that cannot be purchased directly but that contribute to most people's sense of well-being—such as clean air and water, security from crime and accident, financial security, and public health; and (3) the extent to which these goods and services—both private and public—are shared among citizens. Economic goals such as growth, higher productivity, lower inflation, and a strong currency are means of achieving a higher standard of living, not ends in themselves. A reduction in a nation's standard of living in order to achieve these economic goals is justifiable, therefore, only to the extent that it is necessary for achieving an even higher standard of living in the future.

The United States emerged from the Second World War as the world's richest nation. While most of the developed world was cleaning the rubble from its devastated cities and bombed-out factories, the United States turned its economy from war production to the creation of a standard of living unprecedented in history. With unlimited confidence, it undertook to create a society of consumer affluence. Its unrivaled prosperity during the 1950s and 1960s rested in part on the abundance of rich farmland, mineral wealth, and timber. But its wealth was also based on the efficiency of its economic organization and its ability to pioneer new inventions and work productively.

Beginning in the early 1960s, many Americans came to realize that a significant minority of citizens was excluded from the fruits of prosperity. Subsequently, in the late 1960s, there developed a growing concern about the impoverishment of many public goods—the environment, mass transit, and public spaces in its cities, as well as a disregard for the health and safety of workers and consumers—due to the country's emphasis on increasing private consumption.

In the 1970s, the United States witnessed a precipitous decline in its capacity to create new private wealth. After 20 years of growing economic prosperity, it experienced a decade of stagnation. Between 1970 and 1979, the real median family income of Americans increased by only 6.7 percent. In 1980 it actually decreased by 5.5 percent. This compared to an increase of 33.9 percent between 1960 and 1970 and an increase of 37.6 percent between 1950 and 1960.[1] The total growth of the U.S. national income per employed person was substantially lower than that of most other industrialized countries over the last 20

EXHIBIT 1
Annual Growth in Real Gross National Product
Per Employed Person

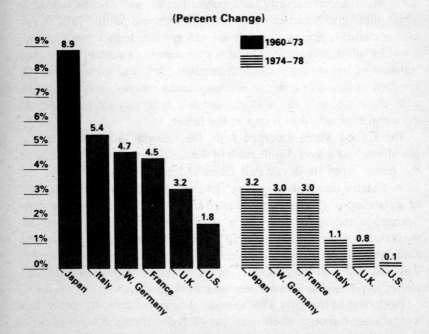

(Percent Change)

Source: OECD Economic Outlook, 1979, Economic Report of the President, January 1979, reported in *European Industrial Policy Past, Present and Future* by Lawrence Franko. Brussels: the Conference Board in Europe, 1980.

years (Exhibit 1). By 1979, many industrialized countries had achieved higher absolute income levels than the United States (Exhibit 2).[2]

EXHIBIT 2
Gross Domestic Product Per Capita as Percent of
U.S. Gross Domestic Product Per Capita

	1960	1963	1970	1975	1979
Switzerland	57	66	70	118	139
Denmark	46	53	67	104	119
Sweden	67	75	86	118	115
Germany	46	53	64	95	116
Iceland	49	56	51	82	103
Norway	45	50	60	99	106
Belgium	44	47	55	90	107
Luxemborg	59	57	66	89	109
Netherlands	47	55	58	90	101
France	47	55	58	90	100
Canada	79	72	81	101	91
Japan	16	22	41	63	82
Finland	40	45	48	82	82
U.K.	48	50	46	58	67

Source: OECD national accounts. For 1979 figures see September 1980, "Main Economic Indicators," p. 169 for GNP, p. 170 for population.

The United States' recent decline relative to other countries cannot be summarized in national income statistics alone. Such data give only an average quantitative measure of the goods and services provided to a nation's people. They do not reflect such important but less quantifiable aspects of life as personal safety, clean and safe environment, availability of leisure time, or the security of guaranteed health care. Nor do they indicate anything about the distribution of wealth. But in these respects as well, the United States compares unfavorably with many other advanced industrial countries.

Quality of life defies easy measurement. In many cases, it relates to personal or societal preference. Nevertheless, the United States' relative decline manifests itself in a variety of ways. For example, workers in the U.S. stand a far greater chance of becoming unemployed (Exhibit 3) without adequate insurance than do workers in other in-

EXHIBIT 3
Average Unemployment Rates for Selected Countries

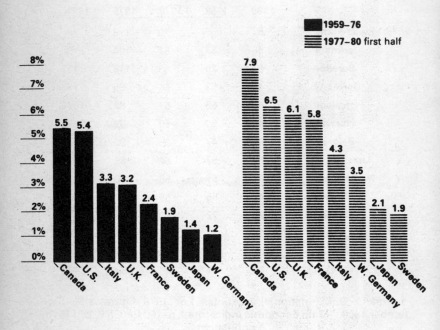

Sources: Social Indicators 1976: U.S. Department of Commerce, Office of Federal Statistical Policy and Standards, Bureau of the Census: December 1977, Washington, D.C., chart 362, p. 393; and "Supplement to Bulletin 1979, International Comparisons of Unemployment;" U.S. Department of Labor, Bureau of Labor Statistics: unpublished, April 1980.

dustrial countries (Exhibit 4). In addition, most workers in the U.S. can be dismissed from their jobs without notice or reason; by contrast, other advanced industrial countries prohibit sudden or arbitrary dismissals. Public expenditures for social welfare are low in the U.S. relative to such expenditures in other industrial countries. France, Sweden, Japan, and West Germany, for example, spend more on social

EXHIBIT 4
Security of Employment Income in Selected Countries

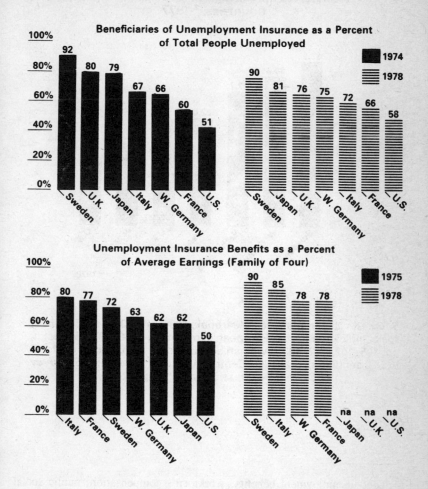

Beneficiaries of Unemployment Insurance as a Percent of Total People Unemployed

Unemployment Insurance Benefits as a Percent of Average Earnings (Family of Four)

Source: U.S. Department of Labor, Bureau of Labor Statistics, "Unemployment Compensation in Eight Industrial Nations," *Monthly Labor Review,* July 1976; updates based on interviews of individual labor ministries and departments.

insurance and welfare benefits as a percent of the Gross National Product (GNP) than the U.S. spends (Exhibit 5).

EXHIBIT 5
Public Collectivized Expenditure on Social Welfare[1] as Percentage of GNP for Selected Countries,[2] 1977

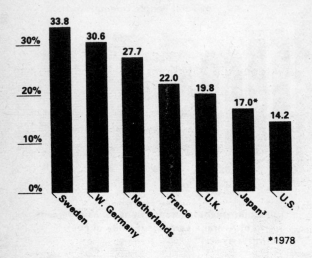

*1978

Sources: Japan Statistical Yearbook, 1980, table 351, pp. 519–521; social indicators for the European community, 1960–1978, Eurostat, pp. 105–109, 182, 183; Swedish social budget (adjusted to conform to EEC definition), Statistical Central Bureau, Stockholm; *U.S. Survey of Current Business,* July 1979, pp. 42–44.

---

[1] Includes unemployment benefits, workmen's compensation, public social welfare assistance (benefits for children, physically handicapped people, etc.,) health care, old age and disability insurance.

[2] Although these countries were chosen for easy availability of data, most other European countries would rank high on the chart.

[3] In Japan, a large portion of the total collective expenditures for social welfare are covered by the companies for which one works. These additional benefits are not included in these statistics. They would increase the Japanese percentage significantly.

European and Japanese workers also have more leisure time than their U.S. counterparts.[3] Even newly hired workers in most European countries receive a legal minimum of four weeks paid vacation. In the U.S., the average yearly vacation is only two and one-half weeks

EXHIBIT 6
Average Paid Vacations in Selected Countries, 1978

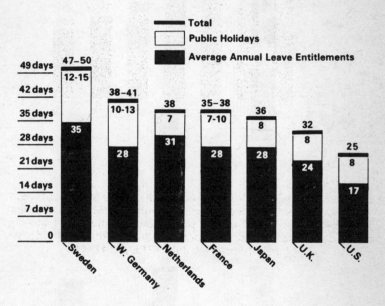

Source: Interviews conducted with the labor ministries and departments of each country, summer and fall of 1980.

(Exhibit 6). After 20 years on the job, only 64 percent of U.S. workers are entitled to four weeks vacation (Exhibit 7).

The United States ranks poorly in life expectancy and infant mortality, fairly reliable indicators of public health. In 1975, fourteen countries ranked ahead of the U.S. in male life expectancy. Seven

EXHIBIT 7
Paid Vacations of U.S. Office and Plant Workers,
1974–1976

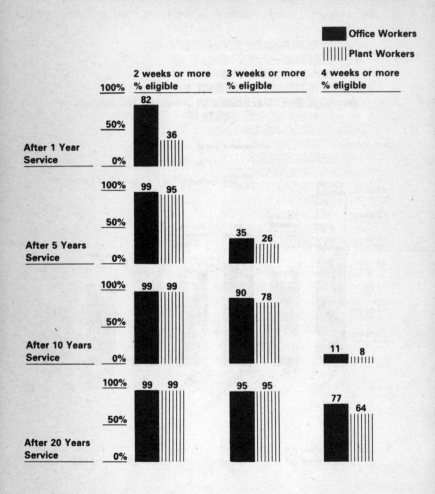

Source: U.S. Department of Labor, Bureau of Labor Statistics, BLS
Bulletin 1627 and unpublished data, June 1978.

EXHIBIT 8
Life Expectancy at Birth, Mid-1970's

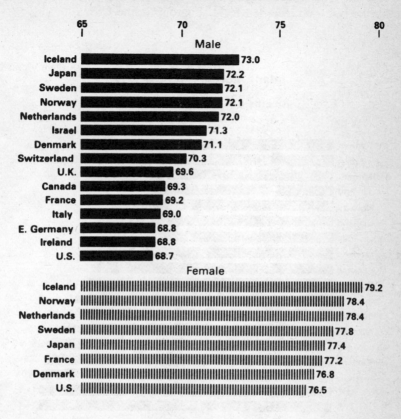

| | 65 | 70 | 75 | 80 |

Male

Iceland	73.0
Japan	72.2
Sweden	72.1
Norway	72.1
Netherlands	72.0
Israel	71.3
Denmark	71.1
Switzerland	70.3
U.K.	69.6
Canada	69.3
France	69.2
Italy	69.0
E. Germany	68.8
Ireland	68.8
U.S.	68.7

Female

Iceland	79.2
Norway	78.4
Netherlands	78.4
Sweden	77.8
Japan	77.4
France	77.2
Denmark	76.8
U.S.	76.5

Source: U.N. Demographic Yearbook, 1978, New York, 1979, pp. 402–414.

were ahead of the U.S. in female life expectancy (Exhibit 8).[4] In 1977, sixteen countries had lower infant mortality rates (Exhibit 9). The U.S. dropped from fifth place in infant mortality in 1950 to eighteenth place in 1977, as most developed countries and even a few underdeveloped ones surpassed it. This poor health record is due in part to the extreme inadequacy of health care for neglected minorities. Alone of all industrial countries, the U.S. lacks a national health insurance system. But even subgroups in the U.S. with access to good medical care do not compare favorably with many foreign countries. Several countries have lower infant mortality rates than whites in the District of Columbia, who, with a rate of 10.1 deaths per 1,000 live births in 1976, have the best rate recorded for a subgroup in the U.S.

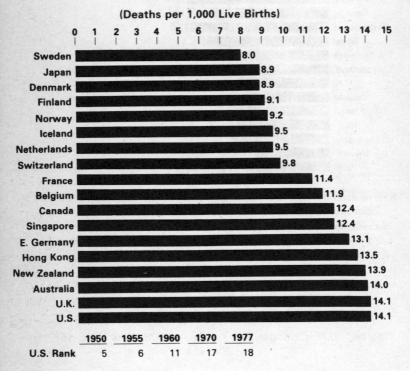

EXHIBIT 9
Infant Mortality Rates, 1977

(Deaths per 1,000 Live Births)

Sweden	8.0
Japan	8.9
Denmark	8.9
Finland	9.1
Norway	9.2
Iceland	9.5
Netherlands	9.5
Switzerland	9.8
France	11.4
Belgium	11.9
Canada	12.4
Singapore	12.4
E. Germany	13.1
Hong Kong	13.5
New Zealand	13.9
Australia	14.0
U.K.	14.1
U.S.	14.1

	1950	1955	1960	1970	1977
U.S. Rank	5	6	11	17	18

Source: U.N. Demographic Yearbook, 1978, New York, 1979, pp. 286–289.

The U.S. also rates poorly on other measures of quality of life. Levels of pollutant emissions into the air are higher in the U.S. than in many other advanced industrial countries (Exhibit 10). Fear of crime is also pervasive in the U.S. A U.S. citizen is ten times more likely to be killed by another person than is someone who lives in the Netherlands, and over two and one-half times as likely as a resident of

EXHIBIT 10
Pollution Levels in Selected Countries, 1975

| | Emissions Per Capita/(Kg) 1975 | | |
	Carbon Monoxide	Hydrocarbons	Nitrogen Oxides
U.S.	402	122	103
Canada	620	101	84
Sweden	171	52	38
W. Germany	na	30	31
U.K.	138	20	30
Netherlands	121	30	30
France	na	na	25
Japan	na	na	20
Austria	129	6	15

| | Emissions Per Unit of Energy Consumed, Tons/103 tons of energy, 1975 | | |
	Carbon Monoxide	Hydrocarbons	Nitrogen Oxides
U.S.	51	69	13
Canada	69	55	9
Sweden	29	15	6
W. Germany	na	8	8
U.K.	38	8	8
Netherlands	29	9	7
Austria	42	2	3
Japan	na	na	7

Source: *The state of the environment in OECD member countries* (1979): OECD, Paris, 1980.

Finland, which has the second highest murder rate among advanced industrial countries (Exhibit 11).

Finally, despite the antipoverty programs of the 1960s, the U.S. still has a relatively inequitable distribution of income. Only France and Canada provide a similarly small share of national income to those at the lower end of the economic scale. The lowest 10 percent of families in Japan, West Germany, and the Netherlands receive about double

EXHIBIT 11
Death by Homicide and Injuries Purposely
Inflicted by Other Persons, 1977

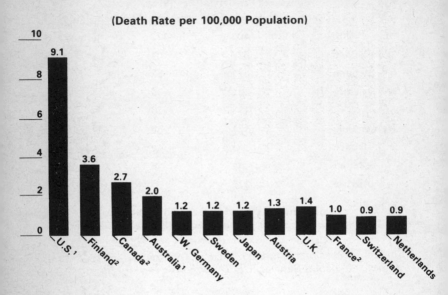

(Death Rate per 100,000 Population)

Source: U.N. World Health Statistics Annual, Vol. 1, Vital Statistics and Cause of Death, 1979, pp. 60, 88, 140, 214, 260, 268, 308, 348, 396, 404, 420, 428, 438.

the share of national income received by the bottom 10 percent in the U.S. (Exhibit 12).

Throughout the postwar period, the incomes of 20 percent of U.S. families have remained less than half of the median family income (Exhibit 13). Moreover, economic growth in the 1950s and 1960s increased the absolute inequality between rich and poor. In constant

[1] 1975
[2] 1978

EXHIBIT 12
Distribution of Income: After-Tax Income Shares*

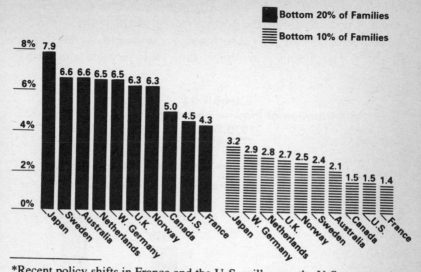

■ Bottom 20% of Families

☰ Bottom 10% of Families

*Recent policy shifts in France and the U.S. will cause the U.S. to move into last place.

Source: Occasional Studies, "Income Distribution in OECD Countries," Malcolm Sawyer, *OECD Economic Outlook,* July 1976.

EXHIBIT 13
Relative Poverty in the U.S.

(Percent of Families with Incomes Less than Half of the Income Median)

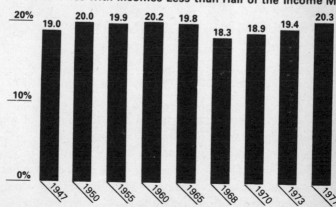

Source: Analysis based on data in U.S. Census Bureau's *Current Population Reports,* Series P-60, Nos. 117, 118, and 119, March 1979.

dollars, the gap between the bottom 20 percent and the top 5 percent of families doubled during the postwar period (Exhibit 14).

Income measures are only a surrogate for assessing overall wealth differences. Though this is extremely difficult to measure, one recent

EXHIBIT 14
Distribution of Income Including Transfers in
1978 Dollars

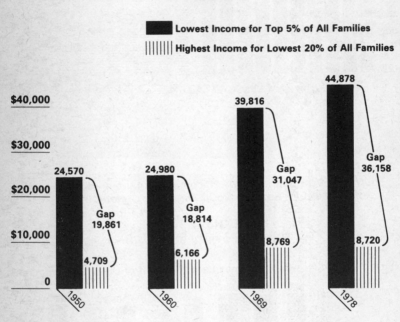

Source: Analysis based on data in U.S. Census Bureau's *Current Population Reports,* Series P-60, Nos. 117 and 118, March 1979.

study showed the U.S. has the most inequitable distribution of wealth among the countries surveyed (Exhibit 15).

These comparisons are not intended to suggest that the U.S. is a worse place to live than other countries, nor that it trails other countries in all aspects of life quality and equity.[5] They are presented only to rebut the commonly held notion that while the U.S. has economic and social difficulties, it is still far ahead of other countries. This may have been true a decade or two ago, but it is no longer so.

Nor have the statistics been recited with the intention of engaging in yet another round of cultural masochism. When faced with these realities, it is all too easy to lay blame on the American character—to point to the decline of the work ethic in the United States, the erosion of public morality, or the collective failure to save and invest. The problem in the United States is less one of national character than of economic organization.

The real purchasing power of U.S. citizens and their ability to invest in more "quality of life" goods depend on the amount of goods and services, or *wealth,* generated. It is also easier to move toward a more equitable sharing of a high living standard if wealth is being created

EXHIBIT 15
Percentage of Wealth Held by Top 1–2 Percent of
Total Householders

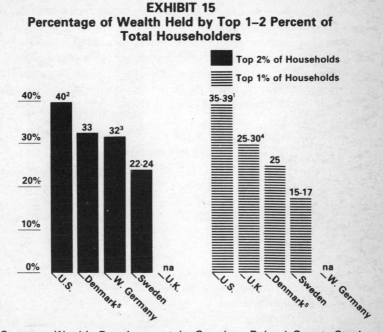

Source: *Wealth Development in Sweden:* Roland Spant, Stockholm, 1980.

[1] Derived from estate inventories, 1972.
[2] Derived from income, 1969.
[3] Derived from 1965 data.
[4] Derived from 1972 data.
[5] Derived from 1975 data.

at a faster rate. Over the last 10 years, the United States' capacity to generate new wealth has been impaired. This is the fundamental problem that must be addressed if the U.S. is to raise its living standard in the total sense.

FOOTNOTES

[1] There are a number of ways to measure national income, none of which is truly satisfactory. A per capita measurement can be misleading since it does not take account of the increasing participation rate in the U.S. labor force. As the postwar "baby boom" generation has entered the labor market and female participation in the labor force has increased, a larger proportion of the population is engaged in producing income. Therefore, the society's per capita ability to generate income inevitably increases even though this does not reflect an increase in the productive power of each working individual. Even by this measure our growth has declined compared to that of the 1960s.

Different measures normally used for measuring national income are shown below. The purpose of these charts is to show the approximate differences in the rate of growth. In the 1970s, income in the United States for an hour's work has increased at a slower pace than in the 1960s.

COMPARISONS OF GROWTH IN REAL INCOME
Real Average Percent Increase

	1950–59	1960–69	1970–79
Gross Domestic Product	35%	47%	32%
Median family income	28	34	7
Wage and salary disbursements per hour worked (index of average hourly earnings)	21	15	3
National income (GNP – depreciation-indirect taxes)	34	47	33
Gross Domestic Product per capita	26	31	22

Sources: Disposable income for 1950 to 1972 and population, *1973 Statistical Supplement to the Survey of Current Business*, pp. 7, 240; National income for 1950 to 1972, *January 1976 S.C.B.*, pp. 12–13; Index of average hourly earnings for 1950 to 1972, *1973 Statistical Supplement to the Survey of Current Business;* National income and disposable personal income, population, average hourly earnings, *Survey of Current Business:* 1978–1979 figures from June 1980, pp. 11, 13, S-13; 1976–1977 figures from June 1978, pp. 7, 9, S-15; 1974–1975 figures from June 1976, pp. 7, 9, S-15; 1973–1974 figures from June 1974, pp. 14, 15, S-15

[2] Gross domestic product per employee is the best measure of gross national income. Better than other measures, it reflects the sum total of goods and services produced per a given amount of work. But there are a number of problems that bias this measure. It reflects only income and not the total stock of wealth. Therefore, it can be misleading as a mirror for living standard. Also, the wealth of resource-rich countries such as the U.S. may be understated because of locally cheaper prices for land and raw materials. On the other hand, the wealth of countries providing health and other services as a public good are understated relative to the U.S. Finally, currency changes can cause these comparisons to fluctuate significantly. The purpose of these data is to indicate approximate trends, not to make a precise quantitative comparison of living standards. Such efforts yield controversial results at best.

[3] Leisure time is sometimes equated with the length of the work week. Statistical surveys showing average work week lengths can be misleading as some take legal maximums that are not usually representative and most do not separate involuntary short-time schedules from the normal work week. Often, overtime work paid at extra rates is not distinguished from normal working hours. Statistics that show a short work week in the U.S. are often related to the higher percentage of involuntary short work weeks. The five-day week is common in all countries, though in Japan, five and one-half days are still present in some businesses. In Japan as well, workers do not always take their full vacation. In this sense, the Japanese figures may be somewhat overstated.

[4] Life expectancy depends on many genetic, cultural, climatic, and social factors. Trends do not change rapidly over time. The quality of health care plays a significant role in the determination of life expectancy, but it is not the only factor.

[5] The U.S. does compare favorably with other countries in some aspects of quality of life, though the distribution of these benefits is not as equitable as in other countries. For example, the U.S. has, on the average, larger homes and apartments with a higher percentage of basic plumbing, heating, and cooling amenities than in other industrialized countries, though this gap is rapidly narrowing. In part, this results from a lower population density and a wealthier immediate past.

The U.S. also has a larger proportion of its population in higher education institutes than in other countries, though this gap is decreasing; a higher proportion of skilled workers and professionals in other countries receive their training through apprenticeship.

2

The Importance of Relative Productivity

The initial response in the U.S. to the stagnation of living standards in the 1970s was to employ fiscal and monetary policies. These policies were aimed at preventing runaway inflation and massive unemployment by moderating the ebbs and flows of the business cycle. During recessions, government deficit spending and tax cuts increased demand, thereby promoting economic activity and employment. During boom periods, high interest rates, restrictions on bank lending, and reduced government deficits dampened demand, thereby reducing inflation. From the mid-1940s through the 1960s, these policies succeeded in "fine tuning" the economy. Although the U.S. traded higher unemployment (5 to 6 percent) for low inflation (2 to 3 percent) in certain periods, followed by lower unemployment (3 to 4 percent) and higher inflation (4 to 5 percent) at other times, it generally managed to maintain a steady increase in economic activity and real incomes.

These monetary and fiscal policies failed in the 1970s. The boom periods became less buoyant and the downturns became deeper and more severe. The lowest rates of unemployment and inflation during the past five years (5½ and 9 percent, respectively) were as bad, on average, as the highest rates during the previous 25 years. In fact, the highest rates (8 percent unemployment and 13 percent inflation) would have been unimaginable a decade ago. With sustained interest rates of 20 percent necessary to bring inflation rates down to 10 percent a year, management of the business cycle could no longer be characterized as "fine tuning."

These solutions have not worked because they address problems different from those the U.S. began to face in the 1970s. Designed to alleviate inflation and unemployment caused by the business cycle, they operate by varying levels of demand. But they do not address the problem of assuring a competitive supply of goods from U.S. industry once demand is stimulated. Indeed, accelerated demand can as easily result in the purchase of more Japanese cars or German machine tools. The problems the U.S. now faces are rooted in its basic ability to create wealth.

Greater wealth for each person in a nation is created by increasing the value added per work-hour in producing goods and services. This is accomplished both by improving the productivity of existing industrial activities and by shifting resources across industrial activities toward those resulting in new and more productive uses. In the first case, for example, methods of building a house can be improved through the use of better equipment so that fewer workhours are required. Wealth can be created, since more houses can be constructed for the same amount of work. In the second case, if making tools or drawing engineering plans can command a higher price per hour of labor than can inserting components in a circuit board—because of the shorter supply of people in the world capable of performing these higher-skilled activities—then shifting the production mix toward these activities can increase the wealth of the society.

In both methods of increasing wealth, the U.S. has been failing. Productivity growth in the United States has declined over the past 15 years (Exhibit 16). Measured as total dollar output of goods and services in the economy divided by the number of hours worked, productivity increased by 3.2 percent per year between 1948 and 1965. It fell to 2.4 percent between 1965 and 1973 and to 1.1 percent between 1973 and 1978. In 1979, productivity actually shrank by -0.8 percent, despite real growth in output that year. Productivity was again negative (-0.8 percent) in 1980. This decline is a major reason for stagnating wealth creation in the U.S.

Even with improvements in efficiency, society is faced with a difficult challenge: The potential for greater wealth can only be realized if workers displaced by efficiency improvements or resource shifts can find work in other productive enterprises. Thus, if fewer people are needed to build a house in a given length of time because of labor-saving machines, this productivity improvement can be translated into greater wealth only if the displaced workers are re-employed (or, if the hours saved by work improvements are divided among workers who are willing to sacrifice their wages for increased leisure time).

Nor has the U.S. met the challenge of transferring its workers who are displaced by efficiency improvements. Over a 15-year period be-

EXHIBIT 16
U.S. Productivity Improvements, 1948–1980

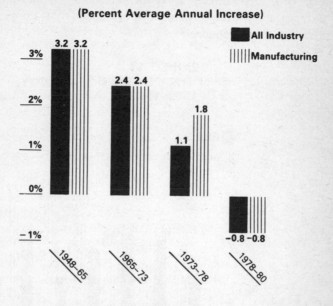

(Percent Average Annual Increase)

■ All Industry

||||| Manufacturing

Sources: The national income and product accounts of the United States, 1929–1974 statistical tables, Bureau of Economic Analysis, U.S. Department of Commerce, pp. 178, 214; *Survey of Current Business,* July 1979; Bureau of Economic Analysis, U.S. Department of Commerce, pp. 52, 56; U.S. Department of Labor *News,* Bureau of Labor Statistics, January 1981.

ginning in 1965, unemployment rates increased to the point that, by 1980, the U.S. had higher unemployment than most other developed countries. Its inability to expand the economy and fully use its people is a second major cause of the United States' problems.[1]

International trade has complicated this picture. Prior to 1970, the United States had only a small proportion of its goods exposed to world trade. That is no longer the case. In 1980, 17 percent of its goods' production was exported (up from 9 percent in 1970) and over 21 percent of its total sale of goods was imported (up from 9 percent in 1970) (Exhibit 17). Almost 25 percent of the total growth in U.S. consumption of goods over the past decade was taken up by imports. Even this rapid rise in imports and exports underestimates the importance of foreign competition in most industries. While 14 percent of our steel is imported today, it is our total steel production that is threatened by foreign competition. If one considers potential exposure to import penetration, over 70 percent of our goods must now operate in an international marketplace.[2]

EXHIBIT 17
The Importance of Trade for the U.S. Economy,
1969–1979

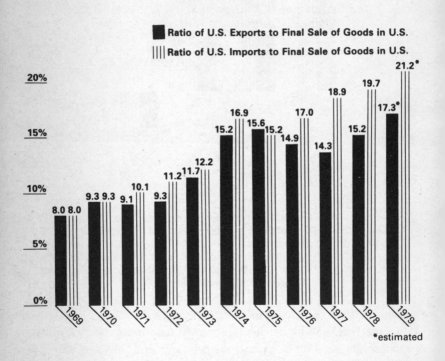

■ Ratio of U.S. Exports to Final Sale of Goods in U.S.

||||| Ratio of U.S. Imports to Final Sale of Goods in U.S.

*estimated

Source: U.S. Commerce Department, *International Economic Indicators* (various issues).

If U.S. productivity falls relative to that of other countries producing the same internationally traded goods, either employment and output in these U.S. industries drop (through increased imports) or people in the U.S. have to accept lower relative incomes (living standards) for producing those goods, or both. By contrast, high relative productivity allows higher real wages to be paid (a manifestation of a higher living standard), while still keeping total costs relatively low and total prices competitive.

For example, if the U.S. can produce steel with a 2 percent increase in productivity every year, and it can use the resources it saves to increase output of steel or some other product, then it experiences an increase in its living standard. But where there is international trade, this result does not necessarily occur.

EXHIBIT 18
The Growth of U.S. Imports in Selected Products
(Imports as Percent of Consumption)

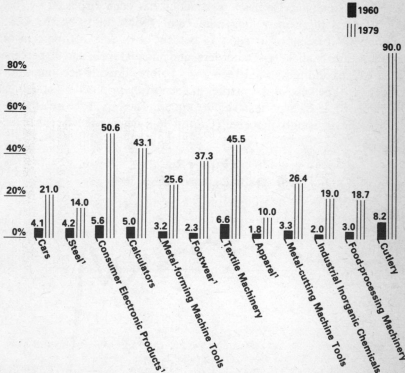

Sources: *Business Week,* June 30, 1980, p. 60; U.S. Commerce Department Trade Series FT 210 and FT 610; and *U.S. Industrial Outlook* (various issues).

---

[1] Areas where U.S. restrictive trade policies have curtailed further imports.

If steel producers in another country improve their productivity faster than the U.S. does and achieve higher levels of productivity, they can choose to export their steel to the U.S. at a potentially lower price than U.S. producers can match. The U.S. benefits from access to lower-priced foreign steel, but this benefit is offset by the penalty of lost employment. If U.S. steel workers find other employment producing goods that are not as highly valued in world markets as steel is, the relative standard of living of the U.S. declines. If these workers remain idle, the standard of living may decline absolutely.

The U.S. has suffered a decline in its ability to be as productive as other nations that produce many of the same goods. Thus, the U.S. derives less income. Domestic production has been displaced by foreign imports in an increasing number of goods. In 1979, the U.S. imported 21 percent of its cars, 14 percent of its steel, 50 percent of its televisions, radios, tape recorders, and phonographs, and 90 percent of its knives and forks. Nineteen years before, imports accounted for less than 10 percent of the market in each of these product categories (Exhibit 18). U.S. exports have not kept up. The U.S. balance of trade has gone increasingly negative (Exhibit 19), despite the fact that the

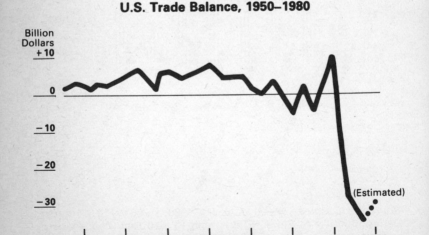

EXHIBIT 19
U.S. Trade Balance, 1950–1980

Sources: Economic Reports of the President, January 1980, p. 316; January 1981, p. 344.

U.S. has lowered the price of its goods (and our relative living standard) through devaluation of the dollar (Exhibit 20).

EXHIBIT 20
Index of Values of Major International Currencies versus the Dollar

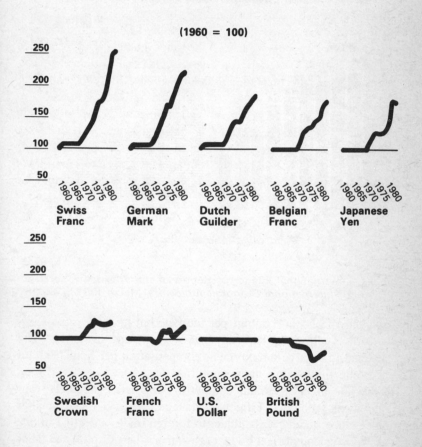

(1960 = 100)

Sources: International Monetary Fund International Financial Statistics, January 1970, January 1976, and January 1981, various pages, International Monetary Fund, Washington, D.C.

The U.S. has lagged behind other countries in productivity improvements for two decades (Exhibit 21). It started in the 1950s with much

EXHIBIT 21
Comparative Productivity Improvements for 11 Industrialized Countries

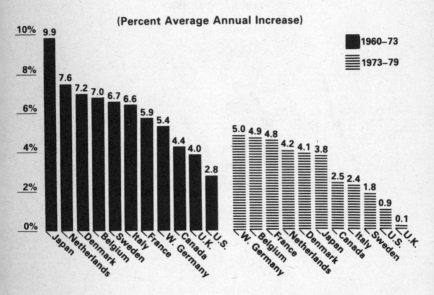

(Percent Average Annual Increase)

■ 1960–73
≡ 1973–79

Sources: International Economic Report of the President, March 1973, p. 81; *International Economic Indicators,* March 1981, p. 64.

higher levels of absolute output per worker, but its slow rate of improvement has allowed others to surpass it in many industries. The U.S. decline in relative employment compensation per hour (Exhibit 22)[3] is a reflection of this phenomenon.

The decline in international competitiveness has exacerbated our unemployment problems. Fifteen years ago, when a much smaller portion of our economy was subject to foreign trade, a decline in one industry was typically offset by increases in another. Capital and labor could shift fairly easily out of old enterprises and into new. But today, with so much of our economy exposed to foreign trade, such adjustments are far more difficult.

Why has U.S. productivity declined? The following chapter examines several conventional explanations and shows why each is unsatisfactory.

EXHIBIT 22
Estimated Hourly Compensation for Production Workers in Manufacturing,[1] 1960–1979

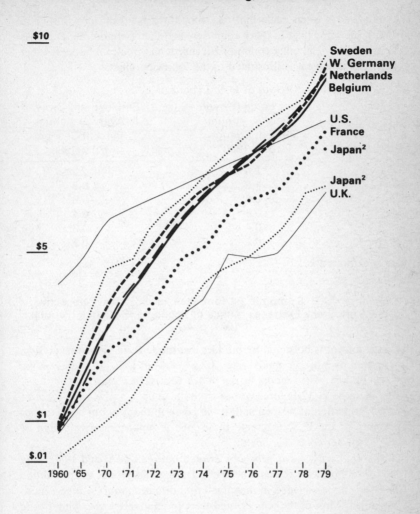

Source: U.S. Department of Labor, Bureau of Labor Statistics, Office of Productivity and Technology, February 1980, unpublished data.

[1] Annual average exchange rate; includes benefits paid to employees.

[2] Japanese firms provide a significant number of extra benefits not provided by Western counterparts, such as low-interest mortgage loans, clinics, recreation facilities, etc.: the higher figure includes these items for 1979.

FOOTNOTES

[1] The argument is often made that the labor force has been growing more rapidly in the U.S. than in other countries, and that therefore the U.S. has performed better than other countries because it has created a larger number of jobs. The argument is illustrated in the following charts:

Growth of U.S. Labor Force

	Labor Force Growth[1] Average Annual Percent Change 1970–1980	Employment Growth[2] Average Annual Percent Change 1970–1980
U.S.	2.4%	2.2%
Sweden	1.0	0.9
Japan	0.9	0.8
France	0.8	0.4
U.K.	0.4	0.3
Germany	−0.2	−0.2

[1]Those seeking work.
[2]Those working.

> Source: "U.S. Economic Performance in a Global Perspective;" New York Stock Exchange, Office of Economic Research, February 1981, p. 46.

This argument is bolstered by the fact that the U.S. increased its civilian employment by a higher annual rate (2.2 percent) in 1970–1980 than in the previous decade, when increases ran at 1.8 percent per year.

This increase in labor force comes from the entry into the work force of a higher proportion of women and of the postwar "baby boom" generation. The ability of the U.S. to create these jobs is not necessarily a sign of relatively greater economic health.

Of the 18.7 million net new jobs created between 1970 and 1980, only about 1.0 million were in manufacturing. During this period, the proportion of the work force engaged in manufacturing dropped from 24.6 percent to 20.9 percent. Most of the jobs created were in relatively low-paying public and private service professions.

Further, within the manufacturing sector, the decline of the U.S. average wage relative to that of other countries (Exhibit 22) shows that we in effect traded off average income levels for more jobs at the lower end of the pay spectrum. One could turn the argument on its head and assert that our unemployment would have been significantly higher had we not suffered real relative wage declines and increased our public sector employment in the 1970s.

Presumably other countries could have created low paying service and even manufacturing jobs had they chosen to do so. Measures of overall wealth and productivity improvement are a better means to gauge the relative success of the economy.

[2] This estimate is obtained by adding up total production of U.S. goods in Standard Industrial Classification six-digit categories where imports equal more than 10 percent of consumption or exports equal more than 10 percent of production.

[3] Comparisons of compensation of U.S. and foreign workers compiled by the U.S. Bureau of Labor Statistics are often misleading. These data sometimes omit benefits that are provided to foreign workers but are not available to U.S. workers. This is especially true in the case of Japanese workers, who receive many benefits in areas such as housing, low interest mortgage loans, and access to company recreation facilities.

3

Common Explanations for the Productivity Decline in the United States

Over 20 different reasons have been put forward to explain the decline of U.S. productivity growth.[1] The most popular explanations are the increasing burden of government regulation and deficits, and low levels of capital expenditure by industry. But even taken together, these arguments fail to supply a satisfactory explanation.

GOVERNMENT REGULATION AND DEFICITS

Those viewing government regulation as the root of the problem contend that laws and regulations in such areas as environmental protection, occupational safety and health, and consumer protection have created operating inefficiencies in industry; have required large capital expenditures (particularly environmental and safety laws) that have diverted funds from productive investment; and have spawned paperwork that has wasted time and dampened initiative.

There is no doubt that such laws and regulations have affected productivity. Recent studies, however, suggest that their effect has been small. Environmental laws usually require capital expenditures but do not significantly contribute to increased operating costs. While safety regulations can add some cost to operations, many companies have found that the time and expense saved because of fewer accidents (not to mention the savings in human terms) offset these extra costs.[2] Some critics, pointing to the dramatic declines of productivity in the mining industry, for example, have blamed regulations. In fact, about 80 percent of that decline has been in oil and gas, and has resulted primarily from higher prices rendering older and less efficient wells economical.[3] Even in coal mining, where regulation has been heaviest, safety regulations have had less effect on productivity than has the opening of formerly uneconomic mines.[4]

Capital expenditures on pollution control and safety, though sometimes overstated,[5] have not been significant (5 to 6 percent of total industrial investment).[6] Even if it is assumed that these expenditures would have been put entirely to productive uses, most economists agree that the expenditures have been the cause of no more than 10 to 12 percent of our productivity slowdown.[7] In fact, pollution control and mandated safety laws are more stringent in many other countries, including Japan, which have still maintained higher rates of productivity growth than the U.S.

Government paperwork, though certainly an annoyance, does not appear to be a primary culprit in the decline of U.S. productivity either. Estimates of the proportion of total work time taken up by industry in filling out government forms has varied from 0.2 percent to roughly 4 percent of total work hours. While this paperwork has undoubtedly burdened industry, especially small business, it appears that about 80 percent of the burden is attributable to tax forms, which have not changed in terms of complexity since 1963. The peak load of paperwork actually occurred in 1944, 1952, and 1973, because of wage and price controls, and has declined since 1973.[8]

A more general argument blames the size of government and accompanying government deficits for the slowdown in productivity. This contention rests on three assumptions: (1) Government deficits "crowd out" private investors from borrowing, or at least raise the interest costs of their doing so. Since this dampens their investment, it hinders productivity. (2) Government spending redistributes income away from those who have a higher propensity to save (the wealthy) toward those who do not save (the poor). This redistribution reduces funds available for saving and investment and thereby hinders productivity.[9] (3) The higher marginal tax rates required to fund government expenditures discourage worker incentive and entrepreneurship.

While these arguments are easy to comprehend in theory, there is no significant evidence demonstrating either that government deficits are the major cause of high interest rates or that the lack of investment in the private sector is in fact caused primarily by high interest rates or a funds shortage.

The period from 1956 to 1973, which saw the largest growth in the U.S. public sector, was also a period of buoyant growth for the whole economy.[10] Since 1973, as growth declined, the government share of the GNP has stabilized. Moreover, the U.S. government sector as a proportion of the GDP is one of the smallest among industrial countries

EXHIBIT 23
General Government Outlays as a Proportion of
GDP for Selected Countries, 1978

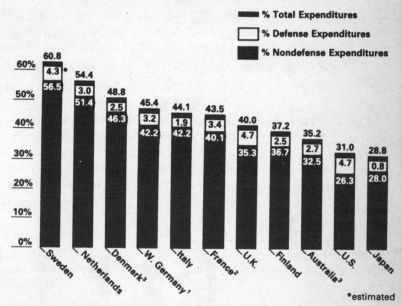

█ % Total Expenditures
☐ % Defense Expenditures
■ % Nondefense Expenditures

Country	Total	Defense	Nondefense
Sweden	60.8	4.3 *	56.5
Netherlands	54.4	3.0	51.4
Denmark[3]	48.8	2.5	46.3
W. Germany[1]	45.4	3.2	42.2
Italy	44.1	1.9	42.2
France[2]	43.5	3.4	40.1
U.K.	40.0	4.7	35.3
Finland	37.2	2.5	36.7
Australia[3]	35.2	2.7	32.5
U.S.	31.0	4.7	26.3
Japan	28.8	0.8	28.0

*estimated

Source: OECD National Accounts, Statistics 1961–1978, Volume II, tables 3A and 3B for each country, OECD, Paris, June 1980.

(Exhibit 23). Finally, as has been shown, other countries spend more than the U.S. does on collective social expenditures. Only in the defense sector is the U.S. expenditure proportionately larger and, in this area, the government often purchases from private industry. Governments in West Germany, Japan, and France have borrowed heavily

---

[1] 1977.
[2] 1976.
[3] 1975.

in the public sector and have larger public-debt-to-GDP ratios than does the United States (Exhibit 24). Finally, no evidence exists showing a relationship between marginal tax rates and entrepreneurial activity or work effort. Although the U.S. has a lower marginal tax rate on personal income than most competitive countries, these countries have managed to achieve higher productivity improvements and increased living standards.

The U.S. government has often failed to conduct its affairs in the most efficient manner—and making government more efficient is, of course, a worthy goal. However, reducing government regulation, cutting government spending, and balancing the budget—while perhaps encouraging the confidence of the industrial and financial communities—do not contribute significantly to increasing national wealth over the long term.

EXHIBIT 24
Total Deficit of General Government as a
Percentage of GDP for Selected Countries 1978

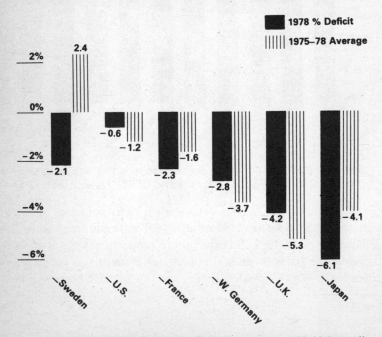

Source: OECD National Accounts, Statistics 1961–1978, Volume II, detailed tables, Annex 1, pp. 240–252, OECD, Paris, June 1980.

THE LEVEL OF PHYSICAL CAPITAL FORMATION

Perhaps the most pervasive explanation of the slowdown of U.S. productivity growth, both absolute and relative, cites the decline in physical capital formation and the concomitant low level of capital expenditures compared to those of our major trading partners. A number of economists have claimed that U.S. capital-to-labor ratios began to decline in the mid-1960s.[11] Others point out that investment as a proportion of the total GNP is low in the United States as compared to that in other countries (Exhibit 25).

EXHIBIT 25
U.S. Capital Formation Compared to Other Countries

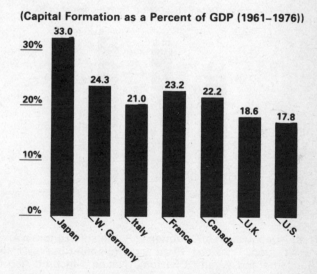

(Capital Formation as a Percent of GDP (1961–1976))

Source: World Business Weekly, September 15, 1980.

While there is probably some relationship between the level of certain types of investment in an industry and the rate of productivity improvement in that industry, levels of aggregate capital expenditure for all industry do not reveal very much. U.S. investment in plant and equipment as a percent of the GNP has remained stable over time, actually showing a slight increase. Between 1951 and 1964, total investment as a percentage of the GNP was 9.4 percent; between 1965 and 1972, it rose to 10.3 percent before dipping slightly to 10.2 percent between 1973 and 1978. In 1979 and 1980, it rose to 10.7 percent.

More significantly, investment in manufacturing as a percentage of the total output of goods in manufacturing has increased substantially (Exhibit 26). The sharp decrease in the ratio of capital to labor in the 1973–1978 period actually occurred only between 1976 and 1978, after the worst recession in postwar history. Previous to this, capital-to-labor ratios had not shown a significant decline, particularly if only plant and equipment investments are considered.

EXHIBIT 26
U.S. Manufacturing Investment as a Percentage of Total Production in the Manufacturing Sector

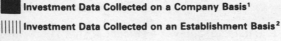

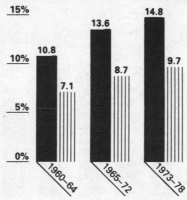

Sources: Department of Commerce, Bureau of Economic Analysis: Business Outlook Division, "Plant and Equipment Survey"; and National Income and Wealth Division, "National Income Accounts," unpublished series.

Moreover, a growing proportion of the total GDP is in service industries, many of which have a lower capital intensity than goods

---

[1] This includes all investment by companies whose primary businesses are manufacturing.

[2] This includes all investments in factories used for manufacturing, regardless of ownership.

EXHIBIT 27 Structure of GDP for Major Industrialized Countries

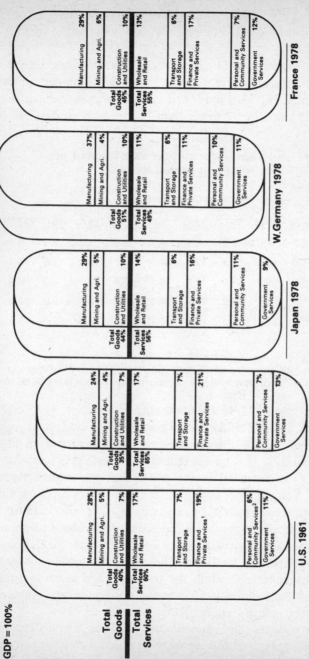

Sources: OECD National Accounts, Statistics 1961–1978, Volume II, detailed tables, OECD, Paris, June 1980, tables 2A and 2B; German National Accounts.

[1] Private services include financial institutions, insurance, real estate and business services, and machinery and equipment leasing.

[2] Community services include public administration and defense, sanitary services, medical, educational, welfare and social services, research and scientific institutes, business, professional and labor organizations, entertainment, libraries, recreational services, repair and laundry shops, etc.

production sectors. Most other industrialized countries have a higher proportion of goods production in the GDP than does the U.S. (Exhibit 27).

Accordingly, if comparisons among countries are made only for investment in the manufacturing sector, the U.S. no longer appears to be as low (Exhibit 28). Data published in 1980 for these comparisons showed the U.S. still slightly lower than European countries, but in

EXHIBIT 28
Gross Fixed Capital Formation as a Percent of Value Added in Manufacturing

(Manufacturing Only)

	1970	1971	1972	1973	1974	1975	1976	1977	1978
U.S.	8.9%	8.0%	7.9%	8.6%	9.7%	8.9%	9.7%	9.9%	9.9%
U.K.	15.0	14.1	12.1	12.5	14.9	13.7	13.1	13.8	12.4
W. Germany	16.2	16.2	13.9	12.0	10.7	10.4	10.2	10.0	9.8
France	15.7	16.5	14.9	14.3	14.5	13.1	13.7	12.9	11.6
Japan	25.2	24.3	24.2	25.3	22.1	21.2	19.8	19.6	19.1

Sources: OECD National Accounts, Statistics 1961–1978, Volume II, tables 2A and 2B and 4A and 4B through 1977 (1976 for Germany), Paris, June 1980; country national accounts series for later data.

fact the data understate U.S. manufacturing investment. U.S. companies undertook a significantly higher porportion of their machinery and equipment expenditures through leases than did companies in other countries (Exhibit 29). This means that these investments were computed as part of the financial sector rather than the manufacturing sector. Also, U.S. companies undertook a much higher proportion of their investments abroad than did companies in most other countries. In 1979, U.S. companies invested 9.5 percent of their total plant and equipment expenditures abroad, compared to 2.7 percent for Germany and France and 1.9 percent for Japan. These expenditures do not show up as U.S. investments.[12] Overall, the statistics used to demonstrate lower investment rates in the U.S. manufacturing industry compared to those of foreign industry are questionable at best.[13]

Whatever the correct figures may be, the U.S. has been undergoing some shifts in the growth of various sectors, which would suggest that

EXHIBIT 29
Value of Machinery and Equipment Purchased for Leasing as Percent of Gross Fixed Capital Formation in Machinery and Equipment, 1976

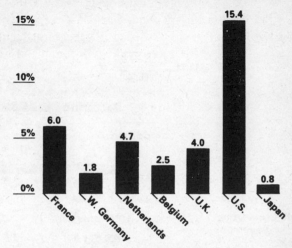

Sources: T.M. Clark. *Leasing* (McGraw-Hill U.K. Ltd.), London, 1978, p. 48; Japanese figures are estimates from a small sample of Japanese companies.

a lower capital investment rate is perhaps appropriate. Industries such as steel, cement, fibers, automobiles, and commodity plastics, which are heavily capital intensive, are mature; they have been growing slowly. Industries providing most of the recent growth—such as computers, industrial machinery, and electronic instruments—tend to be far less capital intensive. During the 1970s, the U.S. invested almost five times as much in steel as it did in computers or aircraft, even though the latter two industries showed much more rapid growth, productivity improvements, and better export performance (Exhibit 30). Indeed, it may well be that capital-to-labor ratios *should* be declining if the right types of industrial investments are being pursued. Just as the shifts in our economy from clothing and textiles to steel and chemicals saw an increase of overall capital-to-labor ratios, it may be that the recent relative shift toward more "knowledge-intensive" industries would involve an overall decrease in this ratio for manufacturing as a whole (even though within each of these industries the United States should strive for higher investment levels than competitors).

EXHIBIT 30
U.S. Capital Investment Levels and Trade Performance

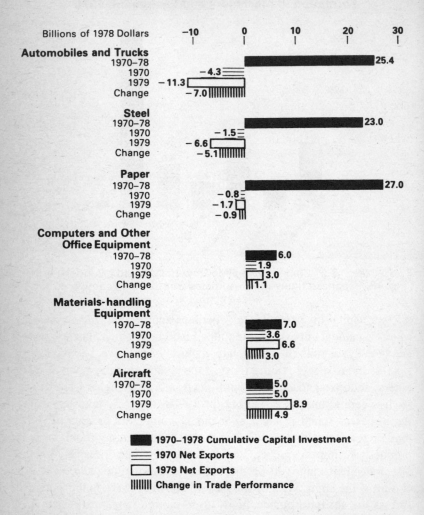

Sources: U.S. Commerce Department trade series FT 610 and FT 210 for various years; U.S. Commerce Department: Annual Survey of Manufacturers and Census of Manufacturers for various years.

This factor may also explain different manufacturing investment levels in different countries, since countries at different stages of industrial growth have different capital investment needs. It is not surprising, for example, that in the late 1960s and early 1970s the Japanese invested more than others, given the mix of industry they were building. During this same period, most European and North American countries were witnessing a maturing of their basic capital-intensive industries; the Japanese were still creating their steel, automobile, chemical cement, fiber, and basic metals industries.

When all of these factors are considered together, it is unclear whether U.S. manufacturing industry as a whole is in fact investing too little to remain competitive. The link between aggregate capital formation figures and productivity rates is ambiguous. Changes in the structure of the U.S. economy and differences in structure between the U.S. economy and that of other countries may explain capital formation differences without explaining productivity differences.

"CATCHING UP"

Another often-heard explanation about why other countries have improved productivity and, therefore, living standards at a faster rate than the U.S. holds that these countries have been "catching up," following the well-known paths that the U.S. blazed rather than trying to break new ground technologically. The argument predicts that once the other countries have caught up, they will no longer be able to maintain the productivity and living standard advances they have enjoyed in the past.

Certainly, there is validity to this argument when describing Europe and Japan in the 1950s and 1960s and perhaps Japan in the early 1970s. But the argument is no longer valid. By and large, Japanese, German, and French goods no longer enter the U.S. based on low-wage rates. Manufacturers in these countries have achieved technological leadership in product design, productivity, and quality in a wide variety of industries—steel, television sets, cameras, numerically controlled lathes, compressors, and power generating equipment. Technical assistance agreements flow more equally between the U.S. and other advanced industrialized countries, and have done so for at least five years. The U.S. patent balance with Germany turned negative in the mid-1960s and with Japan in the mid-1970s (Exhibit 31).

EXHIBIT 31
Patent Balance
(Number of Patents Granted
to Companies or Individuals)

	1966	1972	1975
W. Germany			
Granted to U.S.	3,733	4,575	3,140
Granted by U.S.	3,981	5,728	6,069
Balance	− 248	− 1,153	− 2,929
Japan			
Granted to U.S.	4,683	5,948	− 4,918
Granted by U.S.	1,122	5,154	6,339
Balance	3,561	794	− 1,421
Total			
Granted to U.S.	45,633	30,520	37,482
Granted by U.S.	9,567	16,839	19,197
Balance	36,066	19,681	18,285

Source: U.S. National Science Board, *Science Indicators 1976*, Washington, D.C., 1977.

It is also sometimes pointed out, particularly with respect to Japan and West Germany, that their internal service sectors have been neglected and that public demands for increased investment in these areas will be made now that these countries are more developed. While the housing stock in these countries has not received as much investment as in the U.S., other key services, such as telecommunications, power generation, internal public transportation, and health services are at least as developed as those in the U.S.

The transition from "catch up" to parity with the U.S. occurred several years ago. The end of this phase has had its effects; for example, Japanese growth is no longer over 10 percent a year as it was in the 1960s, and Germany no longer has labor shortages as it did in the 1960s. However, these countries still enjoy wealth increases that are more rapid than that of the United States. Accordingly, "catching up" is an argument whose time has passed.

OTHER EXPLANATIONS

The proportion of the GNP spent on research and development has been declining in the United States, while other countries have been increasing their R&D expenditures rapidly (Exhibit 32). Some analysts point to this as a major cause of declining productivity and competitiveness.[14] But this argument does not provide a convincing explanation for declining productivity growth in the United States.

EXHIBIT 32
R&D as Percentage of GNP for Selected
Countries

	1962	1964	1966	1968	1970	1972	1974	1976	1978
U.S.	2.73	2.97	2.90	2.83	2.64	2.43	2.32	2.27	2.25
Japan	1.47	1.48	1.48	1.61	1.79	1.85	1.95	1.94	1.98
W. Germany	1.25	1.57	1.81	1.97	2.18	2.33	2.26	2.28	2.28
France	1.46	1.81	2.03	2.08	1.91	1.86	1.81	1.78	1.85
U.K.	na	2.30	2.32	2.29	na	2.06	2.0	2.1*	2.1*

*estimated

Source: National Science Foundation, 1979, quoted in Mansfield, Edwin, "The Competitive Position of U.S. Technology," unpublished p. 7.

The decline in research and development has stemmed mostly from the slowdown of publicly financed defense and space programs. One can argue that these programs have an effect on overall productivity through spin-offs to industry, but the effect is probably not as direct as targeted investment by industry itself.

Although R&D expenditures as a proportion of the GNP have been falling, they are still higher absolutely than those of U.S. competitors. Further, in 1980, the U.S. still had a much higher proportion of scientists and engineers in its total mix of industrial employees than had other industrialized countries.[15]

Technical innovation plays an important role in fostering long-term economic growth and productivity improvement, but a decline in aggregate R&D expenditures does not appear to have been a major cause of the decline in U.S. productivity growth during the 1965–1980 period.

Some people argue that the real culprit in productivity decline is energy prices. Increases in energy prices have given successive jolts to inflation since 1973. These events may have contributed to declining productivity rates either because increased energy costs have dampened demand growth or because they have increased economic uncertainty. Energy price hikes, however, do not explain why the downtrend has been so severe, nor why it has disproportionately affected the U.S. and the U.K., both of which have greater energy resources than other countries. The decline in productivity growth and the low relative-growth rates of the United States predate the energy crisis. While the U.S. may work toward energy independence, it seems doubtful that these measures in themselves will significantly improve productivity.

In every country, business executives complain that productivity rates are declining because "people don't want to work anymore." More sophisticated arguments attribute the decline in productivity to changes in the composition of the work force as it becomes distinctly younger and more female. These arguments are usually based on historical trends showing that these workers are less productive.

It is no doubt true that the ability of managers to impose strict discipline upon workers no longer exists to the degree it once did. Laws and contracts now give workers more freedom. But it is questionable whether this freedom reduces productivity; no studies substantiate such an effect. Other countries, such as Japan, Germany, Holland, Denmark, and Sweden, with better productivity rates have given workers more freedom and discretion than the United States has.

As for the composition of the labor force, studies have shown offsetting effects of age, sex, and level of education.[16] The fact that women and young employees receive the lower-paying jobs is probably an effect of their more recent entry to the labor force, residual discrimination and the economy's inability to generate higher value-added jobs rather than a cause of lower productivity.

GENERAL SHORTCOMINGS OF CURRENT EXPLANATIONS

Conventional diagnoses of U.S. productivity problems have been presented in summary fashion. Although their complexities and subtleties do warrant closer attention, these explanations all suffer from two overriding deficiencies: (1) their definitions of productivity do not measure living-standard improvements; and (2) they overemphasize the importance of the aggregate level of various inputs, i.e., government expenditure, capital, research and development.

The common measure of productivity (total dollar value of output divided by total hours worked) is inadequate. It does not measure new product modifications or improved reliability in existing products unless they are accompanied by real price increases. Accordingly, such improvements are not registered as productivity improvements, even though they enhance the wealth of society.

Also, because the total value of output is measured in price terms, these data do not fully account for productivity improvements that reduce real prices. Thus, if cost-reduction benefits from greater productivity are passed directly on to consumers as lower prices, they are not registered in the statistics. Yet it is precisely in this way that newly created productive wealth is distributed to society.

Nor do productivity statistics indicate anything about *competitive* productivity. At any given time, certain businesses have higher productivity rates worldwide than others. But merely participating in these faster-moving industries without achieving a competitive advantage in productivity does not produce growth in wealth over the long run in the large portion of the economy exposed to world trade. For example, the U.S. radio and television receivers industry showed a productivity improvement of 6.9 percent per year between 1959 and 1976, well above the 2.7 percent average for all manufacturing during that period. Yet, U.S. radio and television manufacturers were liquidating their position because foreign competitors were improving far more rapidly during the same period. By contrast, the U.S. aircraft industry improved productivity by only 1.8 percent per year during the same period, yet the industry remained a successful, competitive exporter.

A more accurate definition of productivity, one that reflects changes in living standards, would measure real cost reductions for comparable quality goods or real quality improvements for comparably priced goods. It would also measure improvements relative to international competitors for specific businesses.

The common explanations of our productivity problem also suffer from an overemphasis on aggregate levels of inputs. Actually, aggregate levels of inputs—labor, capital, research and development, and government expenditure—reveal little, particularly about competitive productivity. Competitive position turns more on how these inputs are utilized. The root cause of the United States' decline has been its failure to utilize its resources correctly, based on a clear understanding of the mechanisms of competition as they work in different types of businesses. In short, the failure has at least as much to do with the pattern of investment as with the aggregate level of investment.

The implications of this explanation are similar to lessons the United States has learned in its military and social ventures. The amount of resources committed to a project does not determine success. The strategies pursued, the effectiveness of the organization, and the allocation of the resources are determinative. Levels of inputs are important, but it is the way they are committed that is crucial.

Subsequent sections of this book will use a different definition of competitive productivity, one that is more closely tied to living-standard improvements than traditional government measurements. The book will also focus on strategies for using labor and capital, not simply on the appropriate aggregate levels of these inputs.

FOOTNOTES

[1] Denison, Edward F., *Accounting for Slower Economic Growth: The United States in the 1970s* (Brookings Institution), 1979, provides a thorough list.

[2] Client study for U.S. manufacturing industry that included an assessment of the effects of increased safety regulations over five years.

[3] Packer, Arnold H. and Brusnahan, Brian P. "The Productivity Puzzle, or The Hounds That Didn't Bark," November 1979, unpublished, p. 12.

[4] Ibid, p. 13.

[5] Sometimes, in order to take advantage of public pollution-control low-interest or tax-free loans, investments not directly related to pollution control are lumped together with those that are related to pollution control in classified company data.

[6] Samuelson, Robert J. "Investment Imagery," *National Journal*, 3/28/81, p. 538.

[7] Denison. *Accounting*, pp. 69–71; Griliches, Zvi. "Productivity: Background Notes," March 1980, unpublished, p. 12.

[8] Denison. *Accounting*, pp. 128–129.

[9] Ibid, pp. 130–133.

[10] Ibid.

[11] Tatum, John A. "The Productivity Problem," (Federal Reserve Bank of St. Louis) September 1979, pp. 6–7; Siegel, Robin. "Why Has Productivity Slowed Down?" (Data Resources Review) March 1979; Bennett, Paul.

"American Productivity Growth: Perspectives on the Slowdown," (Federal Reserve Bank of New York, Quarterly Review) Autumn 1979, p. 29; Kopcke, Richard W. "Potential Growth, Productivity, and Capital Accumulation," (New England Economic Review) May/June 1980, pp. 22–36. The following chart shows the type of comparison normally made.

Annual Growth Rates of U.S. Capital and Labor
Inputs to Production Between Cycle Peaks

(Percent Per Year)

	Capital	Labor Hours	Capital/Labor Rates
1948–53	4.59 %	0.36%	4.21%
1953–57	4.15	0.10	4.05
1957–60	2.68	−0.21	2.91
1960–69	4.65	1.32	3.29
1969–73	3.71	1.18	2.50
1973–78	2.69	1.35	1.32

Source: Bureau of Labor Statistics, quoted in Zell, *Productivity in the U.S. Economy: Trends and Implications* (Economic Review, Federal Reserve Bank of Kansas City) November 1979.

[12] If a U.S. power generation equipment manufacturer invests in assembly facilities in Brazil in order to help secure business that will allow it to expand production in the U.S., this investment is not included as U.S. capital investment. On the other hand, investment by a Japanese television producer in assembly facilities in the U.S. would be counted as U.S. capital investment, even though it reduces U.S. participation in some components businesses and may reduce current U.S. output.

[13] Methods of collection of investment data vary widely among countries and must be carefully scrutinized. For example, the U.S. has two means of collecting statistics on investment in the manufacturing sector that vary considerably (50 percent) in their estimates. The first surveys specific establishments actually performing manufacturing functions; warehouses, distribution networks, raw materials supplies, financing companies, or other investments that might be integrally connected with a company's manufacturing strategy are not included. The second method classifies companies by their major activity. If the company is primarily a manufacturing company, all investments it makes are included, regardless of whether it has invested in real estate or some other unrelated area. The results from both methods are as follows on page 58.

Methods of data collection in other countries are similar in theory; in practice, they occasionally combine company and establishment data.

Prior to 1980, had one looked at the statistics published by the Organization of Economic Cooperation and Development to compare investment rates in manufacturing, one would have found that the U.S. had considerably

	Plant and Equipment Expenses in Manufacturing by Company Percent GNP	Plant and Equipment Expenses in Manufacturing by Establishment Percent GNP
1975	15.6%	8.9%
1976	14.8	9.7
1977	15.3	9.9
1978	15.7	9.9
1979	15.9	10.1

higher investments as a proportion of goods output than any country reporting, except Japan. But in the 1980 data, the U.S. fares much worse. Indeed, all the U.S. data for the previous 20 years have been now recast because mistakes were found in the previous methodology used by the U.S. Department of Commerce to compute the data.

New and Old Means of Reporting U.S. Investment Data to OECD

	Old Method	New Method
1970	17.3%	8.9%
1971	16.8	8.0
1972	16.5	7.9
1973	16.6	8.6
1974	17.5	9.7
1975	16.5	8.9
1976	15.6	9.7
1977	16.4	9.9

We therefore caution the reader against drawing too many significant conclusions from the data as they now stand.

[14] Mansfield, Edwin. "The Competitive Position of U.S. Technology" (paper presented at the conference on U.S. competitiveness at Harvard University, April 25–26, 1980); Klein, Burton H. "The Slowdown in Productivity Advances: A Dynamic Explanation," in *Technical Innovation for a Dynamic Economy,* MIT Press, 1979.

[15] The U.S. still employs proportionally more scientists and engineers in its work force than other countries, though it is the only country to show a decrease over the past decade.

Scientists and Engineers per 10,000
in the Labor Force

	1965	1977
France	21.0	29.9[1]
Germany	22.6	40.5
Japan	24.6	49.9
U.K.	21.4	30.6[2]
U.S.	64.1	57.4

[1]1976.
[2]1975.

Source: U.S. National Science Borad, *Science Indicators 1978*, Washington, D.C. 1979.

[16] Denison, Edward F. *Accounting for Slower Economic Growth: The United States in the 1970s* (Brookings Institution), 1979, p.

4

The Inadequacy of Current Economic Policies

The solutions to U.S. economic problems that are most often proposed today quite naturally correspond to the common diagnoses of the problem expressed in the last chapter. These proposals ultimately focus on increasing aggregate levels of investment, though they approach this goal from two different directions.

One group argues that the U.S. cannot improve its standard of living unless it first cuts its inflation rate. This group proposes that both government and individuals curtail spending and borrowing. These measures, combined with careful government control over the money supply, allegedly would slow inflation. Once inflation was under control, businesses would have greater confidence in the future and would increase their investment. Higher investment in turn would lead to greater productivity, which would improve the country's competitive position internationally, strengthen the dollar, and provide more jobs.

There is no doubt that an environment of predictable, low levels of inflation contributes to industrial confidence. The primary problem with this approach lies in the methods chosen to reduce the rate of inflation. Restrictive fiscal and monetary policies are slow to affect inflation, both because many wage contracts are now indexed to the cost of living and because many corporations can rely on retained earnings or foreign sources of capital to help them through the crunch. These restrictive measures have counterproductive side effects as well. Because they reduce overall demand, they result in excess capacity and higher unit costs of production. They thereby reduce the competitiveness and profitability of many industries, and actually fuel inflation in the short term. High interest rates also attract foreign currency into the U.S., thereby adding another spur to inflation.

Even if these efforts to lower the inflation rate were to succeed, they still depend upon the assumptions that lower inflation inevitably would result in higher investment and that greater levels of capital expenditure as a whole inevitably would improve competitive productivity. As we have pointed out, these assumptions are questionable.

Another group advocates increasing business investment by cutting government spending and taxes, particularly for individuals at the upper income levels who normally save more, and for businesses. This group also advocates reducing government regulation of industry—such as controls over pollution and safety—so that business investment can focus upon expansion and productivity improvements. Such expansion and productivity improvements allegedly would lead to lower inflation and improved competitiveness, which in turn would increase the value of the dollar and create employment.

This proposal is also premised on several questionable assumptions. First, it assumes that a reduction of government spending and taxes would necessarily lead to more savings in a form that would be available for productive investment in this country. On the average, Americans save only 5 percent of their total disposable income. Undoubtedly, wealthier individuals save a higher proportion, but certainly a large portion of their windfall from reduced taxes would be used for consumption. An additional amount might be saved and used in a manner that did not add to productive investment, for example, funds could flow into speculative investment.

Finally, like the first proposal, this one assumes that increased aggregate levels of investment would be sufficient to improve competitive productivity in our industry.

Both of these proposals would require that low- and middle-income individuals reduce their living standards in the short run in order to improve them in the long run. It would be necessary for private consumption to fall, as well as the provision of government services. In addition, both proposals—particularly the second—would be likely to reduce the equity of income distribution and the availability of public amenities such as clean air, social security, and worker safety. Such sacrifices could perhaps be endured if they were temporary and would ultimately result in greater wealth and high living standards in the long run.

Unfortunately, these proposals are unlikely to have the desired effect because they ignore the strategic aspects of the international competitive process. They posit a "black box" (private investors and industry) out of which would flow more productive processes, more competitive products, and therefore greater wealth, if only more resources were fed into it, unencumbered by government meddling.

But the economy is not a "black box" that responds simply to increases in private-sector resources. It is instead a set of institutions, both private and public, which inevitably affect each other in highly complex ways.

Within the international competitive system are companies and governments, both of which affect international competition. Since the economic decline of the United States has its roots in the failure of both business and government to utilize resources most productively, greater resources put into this system for U.S. companies might or might not result in greater wealth for the American citizen, depending upon the effective use of these resources.

Analysis of the international competitive system and optimum corporate and national industrial strategies is in its infancy. Yet it is precisely in this type of approach—melding the concepts and tools of the business strategist and the policy analyst—that solutions to U.S. economic problems must be sought. Solutions based on this type of analysis are complex and do not easily lend themselves to slogan or diatribe. The competitive process differs from one business to another, as does appropriate corporate and national strategy.

In the following chapters, the international competitive arena and the shortcomings of U.S. strategies are analyzed first at the business level and then at the government level. After this presentation of the roots of our economic problems, it will be possible to return to solutions and offer an alternate direction for long-term U.S. economic policy.

II

THE ROLE OF BUSINESS

The United States economy is organized primarily through private companies whose legitimacy rests on their ability to generate growth in the overall standard of living by efficiently harnassing human, natural, and financial resources. This is accomplished by providing more and better goods at lower real prices, employing more people in productive work at increasing real incomes, and providing satisfactory returns to those who have invested their personal resources in the future prosperity of the society. Corporations are the agents of society. As they formulate and implement decisions about how resources should be utilized, company executives, no less than elected officials, are the custodians of a society's living standard.

In theory, discipline is imposed on a corporation by the competitive marketplace. Prices cannot be set nor can surpluses be generated at will. To be successful, a company must allocate its resources efficiently to pioneer new products and improve its overall productivity. Competition can ensure greater efficiency in the use of resources, resulting in better quality and lower prices for consumers as well as increased rewards for investors and workers. Earnings can provide a feedback mechanism for judging how well the firm has made use of its resources. Long-term, sustainable growth in earnings relative to cash invested should reflect the contribution of the business to the standard of living of the society.*

When an economy is relatively isolated from world trade, competition among firms helps ensure high performance for the economy as

---

*This is true as long as increases in earnings come from productivity increases, new products, and market development rather than from companies colluding with each other, defrauding or endangering the public, or subjecting workers to economically or socially unacceptable conditions or lowering real wages.

a whole. Mismanaged companies lose business to those that are better managed. Although this can cause regional dislocations and the relative decline of one group of owners and workers, the overall wealth of the economy is increased as the more efficient replace the less efficient.

In today's world of increased international trade, however, the entire economy may be penalized by poor management. If U.S. companies lose out to their Japanese or German competitors, the world economy may become more efficient, but the U.S. economy will suffer. U.S. company executives' decisions about strategic resource allocations are therefore crucial determinants of the nation's long-term economic success.

5

Achieving Competitive Advantage

Since the competitive process is the prime mover in the achievement of productivity improvements and growth, it is extremely important to understand this process before prescribing remedies for U.S. economic ills. The competitive process differs significantly across businesses.* A disaggregation of business activities in the economy according to the key elements of the competitive process forms the basis for this understanding (Exhibit 33).

---

* One of the mistakes most often made by corporate officials, economists, and government policymakers is to confuse the definitions of "businesses" and "industries." Boeing, for example, is in the airplane "industry" and so is Cessna, but the two companies are in different businesses. Their markets are different, as are their technologies and production methods. Their cost structures differ, as do the potential barriers to new entrants. It would be extremely difficult for one to enter the other's products and markets—Boeing in the large aircraft business and Cessna in small aircraft.

The production and sales of motorcycles, on the other hand, is all one "business," although it includes both large and small products. Many manufacturing processes can be shared, distribution is performed in roughly the same manner, and technologies are similar for small and large motorcycles.

The definition of a business is extremely complex and beyond the scope of this book. The significant point is that one is on dangerous ground when one speaks of whole industries, such as steel or chemicals, in the aggregate. The basis for competitive productivity improvements varies significantly across various businesses within each of these industries. For example, the chemical industry is divided into seven industrial groups and more than 700 trade categories by the international statistical authorities. In many cases, however, none of these classification schemes captures the economically significant distinctions among various businesses in the industry.

For some businesses, such as basic petrochemicals like low-density polyethylene, raw materials procurement and manufacturing process and scale

EXHIBIT 33
Division of Business According to Key
Competitive Cost Factors

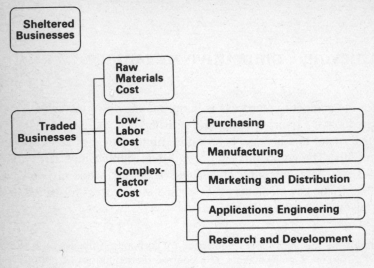

Source: Client study.

are the most important determinants of competitive cost position. For other businesses, such as formaldehyde or industrial gases, transportation costs outweigh potential scale economies, making them sheltered businesses.

Applications engineering and marketing costs play a more important role for many traded specialty chemical products. The costs associated with creating an individual formulation to solve a special problem—the applications engineering costs, for example—are the key points of competitive leverage. Examples include process chemicals to meet the varying characteristics of pulp and paper mills, specialty food additives, or nitration products for the pharmaceuticals industry. For other special chemicals, such as surfactants sold to compounders, the critical factor is the ability to serve the needs of a large fragmented group of customers who purchase in smaller volumes. An elaborate distribution network cutting selling and delivery costs is crucial for these types of businesses.

The lesson to be learned is more one of discipline of analysis than one of prescription. When considering the competitive process and how to achieve greater competitive productivity, one should be wary of superficially discussing this or that industry or subindustry. In terms of the requirements for competitive success, the nature of the product or the industry per se may be less relevant than the key elements of cost structure. For example, a

At the outset, it is crucial to distinguish between businesses that are sheltered from international trade and those that are not. As we pointed out in Part I, while absolute productivity improvements can raise living standards in purely domestic businesses, such improvements may not be sufficient in traded businesses if foreign competitors are improving their productivity at a faster rate.

SHELTERED BUSINESSES

Sheltered businesses include services such as health care, goods distribution, public transportation, and housing construction. They also include certain manufactured goods where productivity improvements achievable through increased production scale are not great enough to offset the increased costs of distributing the product to a foreign country. Manufactured goods in this category include milk and sulphuric acid, which are hard to transport, and steel beams or plastic mouldings, which are expensive to transport compared to the value of the product.

While an increase in the productivity of sheltered businesses increases national wealth, a slower increase in productivity relative to that of other countries does not necessarily jeopardize U.S. living standards. For example, if barbers in the U.S. are less productive than those in other countries, U.S. consumers may pay a higher price for haircuts than foreign consumers. But because there is no international trade in haircuts, the U.S. will not run the risk of losing many jobs in this industry or of losing its ability to import other goods that it needs.

For this reason, economic policy concerns are different for sheltered and traded businesses. For sheltered businesses, national policymakers have an interest in ensuring that the competitive process functions

chemical business such as food additives (where the selling of applications packages to meet different users' needs is crucial) might have more in common with a process control instrument business (where applications engineering is also a key to overall cost position) than it does with another chemical business such as polyethylene, where manufacturing and raw materials costs are more important.

smoothly to encourage efficiency improvements and to determine special cases where scale economies may dictate a regulated monopoly or a government-owned company as the best means to ensure the greatest efficiencies. National economic interest is not concerned with which companies succeed and fail. As long as basic rules of market competition operate, overall productivity in sheltered businesses as a whole should improve. It is also easier to control developments in these businesses since their progress depends entirely on decisions taken within the nation's borders.

TRADED BUSINESSES

Internationally traded businesses offer a different picture. U.S. success in these businesses depends not only on what companies in the U.S. do but also on what foreign competitors do. U.S. officials must better understand the competitive process in these internationally traded businesses since failure in these businesses has wide-reaching effects throughout the economy. The integration of the U.S. into the world economy has hastened dramatically over the past decade, and it is within this process that the seeds of the country's economic difficulties lie.

Generally speaking, economists attempt to explain patterns of international trade by looking at the relative abundance of productive factors—land, labor, and capital—among nations. The theory of comparative advantage hypothesizes that a country exports those goods whose production requires factors that are in relative abundance. Unfortunately, this aggregate level of analysis is too general and abstract. It does not really distinguish among the different types of cost structures characterizing the various businesses that compose an economy. Analyzing cost structures in detail is important for the business strategist since the character of these costs and how they differ among competitors largely determine the strategic options open to a firm. These distinctions—and the different types of competitive strategies that evolve from them—are also critical in evaluating government programs to promote industrial development. Promotional policies are useful only to the extent that they reinforce and complement the competitive strategies of firms within an industry.

The goal of a firm is to establish a sustainable competitive advantage over others in the same business. Usually, the essence of such a competitive advantage is having lower costs than other firms. This "competitive cost position" is the key determinant of a company's chances for long-term success in a business.

Having lower total costs than competitors can result from lower cost of raw materials, lower wages and salaries, or higher productivity. All businesses can benefit from each of these factors, but their relative importance differs from business to business. In analyzing the competitive position of the U.S. in traded businesses, it is useful to divide U.S. businesses according to their key competitive cost elements: raw materials businesses, wage-rate businesses, and complex-factor cost businesses.

Raw materials businesses depend on the physical endowments of a country. When these products are traded, competitive position is usually based on natural factors such as geology and climate. For example, Australian iron ore is of high purity and lies near the surface in very thick deposits. But Swedish iron ore is one mile underground in thinner deposits where it is mixed with considerable phosphorous impurities. It is not surprising that Australian iron ore mining is more productive than Swedish iron ore mining. Similarly, American Midwestern soil and climate are more favorable for growing grain than is the rocky, mountainous soil covering most of Japan. Again, not surprisingly, U.S. agricultural exports far exceed those of Japan. Efficient mining or farming methods or improved technology in the processing of the raw material can contribute to better competitive costs, but the basis for competitive success in these commodity businesses is a country's natural endowment.

In low wage-rate businesses,* developing countries can compete successfully because of their low labor costs, even though their pro-

---

* It is important to realize that whole industries do not become low-wage businesses. Usually, only specific products or parts of the production process become low-wage businesses. In many businesses, certain processes require highly skilled labor, while others do not. Where transport costs are low, it often makes sense to move the unskilled labor-intensive process to low-wage countries, while keeping the higher-skilled operation in a developed country. Integrated circuit assembly, for example, is a low-wage business

ductivity may be below that of developed country producers. Korean shipyards, for example, are only one-third to one-half as productive as major European yards, but their wage levels are one-eighth to one-tenth of those in Europe. As a result, Korea can construct ships at a cost competitive with that in Europe.

Complex-factor cost businesses involve products whose raw materials represent only a small part of the total product cost. The level of sophistication required for these businesses to be competitive is relatively high. Developed countries are the major participants in complex-factor cost businesses. Competitive success in these businesses depends on productivity advantages achieved through an effective strategy and organization within the firm. Relative productivity often depends upon factors such as production scale, production run lengths, distribution structure, product mix, and product or process engineering capability. Japanese companies, for example, assemble a television set in one-third the time required by their European or American competitors. This advantage is derived from such factors as product designs that incorporate fewer components; machines that automate board assembly and transfer; and designs that use only one main printed circuit board, thus avoiding the need to connect multiple boards.

Raw Materials Business

The biggest single blow to the U.S. economy in recent years has been in raw materials, particularly oil (Exhibit 34). The rapid escalation in oil prices since 1973 has directly increased U.S. imports by about $32 billion a year. Higher oil prices have also directly affected the disposable income available to the average American by causing price rises in a whole range of products, from gasoline to food and fibers. In the short run, these price rises have resulted from the actions of a cartel that restricts competition. In the long run, because U.S. petroleum resources are limited and costly to obtain, the country will inevitably have lower rates of productivity and higher cost production than

---

performed historically in Singapore, Taiwan, or Korea and more recently in Malaysia, the Philippines, and Sri Lanka. Integrated circuit design and fabrication, however, are among the most advanced processes in developed countries.

EXHIBIT 34
Deterioration of U.S. Raw Materials Trade Balance

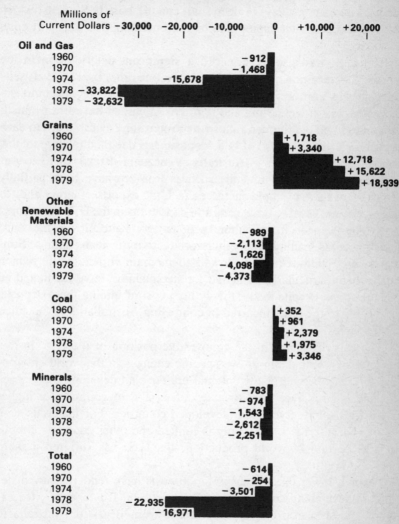

Millions of Current Dollars   −30,000   −20,000   −10,000   0   +10,000   +20,000

Oil and Gas
1960 −912
1970 −1,468
1974 −15,678
1978 −33,822
1979 −32,632

Grains
1960 +1,718
1970 +3,340
1974 +12,718
1978 +15,622
1979 +18,939

Other Renewable Materials
1960 −989
1970 −2,113
1974 −1,626
1978 −4,098
1979 −4,373

Coal
1960 +352
1970 +961
1974 +2,379
1978 +1,975
1979 +3,346

Minerals
1960 −783
1970 −974
1974 −1,543
1978 −2,612
1979 −2,251

Total
1960 −614
1970 −254
1974 −3,501
1978 −22,935
1979 −16,971

Source: U.S. Commerce Department, trade series FT 210 and FT 610 for various years.

---

[1] Other agricultural products, plus fishing and forest products.

some other countries. For example, Saudi Arabian wells, each producing a few thousand barrels a day, have significantly higher productivity than either marginally productive onshore U.S. wells (averaging 20 barrels a day) or deep shaft and offshore U.S. wells, which require much greater capital and higher operating and transport costs to exploit.

The U.S. has also experienced a significant deterioration in the competitive position of other minerals. At one time, the U.S. was self-sufficient in iron ore; over a period of years, however, the most accessable ores in Minnesota and northern Michigan have been mined. The purity and overburden ratios (the proportion of usable ore to each ton of rock to be cleared) of U.S. deposits has declined relative to new and abundant resources in Australia, Venezuela, Brazil, and Liberia. The trends in oil and minerals such as iron ore have been partially offset, however, by rapid increases in U.S. exports of grain and, to a lesser extent, coal. Climate and soil conditions in the U.S., combined with improvements in agricultural productivity, have allowed the country to develop leading competitive productivity in many grains. Similarly, the qualities of U.S. low- and medium-volatile coals, which make them particularly attractive for steelmaking, have facilitated an export boom, despite the relatively high cost of mining these deposits compared to the costs incurred in competing Australian and Canadian coal sources.

The overall change in the competitive position of the U.S. in raw materials is attributable to two specific changes in the world environment. First, the end of the colonial era enabled developing countries to gain control over their own resources and to command a higher price for their reserves from developed countries. For materials such as oil, because the U.S. supply is limited and other countries control a large portion of world production, the U.S. has suffered a sharp increase in price.

Second, lower ocean transportation costs have rendered raw materials in developing countries more competitive. It is cheaper, for example, to ship iron ore by supertanker from Brazil or Australia to Japan than it is to ship it from Minnesota to Pittsburgh. Concomitantly, the opening of previously inaccessible mining areas in Brazil, Venezuela, Zambia, central Australia, and northeastern Canada have made vast new deposits of raw materials available. As a result, extraction costs have become more important than transport costs for many resources. Countries such as the U.S., where the most accessible resources have already been depleted and the remainder have high extraction costs, are potentially less competitive.

To be sure, all other developed countries, except the U.K., Canada, and Norway, have faced the oil crisis. In addition, France, Germany, and Japan have seen a deterioration in their competitive position in coal; Sweden and Belgium have seen the same result in their iron ore industries. But, to a significant extent, these countries have been able

EXHIBIT 35
Trade Effects of OPEC Oil Price Rises and OPEC Goods Purchases, 1973–1979

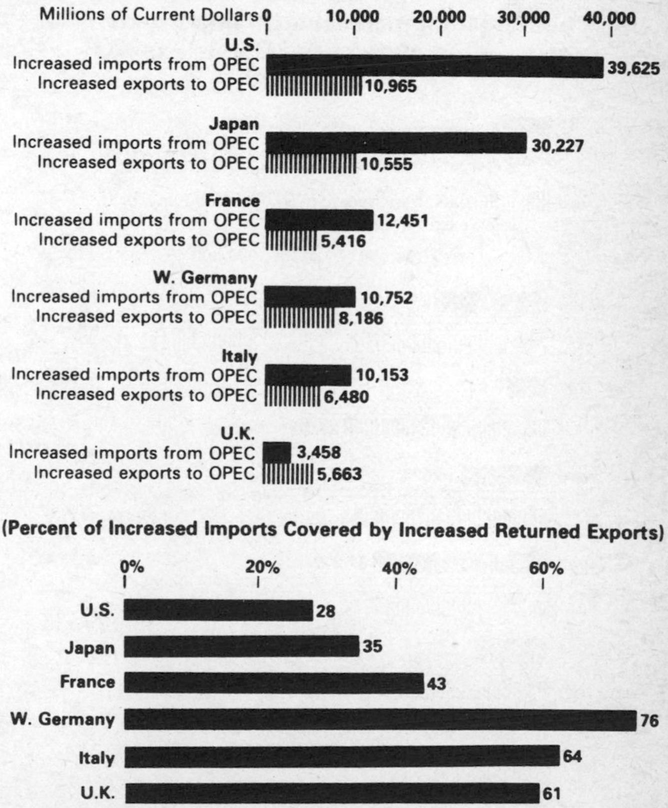

Sources: U.S. Commerce Department, trade series FT 210 and FT 610 for various years; OECD trade series B for various years.

to offset the increased price of oil by increasing their manufactured exports. Interestingly, other developed countries have been more successful than the U.S. in improving their exports to oil-producing countries and their exports of manufactured goods in general. All major developed countries have increased their exports to OPEC countries at the same time that they have had to increase oil imports. As Exhibit 35 demonstrates, the U.S. has covered only 28 percent of its increased oil bill with increased exports, while the French have covered 43 percent and the Germans 76 percent. Perhaps more significantly, major U.S. trading partners have counteracted increased oil imports by overall increases in manufactured goods exports. As Exhibit 36 indicates, the

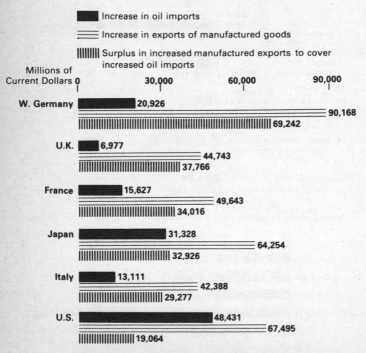

EXHIBIT 36
Counteracting Increased Oil Imports with
Increased Manufactured Goods Exports
(1973–1979)

■ Increase in oil imports

≡ Increase in exports of manufactured goods

||||||| Surplus in increased manufactured exports to cover increased oil imports

Millions of Current Dollars

	0	30,000	60,000	90,000	

W. Germany 20,926 / 90,168 / 69,242

U.K. 6,977 / 44,743 / 37,766

France 15,627 / 49,643 / 34,016

Japan 31,328 / 64,254 / 32,926

Italy 13,111 / 42,388 / 29,277

U.S. 48,431 / 67,495 / 19,064

Sources: U.S. Commerce Department, trade series FT 210 and FT 610; OECD trade series B for various years.

U.S., of all major countries, has performed most poorly by this measure. The shock given to all developed countries by the oil crisis may have been unavoidable. The fact that other industrialized countries compensated better than the U.S. is disquieting, especially at a time when U.S. currency devaluations should have been making U.S. manufactured products more competitive in world markets.

Low-Wage Businesses

Over the past 15 years, the United States has also seen a substantial increase in imports from developing countries (Exhibit 37). These imports have included a wide variety of products, such as shoes, clothing, electronic assemblies, and metal products. The increase of U.S. imports from these countries is based primarily on lower costs, which is due to their low wage rates.

However, four additional factors have contributed to rising U.S. imports. The first is the increasing free flow of world capital because of the expanded international activities of European, U.S., and Japanese banks. Developing countries have access to capital to develop a competitive position in a variety of low-wage-rate industries. A second factor leading to the emergence of developing country exports is the increasingly free flow of technology. In many product areas, technology is held by engineering or capital equipment firms that will sell it to any purchaser. A developing country can buy the world's most modern steel-rolling mills, paper machines, numerically controlled machine tools, or fertilizer plants. In addition, it can purchase training and technical supervision. A third factor that has helped developing countries is the increasing concentration of retail outlets in developed countries. The growth of large-scale retail institutions has enabled developing countries to sell their goods at a competitive price in developed country markets. A Korean monochrome television manufacturer, for example, can gain a reasonable share of the U.S. market by selling to only a dozen large American department store chains.

Finally, all these changes have been accelerated by more rapid, less expensive transportation and communication. In some small appliance businesses, for example, almost all the world's production—whether labeled Panasonic, Philips, G.E., Sony, Zenith, or unrecognizable brands—is centered in Hong Kong, Korea, Singapore, and Malaysia.

EXHIBIT 37
U.S. Imports of Manufactured Goods from Low-Wage Countries,[1] 1970–1979

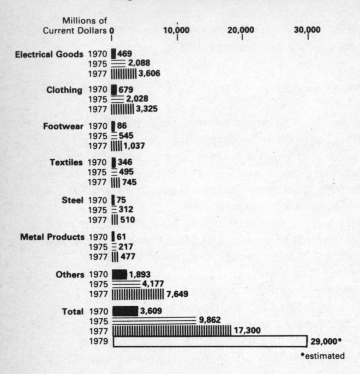

Sources: U.S. Commerce Department, trade series FT 210 and FT 610; OECD trade series C for various years.

Components and product designs are purchased from major companies; financing is arranged through Japanese, U.S., and European banks; and distribution is handled directly through large retailers such as Sears or through the established distribution channels of large Japanese or American consumer electronic companies. Lower wages in the Far East more than offset the additional freight and duty costs (Exhibit 38).

Similarly, most of the growth in world shipbuilding is occurring in shipyards located in developing countries, even though European yards

---

[1] Not including centrally planned economies.

EXHIBIT 38
Cost Comparison of Small Appliances Made in Southeast Asia and the U.S.

	Plant in Southeast Asia	Plant in U.S.
Materials	$10.53	$10.90
Labor Hours (Direct and Overhead)	2.03 hours	1.65 hours
Wage Cost	$1.20 per hour	$7.50 per hour
Total Labor Cost	$ 2.44	$12.38
Other Overheads	$ 2.18	$ 1.90
Duty	$ 1.50	
Transport	$ .50	
Delivered Cost	$17.15	$25.18

Source: Client study.

often receive large subsidies from their governments. In 1970, developing countries supplied only 2.7 percent of world shipbuilding tonnage. By 1979, they supplied 15.9 percent of all ship tonnage launched.

These changes in the world economy have enabled developing countries to move gradually toward higher value-added industries. This evolution is depicted in Exhibit 39, which represents Japan's industrial strategy and provides a paradigm for developing countries. The diamond shape represents Japan's mix of total exports among four different categories of industry, each presenting different requirements for competitive success. The bottom point of the diamond represents the percentage share of Japan's total exports in unskilled-labor-intensive industries, such as clothing, footwear, and toys. These industries require relatively little capital investment or technology. The right point represents the share of capital-intensive processing industries, such as steel and fibers. Competitive success in these industries requires a heavy capital investment and raw materials, although in most cases industry technology is relatively mature and not subject to major innovations. The left point of the diamond represents capital-intensive machine industries, such as televisions and shipbuilding. Competitive success in these industries requires a considerable investment in plant and equipment and substantial technological sophistication. The top of the diamond represents knowledge-intensive industries, such as computers, fine chemicals, and sophisticated machinery. Competitive success in these industries requires a substantial investment in research and development, applications engineering, and sophisticated marketing.

EXHIBIT 39
Evolution of Industrial Structure

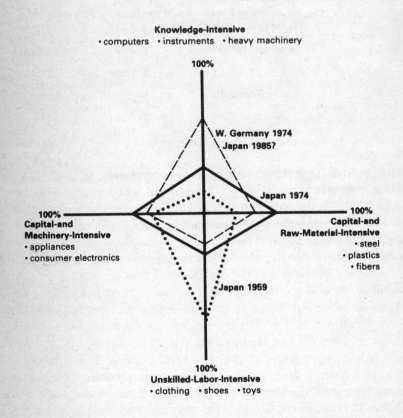

Source: Japanese Economic Planning Agency.

The shape of the diamond represents the mix of products composing Japan's total exports at a single point in time. In 1959, Japanese exports were mainly unskilled labor intensive, and the diamond was skewed toward the bottom. Throughout the 1960s, Japan's exports became more capital intensive. Industries such as steel, motorcycles, and ships increased their share of exports. By the middle 1970s, more complex products in the middle to upper areas of the diamond, such as cars and color televisions, became significant exports. By the end of the 1970s, Japan's export mix began shifting toward high-technology machines and electronic products. The Japanese Economic Planning Agency hopes that by 1985 Japan will have an export structure similar to the structure of Germany's exports of manufactured goods in the mid-1970s.

A second group of countries is now trying to follow Japan up the diamond. Korea, Hong Kong, Taiwan, Singapore, Brazil, and Spain began exporting textiles, shoes, and toys in the late 1960s. In the mid-1970s, they made competitive gains in a wide range of industries: shipbuilding, fiber, and steel. Meanwhile, shoe, textile, and electronics assembly businesses are now migrating to Malaysia, Thailand, and the Philippines, where there are even lower wage rates.

Developed countries have an interest in encouraging this evolution. As Mr. Y. Ojimi, Vice Minister of International Trade and Industry of Japan, said in a speech to the OECD industrial committee in Tokyo on June 24, 1970:

Industrialization in developing countries will stimulate competitive relations in the markets of advanced nations in products with a low degree of processing. As a result, the confrontation between free trade and protectionism will become more intense.

The solution to this problem is to be found according to economic logic, in progressively giving away industries to other countries, such as a big brother gives his outgrown clothes to his younger brother. In this way, a country's own industries become more sophisticated.

A solution of the North-South problem depends not only on internal development for developing nations but also in giving them fair opportunities in the area of trade. To do this, the advanced nations must plan for sophistication of their industrial structures and open their market for unsophisticated merchandise as well as offer [aid in the form of] funds and technology.

EXHIBIT 40
Hourly Compensation by Industry, 1979

Dollars Per Hour	U.S.	W. Germany	France	Sweden	Japan	U.K.
$14	· Iron & Steel					
	· Motor Vehicles					
$12		· Motor Vehicles · Chemicals · Iron & Steel		· Iron & Steel · Paper		
$10	· Chemicals · Machinery · Paper · Fabricated Metal	· Machinery · Fabricated Metal · Equipment · Paper · Instruments		· Motor Vehicles · Chemicals · Machinery · Equipment · Instruments · Footwear · Apparel		
$8	· Equipment · Instruments		· Iron & Steel · Chemicals · Motor Vehicles · Paper · Machinery · Equipment · Fabricated Metal · Instruments		· Iron & Steel · Chemicals · Motor Vehicles · Machinery	
$6		· Apparel · Footwear			· Paper · Fabricated Metal · Instruments · Equipment	· Iron & Steel · Motor Vehicles · Chemicals · Paper · Machinery · Fabricated Metal · Equipment · Instruments · Footwear · Apparel
$4	· Apparel · Footwear		· Footwear · Apparel		· Apparel	
$2						

Source: U.S. Department of Labor: Bureau of Labor Statistics, Office of Productivity and Technology, unpublished data, February 1980.

Unfortunately, most developed countries have taken the more expedient but shortsighted course of limiting imports from developing countries. The U.S. has maintained a series of tariffs and quotas for this purpose. It has also maintained low wages in certain industries in an attempt to remain competitive. As Exhibit 40 shows, the U.S. has a much larger wage differential between its lowest and highest wage industries than do other developed countries. Its minimum wage plus benefits in the clothing industry, for example, is only three times the rate in Korea, compared to six to eight times the Korean labor rate in the German and Swedish clothing industries.*

In the long term, it is self-defeating to remain in businesses that are becoming dominated by developing countries. As businesses migrate to low-wage countries, developed countries can remain in these businesses only if they erect costly protective tariffs and quotas, or if they keep their own wages artificially low. To some extent, the U.S. has followed both policies. But wide differentials between low- and high-wage industries can cause social unrest, because the differential tends to skew income distributions. Artificially maintained competitive positions in low-wage industries are also expensive for the U.S. consumer, who must pay a higher price for protected goods. Finally, the failure of developed countries to manage an orderly transition out of low-wage business can hinder the economic development of poorer countries whose opportunities to invest in new industry (and purchase additional capital goods from developed countries) are thereby limited.

Complex-Factor Cost Businesses

The U.S. has suffered a major decline in competitive productivity—and, therefore, in its trade balance—in complex-factor cost businesses whose competition is primarily from developed countries. Although the U.S. remains strong in certain market areas, such as industrial

---

*This does not include the many examples of subminimum wage employment being carried out in the U.S. by illegal immigrants or through homework.

84

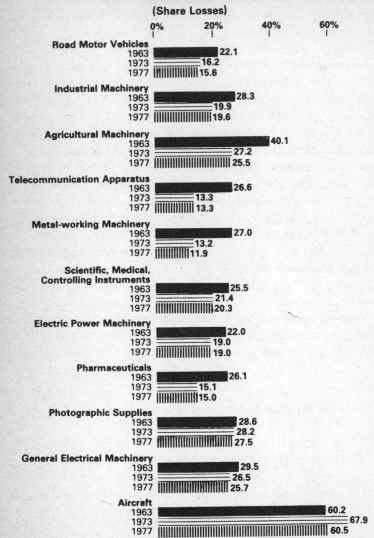

EXHIBIT 41
U.S. Export Shares in Selected Complex-Factor Cost Industries

(Share Losses)

| | 0% | 20% | 40% | 60% |

Road Motor Vehicles
1963   22.1
1973   16.2
1977   15.6

Industrial Machinery
1963   28.3
1973   19.9
1977   19.6

Agricultural Machinery
1963   40.1
1973   27.2
1977   25.5

Telecommunication Apparatus
1963   26.6
1973   13.3
1977   13.3

Metal-working Machinery
1963   27.0
1973   13.2
1977   11.9

Scientific, Medical, Controlling Instruments
1963   25.5
1973   21.4
1977   20.3

Electric Power Machinery
1963   22.0
1973   19.0
1977   19.0

Pharmaceuticals
1963   26.1
1973   15.1
1977   15.0

Photographic Supplies
1963   28.6
1973   28.2
1977   27.5

General Electrical Machinery
1963   29.5
1973   26.5
1977   25.7

Aircraft
1963   60.2
1973   67.9
1977   60.5

Source: Bowen, Harry and Pelzman, Joseph. "A Constant Market Share Analysis of U.S. Export Growth," unpublished report, 1980.

machinery and aircraft, it has serious negative trade balances in many other sectors: vehicles, steel, machine tools, and consumer electronics, to name a few. Even where the U.S. trade balance is positive, its world export share in complex-factor cost businesses is often declining (Exhibit 41). The U.S. manufactured goods trade balance with Japan and the European community, the other major producers of complex-factor goods products, is consistently negative. Ironically, it is precisely in this category of tradable goods that the U.S. economy's problem of a deteriorating competitive position could—and should—have been avoided. While the U.S. decline in raw materials businesses and low-wage developing country businesses was to a large extent inevitable, its failure to keep pace in complex-factor cost businesses is due to failures of competitive strategy.

Traded Services

Some commentators would say that this analysis is too narrow, since it does not take into consideration the U.S. balance of trade in service industries, such as insurance, banking, and consulting, plus income from investments abroad. This service balance is positive ($34.8 billion in 1979) and makes the nation's current account consistently better than its merchandise trade. Is the true comparative advantage of the U.S. moving toward service exports rather than goods exports? A decade ago, one heard this argument in Great Britain, but as events in Britain have shown, most of what constitutes a service balance is in fact dependent, in the long run, on a successful manufacturing base.

The greatest portion of the positive U.S. service balance derives from investment income of American manufacturing firms and, to a lesser extent, individuals. This income amounted to over $32 billion in 1979 (Exhibit 42). But the ratio of receipts to payments in this account has declined significantly since the mid-1960s. The U.S. received five times as much income as it paid out in 1955 and 3.6 times as much in 1965. By 1978, the ratio of investment income receipts to payments was down to 1.8 to 1. As foreign firms become stronger relative to their American counterparts in merchandise businesses, this trend is likely to continue.

EXHIBIT 42
U.S. Service Balance, 1979

	Billions of Dollars
Investment Income	32,314
Fees and Royalties	5,661
Net Military Transactions	(1,181)
Net Travel and Transportation	(2,743)
Other Services	729
Total Service Balance	34,780

Source: U.S. Commerce Department, Bureau of Economic Analysis, *Survey of Current Business,* March 1980, p. 50.

A second major component of the service balance is fees and royalties paid from subsidiaries abroad. This balance also has deteriorated rapidly as American merchandise firms have lost their competitive strength. The third component includes service exports such as banking, insurance, and consulting services of various sorts. These services are also directly linked to the merchandise base of the country, and will surely decline over the long term as the merchandise balance declines. For example, German, Japanese, and Middle Eastern banks have supplanted British banks as their economies have become relatively stronger. Similarly, expertise in engineering services derives from firsthand experience in building plants. If a greater proportion of plants are being constructed in other countries or are being built with equipment from other countries, competitive engineering firms will quickly develop in these countries. Accordingly, if American merchandise businesses do not fare better in the 1980s, a declining service balance is sure to follow.

SUMMARY: THE U.S. COMPETITIVE POSITION IN TRADED BUSINESSES

The U.S. has experienced its most serious decline in trade balance in the raw materials businesses mainly because of oil price increases. Much attention has been focused on this issue and on proposed means of achieving energy independence to reduce the import bill. More ominous and less well understood is the problem of declining competitiveness in the rest of U.S. industry. Despite a sharp drop in the U.S. currency level, and a series of artificial barriers to imports, the U.S. has seen an increase in imports from developing countries and a deterioration of world market shares and trade position in complex-factor cost businesses. Other industrialized countries have compensated for their oil imports far more successfully than has the U.S. by increasing their competitiveness in complex-factor cost goods. They have been able to continue to improve their living standards at a better pace than has the United States.

The U.S. will continue to experience competitive challenges from abroad. Its competitive position in low-wage businesses will not improve. Competitiveness in these businesses depends on a low living standard. In raw materials businesses, the U.S. can develop its agricultural and coal resources further and may expect improved prospects in these businesses, though in other businesses its competitive position may continue to deteriorate as deposits are depleted. Raw materials exports constitute only 25 percent of U.S. total exports. While expanding production and productivity will be useful, they alone cannot provide the living standard improvements the U.S. seeks.

Thus, the greatest threat to the U.S. living standard and the greatest opportunities for living-standard improvement will come in the complex-factor cost businesses. These constitute almost 75 percent of current exports. The danger is that other countries will continue to improve their competitive productivity in a wide variety of businesses, many of which have been dominated by the U.S. in the past. This will jeopardize U.S. exports and leave the country exposed to an increasing wave of job-endangering imports. But this is not an unavoidable fate. The U.S. can substantially expand these businesses and improve their productivity. Along with some of the nation's raw material endowments, these complex-factor cost businesses hold the greatest promise for improving U.S. living standards.

In the following two chapters, we discuss the basic principles of successful competition in complex factor cost businesses.

6

Establishing A Leading Position

Competitive success in complex-factor cost businesses depends on the particular economics of a given business and on the characteristics and growth rates of different parts of the market. Competition is complex because of the many factors that must be considered in order to gain strategic advantage over competitors: manufacturing, marketing, design, pricing, and distribution investments.

Nevertheless, there are guidelines to competitive success, as well as techniques to analyze the series of dynamic interactions that constitute the international competitive marketplace. Through a combination of experience and analysis, managers can develop an understanding of the nature of competition in the markets they serve and devise corporate strategies to improve the competitive position of the firm. Government officials who hope to address the key economic issue facing the country—the long-term decline in U.S. competitive productivity—must understand the elements of successful strategic planning for the firm and appreciate how these strategies must change as conditions in the world economy shift.

It is a basic fact of business economics that costs usually differ among competitors. At any time within a given business segment, there are typically several competitors who have different costs of production and distribution, although their products may be very similar. The fact that their costs differ for performing essentially the same activities is understandable and has been explained by the "experience curve."[1] That is, costs differ among competitors, and for a single competitor between points in time, because in many businesses the costs of producing a unit of product decline with accumulated experience. A corollary is that the larger a company's share of a business, the faster it can accumulate experience relative to its competitors.

Thus, its costs can decline faster, leading to a superior competitive position. If market-share leadership is sustained, that cost advantage can be maintained. Because of this, there is a linkage between the two key goals of growth and productivity improvement.

The advantages to obtaining a lower cost position relative to others in a business are obvious. If two competitors sell a product at the same price, the lower-cost competitor is clearly able to earn a greater return on the product than a competitor whose costs are higher. If this higher return is reinvested in the business, it can enable a low-cost competitor to grow faster than others, thereby continuing to accumulate additional volume and realizing further cost reductions relative to others. The higher return can also enable the low-cost competitor to expand into new business areas.

A low-cost position can also allow a competitor to sell at a lower price than others when necessary, while still remaining at least as profitable as they are. A low-cost competitor is therefore better able to withstand cyclical downturns in the market than are higher-cost producers.

To be sure, high market share only provides the opportunity for attaining a low-cost position. It does not guarantee it. Unless appropriate investments are made to take advantage of the possibilities for rationalization that the increased volume affords, a dominant market position may not yield further advantages in cost. U.S. Steel, for example, lost its position of cost leadership, despite being the largest basic steel producer in the world, because of its failure to invest properly to take advantage of its large size. Others did invest wisely, and eventually overtook U.S. Steel's leading position.

A company's competitive success in a business, therefore, does not depend on improvements in its absolute levels of cost. Rather, success is a function of the company's ability to improve its cost relative to others, and to maintain the advantage once it is achieved. In this sense, competitive cost advantage is similar to the leading position in a race. It is not enough to gain the lead and stop, since others may still be in the running. The leader must continually work to maintain the lead. Moreover, it is the total cost that is relevant, not merely factor costs. Costs of raw materials, manufacturing value added, research and development, transportation, distribution, and service must all be considered. A geographically distant competitor, for example, may still be the low-cost supplier of a product if its higher transportation costs can be offset by economies realized from a larger scale, highly automated manufacturing process.

To achieve a low total-cost position, a producer need not be the lowest-cost competitor in every element of the cost structure of a product. Nor must the producer be the lowest-cost competitor in the largest elements of the cost structure, since it may not always be possible to attain significant cost differences in these areas. Instead, the most critical areas of cost are those that offer possibilities of competitive leverage—opportunities for gaining large cost advantages relative to competitors. For example, in certain segments of the plastics conversion business, all competitors can readily achieve equivalent materials and manufacturing costs, which together represent more than 80 percent of the product cost. But cost advantages can be gained by one competitor over another in warehousing and distribution. Since these costs account for a relatively small percentage of the total product cost, they are easily overlooked as areas in which competitive advantages might be gained.

There are five main ways in which cost advantage can be gained in complex-factor cost businesses, classified according to that part of their cost structure in which opportunities for competitive leverage are greatest.[2]

PURCHASING

In some businesses, the cost of materials offers an opportunity for competitive leverage. In these cases, a competitor's total purchasing volume becomes important, since unit-price reductions are often offered to large-volume customers. A supplier may offer these discounts because it is cheaper for the supplier to deal with a few large customers than with several small ones, which together purchase the same total amount of goods. This is due to manufacturing economies of scale or lower total marketing costs.

For example, one European company has a world market share of approximately 50 percent in a certain heat exchanger business. In this business, materials account for more than 60 percent of total product cost. Because of its large size, this company is the only competitor in the world in this segment that is able to secure significant price discounts in titanium, the key raw material. It thereby enjoys a considerable competitive cost advantage worldwide.

MANUFACTURING

There are many businesses in which manufacturing costs are the key area in which competitive advantage may be gained. Depending on the specific characteristics of these types of businesses, advantages may be realized from scale, yield, run length, or proprietary technology.

Overall plant scale can be a source of competitive advantage in some businesses because of the savings it allows in direct labor and manufacturing overheads. For example, the production of ethylene oxide is a continuous process; therefore, the unit cost of manufacturing decreases directly as the size of the plant increases. This stems from the fact that it does not require twice as many personnel to operate a plant capable of producing twice as much of the product. Rather, only a few extra people are required to run a plant capable of producing more, thereby lowering the labor content per unit produced. Thus, a producer with a plant capacity of 150,000 tons realizes direct labor cost savings in the vicinity of 30 percent over a competitor with a capacity of only 75,000 tons.

Machine scale, as opposed to total plant scale, can have a similar effect in other businesses. For example, in various parts of the paper industry, wider and faster machines yield more paper per unit of labor and energy than do more standard machines. The fixed cost of a machine making Kraft liner paper can be $50 less per ton for a 300,000-ton machine than for a 150,000-ton machine.

Producers can also gain manufacturing cost advantage from superior raw materials yields. For example, although U.S. steel producers have access to lower-cost coking coal (and therefore a possible materials cost advantage), Japanese steelmakers require 20 percent less coke per ton of pig iron produced because of greater blast furnace efficiency and better coal-blending techniques. Their technology gives the Japanese an overall production cost advantage.

In some businesses, run length can be a critical determinant of manufacturing cost advantage. This is especially true if the time to set up the production machinery is very long. The lot size, or "run length," of the product therefore becomes important; a longer run length allows costs incurred in the set-up phase to be spread over more units. Ball bearings produced in run lengths of 500,000 may have labor productivity that is 20 percent higher than bearings produced in run lengths of 50,000. Besides lower set-up costs, longer run lengths can lower manufacturing costs in less direct ways, such as reducing the costs of quality control and generating a higher yield because of more uniform production. A longer run length can also facilitate more efficient materials flow, require less complex supervision, and result in less unused production time—all of which result in lower unit costs of production and a consequent competitive advantage relative to other producers.

Finally, manufacturing cost advantage can be gained in some businesses through development of proprietary process technology. For example, one U.S. producer has lower costs of production of low-density polyethylene because of its investment in a proprietary low-pressure process to produce the resin. This process incurs less operating costs than does the traditional one, especially with regard to energy. As a result, the company enjoys an overall cost advantage in this business segment.

MARKETING AND DISTRIBUTION

A third way in which cost advantages can be gained is in the marketing and distribution areas. Typically, this occurs when there is a fragmented customer base, in which many small customers have significant requirements for information, after-sales service, and/or spare parts.

In these cases, a low cost position can be achieved by obtaining a high share of sales in a given geographic region. Share of sales within a region, rather than total world market share, is significant for two reasons: (1) economies of scale can be realized at the dealer level in the selling function; and (2) after-sales services to customers can be provided at lower unit cost.

A high share of regional sales enables a dealer or distributor (whether a subsidiary of a manufacturer or independent) to incur lower operating costs per unit sold than low-share competitors in the region. This stems from higher sales by each salesperson and the ability to spread advertising and marketing costs over a larger number of units.

In addition, a higher share of regional sales can facilitate higher inventory turnover for a dealer, thereby lowering the dealer's working capital requirements per unit sold. "Inventory turn," measured by dividing total annual sales by the average size of the inventory on hand at any given time during the year, refers to the number of times in a year that a dealer can empty a warehouse by selling the product. The higher the number of inventory turns, the lower the cost of keeping inventory on hand between sales. A higher inventory turn can therefore reduce unit costs.

A high share of regional sales can also reduce a dealer's service costs per unit sold. A high share of regional sales enables a dealer to open more service depots. With more depots in a given region, service people travel shorter distances to make each call. Shorter travel distance per service call permits the distributor to provide repairs or maintenance at lower cost; this can be passed on as a lower service price to the customer. At the same time, the customer has use of the product for a much higher proportion of the time.

This savings in selling and service costs per unit sold can be a source of competitive advantage to a producer. Lower costs can enable the producer to earn a return equal to that of smaller competitors while charging a lower price. This, in turn, may help the producer increase market share in a region, which again can help to further the competitive cost advantage by allowing the producer to open more service depots, reduce service costs, realize selling economies, and therefore reduce prices. A virtual cycle of cost reductions may ensue, to the continued advantage of the low-cost producer.

Marketing and distribution scale can affect overall profitability in another way. As a company's share of the local market increases, so does the number of machines relying on the company's distribution system for service and spare parts. Service and parts may make up a key portion of both the manufacturer's and the dealer's sales and profits—20 to 40 percent of total sales for the manufacturer and 40 to 60 percent of total profits. The dealer's service and parts business is an important marketing tool for replacement sales, as well as a profitable business in itself.

APPLICATIONS ENGINEERING

Another means of gaining cost advantage in complex-factor cost businesses is through "applications engineering." Applications engineering costs are those incurred in tailoring basic equipment or software to the specific requirements of a customer. These costs are not generally classified as such in a company's accounting system but rather are mixed in with general marketing, selling, and engineering expenses.

In businesses where these costs are the key to competitive success, high market share per application provides the opportunity to gain competitive advantage. There are two steps necessary to improve one's cost position. First, it is necessary to correctly identify and focus on specific end-use applications that require customized products or systems and sophisticated selling processes. For example, one "application" in the materials handling business is the computerization of conveying systems for car assembly, as opposed to general all-purpose conveyor systems; another "application" might be a chemical cleaning formulation for an industrial machine that is different from that required by other machines.

Having identified a particular application, the second step in building a low-cost position is to standardize modules of the product or system. Through standardizing modules, the engineering time needed for developing an individual system can be dramatically reduced at both the design and the selling stage. Standardization may take place in software packages, blueprints, chemical formulations, or pieces of hardware, depending on the precise nature of the particular business.

Parts of the telecommunication switching business offer a good example of applications engineering. In this industry, each installation requires a sophisticated software system. One successful competitor has been able to lower its overall cost of installing a site by developing standardized software modules for use in succeeding installations, thus lowering software costs per installation. Since software represents 60 percent of a total systems cost, the savings, and competitive cost advantage, are significant.

Applications engineering is also an important source of competitive advantage in sales of dairy plants. For example, a European company has been able to achieve substantial engineering cost advantages over an American competitor by gaining more orders (15 per year versus 4 for the American company) and by standardizing hardware. Its engineering costs per installation are only 40 percent of those of the American competitor because of the experience gained.

Applications engineering has become increasingly important as the technology of products has become more complex. The introduction of computer and microelectronic technologies into many businesses has increased the integration potential of products and customer needs and lowered the costs of customization. This development has created a proliferation of applications-based businesses in industries as diverse as chemicals, office equipment, and industrial machinery.

RESEARCH AND DEVELOPMENT

Innovation alone seldom provides a basis for long-term competitive advantage. While often necessary, it is rarely sufficient to gain and maintain cost leadership. If innovation is to contribute to a sustainable competitive position, it is usually accompanied by cost advantages in marketing, distribution, manufacturing, purchasing, or application engineering. In a business where the pace of technological change is relatively slow, a leader can often maintain a market share lead, even while lagging behind in product development, by duplicating the innovations of smaller competitors. In many businesses, the technical leader in product development is not the most successful company.

In some businesses, however, research and development can constitute the key area of competitive leverage. These include businesses in which designs cannot quickly be copied because of technological complexity, as well as businesses characterized by a small total market for the product, a high purchase price, and low purchasing frequency. Customers in such businesses choose a particular product on the basis of its performance and cost of operation, and only secondarily on its purchase price. The competitor whose R&D produces a machine with the best performance-for-value will capture the greatest share of the market; a competitor with a poorer performing product cannot enlarge its market share simply by lowering its price. Examples of businesses where the R&D is a key cost include jet aircraft, steel-rolling mills, and paper machines.

In these businesses, because it usually takes a long time to carry a product through from design to commercial production, competitors find it difficult to merely copy another's design. In addition, because the total market is small and customers are large and scattered, businesses of this type cannot easily take advantage of lower manufacturing or distribution-scale costs. Rather, cost advantages stem from a competitor's ability to capture a large share of the market for a product generation, since a large relative volume enables the producer to spread the R&D costs over a larger base, thereby lowering unit costs and maximizing return. This, in turn, enables the producer to fund the next product generation sooner than others are able to fund theirs.

PRICE PREMIUM

In addition to cost advantages, in certain businesses it is possible to attain a sustainable price premium over competitors. This can occur through better quality or performance in products, better after-sales service and strong distributor coverage, or through the creation of a brand franchise.

Product design leadership can sometimes result in products that are more reliable or that perform better than those offered by competitors, or that have special features. On occasion, though not always, consumers are prepared to pay a price premium for this extra quality or performance. In these cases, if the price premium exceeds the costs of implementing the extra quality or performance, then a strategic competitive advantage can be gained.

Sometimes consumers are willing to pay a price premium if the distribution network is more convenient or the after-sales service is more reliable. Rather than travel to the larger city 50 miles away, they will pay extra to buy in their own town. Also, rather than rely on a distant service depot, they would prefer to pay a premium and have service more easily available. A company that has invested to establish a more widespread distribution or service support network may therefore be able to command a price premium. Again, the price premium is a strategic competitive advantage only when it more than offsets the extra costs of establishing the more elaborate distribution network.

Companies can also sustain a price premium by outspending competitors in advertising or promotion schemes or by gaining wider "shelf space" access than competitors in retail outlets. Customers may seek out and pay more for the brand name. Again, this is a strategic advantage only when the price premium exceeds the extra costs of the promotional activity.

The extra return from price premiums can be put to the same strategic use as that obtained from being the low-cost producer in a business—reinvestment to sustain leadership.

FOOTNOTES

[1] The concept was pioneered by The Boston Consulting Group. A more complete explanation of "experience curve effects" can be found in the *Perspectives* pamphlet series published by The Group.

[2] A more detailed description can be found in Magaziner, *et al.,* "A Framework for Swedish Industrial Policy," Liberforelag, Stockholm, 1979. Early work on this framework is partially attributable to work initially done by David Hall, Tom Hout, Eric Vogt, and Eileen Rudden on this study.

7

Maintaining the Lead

Once a competitor has successfully established a leading cost or price position, it must ensure that its advantage can be sustained over time. As discussed earlier, a low-cost position is similar to the leading position in a race. It can be lost to other, more aggressive competitors unless continuing efforts are made to defend and increase the lead.

INVESTMENT BARRIERS

Low-cost advantages are maintained and defended through investment "barriers." They serve not only to defend one's own leading position from existing competitors but can also discourage potential competitors from entering the business. The barriers that are required to maintain a cost or price advantage in complex-factor cost businesses vary according to the cost characteristics of the business. Generally speaking, there are five types of investment barriers: skilled labor, proprietary technology, sophisticated selling, marketing and distribution, and manufacturing scale.

Skilled Labor

In some complex-factor cost businesses, skilled labor can provide a barrier against competition from low-wage-country producers. This is because developing countries may find it difficult to establish a skilled labor force in relatively short periods of time.

It is commonly believed that the best way for a developed country to defend itself against low-wage competition from developing countries is to substitute physical capital for labor in production. But this is not the case. Sophisticated machinery can migrate to low-wage countries more easily than sophisticated workers. In the manufacture of ball bearings, for example, a fully automated plant requires only 30 percent fewer workers than a standard plant of the same size; low-wage labor can still be a determining factor in competitive cost position. This is true in many other industries as well. In fact, some of the most automated clothing plants in the world can be found in low-wage areas, such as Hong Kong.

Number of Workers Required
To Make Ball Bearings

	Standard Plant	Automated Plant
Operators	204	137
Set-up Operators	76	59
Maintenance	20	59
Transport	20	10
Control	40	23
Total	360	288

Source: Client study.

The best defense against low-wage competition is often a manufacturing process that requires a skilled labor force. In the precision castings industry, for example, highly skilled labor is required in the dyemaking, toolmaking, forming, finishing, and correcting stages of the production process. Because the highly skilled jobs must be performed in the same place as the rest of the production, and because they involve a significant percentage of the total labor required to

Functions of Precision
Casting Production Labor

	Number of Employees	Nature of Task
Dyemaking and Tooling	21	Highly Skilled
Forming and Attaching Wax Pieces to Trees	70	—
Finishing and Correcting Forms	96	Judgment and Experience Required
Other Production Labor	200	—

Source: Client study.

produce precision castings, the whole production process is protected against low-wage competition.

Mass production has reduced skill requirements in many industries. The development of numerical computer control has accelerated this process. Significant business segments remain, however, where short run length, special production, and complex testing, maintenance, or process engineering require skills available only in a developed country. These skills typically can only be acquired over a period of time in the work environment itself. Conditions in many newly industrializing countries do not permit this sort of learning.

Machining operations, for example, usually provide significant opportunities for erecting a skilled labor barrier. Generally, products that are highly standardized and have long run lengths tend to be robotized. Products of medium run length with a limited number of varieties tend to rely on programmed, numerically controlled machine tools. Both processes require only low-skilled production labor. But products with short run lengths, in which each small batch requires different machining steps, may depend upon manual-control, high-precision machine tools. These tools require highly skilled operators.

A skill-level barrier against low-wage competition also can exist in assembly functions where calibration, testing, and repair are likely to be necessary. This is frequently the case where the product is costly and requires fine mechanical adjustments. For example, the calibration of a separator bowl for the dairy industry requires high-skilled labor. By contrast, in circuit board assembly, a simple semiconductor can be thrown away if it does not work. Similarly, the assembly of a process-control device may require fine mechanical adjustments, whereas the production of a pocket calculator merely involves the assembly of components, which can be discarded and replaced if defective.

Finally, maintenance and process-engineering functions can create a skill-level barrier against low-wage competition. This is the case where complex, delicate equipment is needed, or when tools must frequently be changed by a skilled operator.

Thus, where skills can be acquired only over a long period of time in the work environment itself, competitors have a skill-level barrier against competition. Although this barrier may not prevent a developed country competitor from entering a business successfully against an established competitor, it can effectively prevent entry of low-wage competitors from newly industrializing countries.

Proprietary Technology

In businesses with rapidly advancing technology, a company that invests in proprietary technology for its product or its production process often achieves a defensible position. Proprietary technology is a barrier since it is proprietary, and thus not available to anyone except its developer. Proprietary technology can also be a source of cash. If a company continues to invest in order to maintain its competitive lead, it will be able to license its old technology as it develops new generations. The revenue from licensing can be used to invest in newer technology. Thus, competitors can be forced to fund the maintenance of a company's competitive technological lead over them, and will remain behind in innovation and cost position.

Nonproprietary technology can be purchased by all competitors, hence yielding specific advantages to none. For example, in order to compete in many commodity chemicals businesses, it is only necessary to purchase a plant designed by Fluor, Kellogg, or another international engineering firm. The fact that a chemical producer may have been in the business 20 years or more will not yield significant economic advantages in engineering, since the key advances are made by the engineering company and are generally available to competitors. These plants can be bought by competitors from developing as well as developed countries.

Sophisticated Selling

Some businesses require a high degree of technical selling and modification of the product to a customers's specific needs. In these businesses, long-term relations and customer confidence in the technical competence of the sales force are critical. It is difficult for a newcomer to become competitive with a company that has been in the business a long time and has gained experience and developed good customer relations. Significant investments through price reductions or special introductory offers are necessary for the newcomer to gain market access.

Businesses that require sophisticated selling include process-control instruments, certain special grades of steel bar, and specialized chemical formulations.

Marketing and Distribution

This barrier exists either where a complex distribution structure for the product is required or where brand image can be established. In businesses where the customer base is comprised of small concerns or where the number of product variations needed to serve them is high, a competitor must invest in an elaborate distribution system capable of efficiently handling many customers and much inventory. Once a competitor has a strong system in place that is capable of meeting these requirements, it is difficult and expensive for a newcomer to duplicate it. A similar marketing barrier occurs when a competitor can build a brand awareness with consumers through advertising or command of retailers' shelf space. The investment in advertising, promotion, or price cutting required to overcome such a leading position can be prohibitive.

Manufacturing Scale

The fifth type of barrier that can exist in complex-factor cost businesses, and one that can be used by a low-cost competitor to maintain its advantage against others, occurs in businesses where manufacturing scale or run length provides cost leadership. It also occurs in businesses where one competitor has a significant share of world volume and can thus supply a high proportion of total world demand from a small number of plants. When these factors converge, no newcomer can build a competitive plant profitably.

BUSINESS EVOLUTION

Categories of investment barriers are not hard and fast. They interact with one another and change over time. For example, the successful exploitation of a cost advantage can establish an investment barrier against advances by other competitors. In a business where marketing and distribution are key cost factors and a company invests heavily in a distribution network designed to sell and service a broad customer base efficiently, the company may increase its regional market share and eventually realize a significant cost advantage over competitors.

At the same time, the very existence of a company's strong distribution network may discourage other competitors from making the large investment necessary to challenge it.

Moreover, individual businesses often show more than one of the cost advantages and barriers discussed above. For example, successful competition in the automobile business may be based on manufacturing scale advantages in key components (engines, transmissions), research and development technology (new model design), and distribution (sales, service, spare parts).

The basis for cost advantage and defensible barriers for a given business evolve over time. A currently reasonable strategy may become obsolete later on. Failure to recognize changes as they occur can virtually ensure the loss of one's competitive position to other, more perceptive competitors. It is this evolution that also offers opportunity for a new entrant or a high-cost competitor to overtake the industry leader.

The cost advantage and investment barriers that constituted a business yesterday may no longer do so today, as technology, customer requirements, and tastes change. For example, historically, businesses in the office equipment industry have been defined by individual pieces of machinery—typewriters, telex machines, and storage files; the economics of competition and the competitors themselves have differed from product to product. But as miniature electronic, computer, and telecommunications technologies evolve, office machines are being sold together as one integrated system. The software that links them is becoming more important. Potential competitors from industries completely unrelated to the traditional office equipment business are positioning themselves for possible entry into this new business. New competitive strategies must be devised by established manufacturers.

The sources of competitive advantage within a business also may evolve over time. This can alter the strategies required for success within the business. Factor costs may change (as with raw materials or energy), and new technologies may be perfected. For example, in the cement business there are three basic types of cement plant: wet process, dry process, and preheat process. Wet-process plants have always been the least efficient, in terms of the fuel consumption in their operation, but were the cheapest to construct. Because of the lower capital costs of these plants and the relatively low cost of energy in the United States before 1973, wet-process plants were favored by U.S. producers to a greater extent than elsewhere. They made up 60 percent of the total U.S. capacity, compared to less than 5 percent in West Germany. Changing energy costs then altered the cost structure of the business dramatically, rendering wet-process plants far less economical than dry- and preheat-process plants, thereby favoring foreign producers that had formerly been at a disadvantage relative to U.S. producers. The competitive position of the existing producers deteriorated, as new entrants using the more process-efficient techniques entered the business.

The telecommunications industry provides another example. Previously, electromechanical technology was used, and manufacturing costs were the key to attaining a low-cost position. When the technology changed to electronic, the basic cost structure also changed. Software costs went from 30 percent of total product cost to 60 percent, and assembly labor decreased from 40 percent of total product cost to 20 percent. The business changed from one where manufacturing costs showed the most significant competitive cost differences to one where applications engineering costs are crucial.

Investment barriers also change as the cost structures of businesses evolve. An example can be drawn from the consumer durables business. In the United States, large manufacturers typically were able to protect their positions by investing in extensive distribution networks, often in the form of subsidiary dealerships operating under the brand name of the manufacturer. These distribution networks often constituted a significant investment barrier against smaller competitors from abroad, since large investments were required to duplicate such networks and to win customers away from the entrenched dealerships.

The distribution structure of the business changed, however, as buying groups and discount stores progressively replaced small independent dealers. For one appliance product, the combined share of these high-volume channels increased from 36 percent in 1973 to 63 percent in 1979, while the independent dealers' share went from 56 percent to 27 percent. Hence, the customer base of the manufacturers became more concentrated. Foreign competitors could enter the market by selling relatively large volumes to a few large customers, thereby avoiding the necessity of maintaining an expensive distribution network of their own. The new entrants could offer lower prices to the high-volume buyers, in part because their costs of distribution were less. What had previously been a barrier in the business—the elaborate distribution structure—no longer afforded any protection against foreign competition.

SUMMARY: COMPETING IN COMPLEX-FACTOR COST BUSINESSES

Complex-factor cost businesses present the greatest challenge to managers and policymakers in developed countries. It is primarily in the success or failure of these businesses, which already represent the majority of U.S. production and exports, that the future prosperity of the United States will be won or lost. It is necessary to understand the cost structures of these businesses and how costs vary for different businesses. For each business, the key levers for corporate strategy and economic policy occur where competitive cost differences are potentially greatest and where investment barriers make these differences sustainable over time. Success also requires anticipating changes in cost structure or investment barriers and capitalizing on them.

There are no direct relationships between aggregate levels of investment and competitive success in the economy as a whole, or in broad industries such as steel, automobiles, or semiconductors. Higher levels of investment can be useful to attain better productivity only if correct strategies are followed in order to gain a competitive advantage. Otherwise, there is a double loss—more funds have been diverted from other uses, and yet competitive deterioration and the accompanying economic stagnation continue.

Over the last decade, the performance of many American companies in traded complex-factor cost businesses has been disappointing. In some cases, the methods by which U.S. firms have organized and managed their businesses have resulted in poor strategic decisions. In other cases, poor decisions have resulted from a failure of analysis. In both cases, the outcome has been a loss of competitive productivity—resulting in the loss of business opportunities and profit for the companies, and the loss of employment, foreign exchange, and income for the nation.

As the international competitive environment has changed, so too have the principles of successful business management. Certain firms are better able to adapt than others. In general, U.S. firms have not adapted to changing conditions well enough.

In the following chapters, we discuss five broad areas in which failures of U.S. management have contributed to declining international competitive positions: investment decisions, cost management, pricing policies, international strategies, and worker-management relations.

8

Investment Decisions

The investment decision is the means by which a company allocates its capital resources. The investment decision is the fundamental management decision for determining the competitive productivity and growth potential of a business. In many U.S. companies, investment decisions are not made strategically. Three failures stand out: an inadequate process for making capital appropriations decisions, a failure to define properly and recognize investment opportunities, and an overemphasis on nonproductive investments.

THE CAPITAL APPROPRIATIONS PROCESS

Many U.S. companies plan investments on a project-by-project basis through a series of appropriations requests. Levels of capital expenditure required for a proposed investment are weighed against the potential for higher profits from increased sales and/or reduced costs. A return on the investment (ROI) is calculated, and inflation is accounted for by discounting the cash flow (DCF) to be received in future years. Approval procedures usually vary according to the size of the investment request. For example, in large companies, appropriations of less than $500 thousand may be approved by a division manager, appropriations of less than $3 million by the internal management committee, and appropriations larger than this by the board of directors. Companies also have different minimum "hurdle rates" of return for judging the acceptability of a request. A real rate of return (after inflation) of 8 to 10 percent is a common minimal hurdle for accepting an investment request.

In a large corporation with many businesses, proposals that accompany appropriation requests usually document how savings or increased sales are to be achieved from the capital expenditure. Documentation includes market projections, engineering diagrams, and financial breakdowns of costs saved and future sales. Division managers, corporate executives, and boards of directors sift through these various requests and often select those with the highest projected return. (Company politics and the individual credibility of the managers making the requests also play a significant role in whether appropriation requests are accepted.)

This approval system can introduce biases that hamper strategic decisionmaking in the company. The system encourages incremental maintenance investments rather than fundamental reinvestments in the business. Investments are tailored to avoid higher approval levels and to meet acceptable hurdle rates, rather than to achieve strategic needs of the business. Projects that can show desired rates of return for relatively small levels of investment are advanced.

If the cutoff for required board submission is $3 million, it is common to see proposals for investments of $2.5 million. If the acceptable "hurdle rate" is 8 percent, it is common to see proposals with 9 percent ROIs.

Return-on-investment calculations encourage a strategy of low investment. High returns can be achieved more easily in the short run by lowering the "I," rather than by raising it with the hope of raising the "R" to an even greater extent in the future. This type of strategy promotes high returns in the short run but can jeopardize competitive business position in the long run. When inflation-discounted return measures are added, this problem can be compounded. Such measures give greatest weight to profits from the early years of an investment. Yet early returns can often jeopardize long-term returns. For example, a company that is prepared to cut prices in order to gain market share to fill a new large-scale, highly automated plant may show poor short-term returns on investment (when depreciation is included). But it is more likely to show better long-term returns than a company that makes superficial changes in its existing machinery.

Investments are often undertaken without sufficient competitive analysis. Although a company's margins depend upon its costs relative to its competitors' costs, investment analyses often assume that the competitive environment is static. Such analyses typically compare current costs to future projected costs, without considering that competitors might be investing to improve their own position at the same time. As previously discussed, competitive advantage is a leading position in a race. Investment to attain a position that a competitor already occupies is often fruitless, since the competitor can also invest and advance its position by the time the project reaches completion.

An example of this type of mistaken analysis is the following investment that was studied and then undertaken by a paper company. The project called for the company to build a 150-thousand-ton paper machine at a cost of $25 million. The new machine was assigned to replace an old 75-thousand-ton machine and add 75 thousand tons of new capacity, bringing total company capacity to 225 thousand tons.

The industry had been at full-capacity utilization for six of the previous eight years, and the company earned a return on sales of 4.9 percent. The ROI analysis by the company showed the following impressive return:

> Replacement of 75,000 tons: New Machine full production cost $268/ton, old machine $290/ton; $22 savings per ton or $1.65 million.
>
> Addition of 75,000 tons of new product; industry price of $305/ton minus cost of $268/ton gives a profit of $37/ton or $2.78 million.
>
> Total investment $25.00 million
>
> Total return $ 4.43 million
>
> ROI 17.7 percent

The problem with the investment, not visible to the company until a few years later, was that other companies with more efficient plants were also investing, so that the industry was later in serious overcapacity. In addition, the company was, and would continue to be, a relatively high-cost producer in the business. Thus, it was the first one to suffer from price cutting associated with overcapacity (Exhibit 43).

Another example is provided by Japanese and U.S. television industries. U.S. companies have followed the Japanese in reducing assembly man-hours and the number of components in their sets for six years without catching up (Exhibit 44). Industry prices have followed Japanese costs. Predicted returns from the U.S. investments have never occurred.

The alternative to this project-by-project approach to investment analysis is followed by most Japanese and many European companies. They view investment decisions not as a series of discrete projects but as aspects of the total competitive position of their entire business.

EXHIBIT 43
Competitive Dynamics in Industry

Current Competitive Situation:
Two large competitors and five small regional competitors

	Current Tonnage (000)	Current Average Cost (per ton)	% Return on Sales
Our Company	175	$290	5
Company A	150	280	8
Company B	250	275	10
5 Regionals	150	280	8
Total	725		

Current Market and Projected Growth: 715,000 tons to grow at 7%

Future Competitive Position

	Projected Tonnage 3 years hence (000)	Average Cost 3 years hence (per ton)
Our Company	225	$275
Company A	225	265
Company B	350	255
5 Regionals	200	265
Total	1,000	

Market 3 years hence: 876

Source:　Client study.

EXHIBIT 44
Productivity in Color Television Assembly and Component Usage

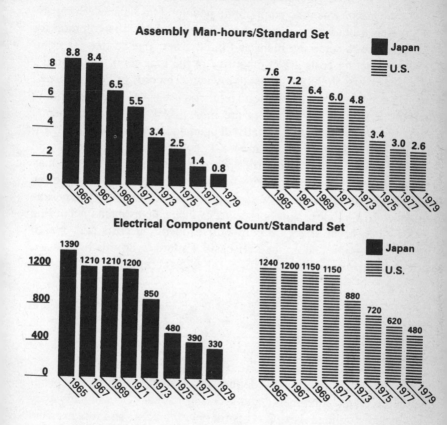

Assembly Man-hours/Standard Set

Electrical Component Count/Standard Set

Source: Client study.

They assess each investment by the extent to which it is likely to advance or retard the competitive position of the whole business. Even minor investments are evaluated for their effect on overall competitive cost position and market share for the whole business over time.

This system does not involve separate decisions on projects, each with its own ROI calculation, nor does it discriminate among projects according to the size of investment. Rather, it aims for overall competitive operating cost or product quality advantage. It assesses what is required to gain this position relative to one's competitors and thereby forces fundamental decisions about the business on a periodic basis.

For example, when the competitive position of a Japanese company is threatened because a plant is becoming obsolete, it is common for the Japanese to scrap the plant and build a new one so that the company's operating costs are competitive in the long term. By contrast, U.S. managers often take a positive view of an old, fully depreciated plant, since it contributes to a good return on net assets even if operating profits are low. U.S. managers are more likely to take incremental steps, leaving plants at a partially depreciated stage rather than committing the large sums necessary for a new competitive plant.

The hazards of the long-term approach are that more capital may be put at risk. However, in high-growth businesses where competition is fluid and the outcome uncertain, this approach is usually superior. In general, it is more appropriate to evaluate investments according to their long-term effect on competitive operating costs and overall business position than on an ROI basis. Failure to do this has caused serious competitive problems for many U.S. companies.

DEFINITION OF INVESTMENT

U.S. companies traditionally define "investment" to include expenditures for plant, equipment, and working capital. Occasionally they also include tooling, start-up costs for new facilities, and research and development. Accounting systems record all other costs as expenses to be deducted from current profits. But an "investment" is more properly viewed as any expenditure of funds associated with creating the capability for future production and sales—including all discretionary expenditures not associated with the day-to-day operations of the existing business.

Indeed, in many knowledge-intensive industries—such as those producing machinery, electronic instruments, and specialty chemicals—plant and equipment comprise only a small part of what could be properly termed investments. Marketing, applications engineering, initial price cutting to enter a new market, and the financing of a new distribution network are also investments. The failure to regard these expenses as investments can hinder strategic planning by discouraging businesses from undertaking them.

For example, a U.S. company that produces test and measurement instruments recently perceived an opportunity to integrate its measuring and display devises with a minicomputer. This new system could be programmed, according to the particular application of the end user, to process information automatically and give immediate data, which formerly would have taken days to develop. This new system did not involve any capital investment nor any significant working capital, except for a small inventory of minicomputer mainframes. But it did require applications engineers, research and development engineers, marketing personnel, and technical service representatives. Applications engineers had to develop appropriate software programs; research and development engineers had to develop modifications in the instrument package to make analog-to-digital conversions and an appropriate input-output structure. Marketing personnel had to call on customers before the product was introduced in order to explain the new product concept to them, gather customers' inputs for product designers, and do some initial promotion. And technical service representatives were required who could do appropriate debugging of the first systems put in the field. Investment was also necessary to price initial orders at a loss so that the earliest customers did not pay for the high costs associated with the development of the first systems. These "expense investments" were to be undertaken over a three- to four-year period. Accordingly, the product would not show positive profits for at least five years, despite anticipated rapid growth and market leadership.

At this time, a West German firm became a competitor. Despite a product of inferior quality, the German firm marketed it aggressively, offering lower prices and better service than the U.S. firm. After two years, the U.S. firm had 80 percent of the market, and the new German entrant had gathered 20 percent. The corporate managers of the U.S. firm, impatient for the product to make a profit, rejected their division's requests for additional price cuts to confront the German competitor and instead opted for price increases. Two years later, the German firm had 50 percent of the market, a new French competitor had 20 percent, another U.S. competitor had 10 percent, and the original company had only 20 percent. After a profitable third and fourth year, the original U.S. company had again become unprofitable.

The U.S. company failed for two reasons. It did not understand that the long-term key to success in the business was in the applications engineering effort to develop standardized applications packages for different industries. These packages could have lowered the cost of the total product to subsequent customers. By raising its price, the company retarded its growth, thus allowing the German firm to gain more experience and a higher cumulative volume of orders around which to develop standard applications packages; this eroded the U.S. firm's cost lead.

Also, the U.S. firm failed to distinguish between current expenses and expense investments. It did not perceive that on a current cost basis the business was in fact profitable, and could have become even more so as necessary expense investments became lower over time. If the investment had been in fixed assets, management's perceptions might have been different. Current profitability would not have been negative for so long. Moreover, it is conceptually easy to recognize when cumulative volume will allow larger-scale plants and greater process automation to create competitive cost advantage; it is harder to visualize when applications engineering experience will allow a standardization of software packages and a savings of the time of marketing, technical service, and engineering personnel on future orders.

Many U.S. companies have failed to understand expense investments or to plan for them when evaluating the long-term prospects of a business. Since many of the businesses that offer the U.S. growth opportunities in the future are of the knowledge-intensive type, this issue is particularly important. Even if tax-accounting conventions do not provide the ability to amortize these types of investment, internal measurements of performance must make the distinction.

NONPRODUCTIVE INVESTMENTS

The misdirected investment strategy followed by many U.S. companies also manifests itself in various asset-rearranging activities. Between 1978 and 1981, for example, over $100 billion in corporate resources were used to acquire existing corporate assets through tender offers.

Most of these mergers were conglomerate, involving unrelated assets. Many were unfriendly, involving significant stock fights. Of course, it often makes economic sense for a company to enter a new business through acquisition. However, there is little evidence to suggest that these arrangements have, on the average, increased the efficiency of merging enterprises.

There has been a rapid increase in speculative investments as well. The number of commodity futures contracts traded in 1980 was 76 million, up from 13.6 million in 1970—a 450-percent gain compared to a 174-percent increase in stock market volume during the same period. Foreign currency contracts, financial futures, and real estate add to the growing list of speculative investments. Indeed, the U.S. collectively invests more money in mortgages than in all U.S. businesses put together, the vast bulk of which goes into inflating the value of existing homes rather than into new home construction.[1] U.S. companies also invest over $10 billion a year in lawsuits among themselves.[2]

While this asset-rearranging activity does not directly use up scarce capital resources—dollars merely exchange hands among speculative players—it is indirectly wasteful. It creates vast service industries in law, accounting, tax consulting, and finance, to which some of the country's most talented and creative citizens are drawn. It also diverts the attention of U.S. corporate executives, who spend their time fending off takeovers, responding to depositions, and devising novel tax and accounting schemes rather than building better products.

By contrast, companies in Sweden, Japan, and West Germany invest a much smaller percentage of their savings in these sorts of nonproductive, asset-rearranging ventures. Unfriendly corporate takeovers are rare. Proportionately far fewer resources flow into futures contracts. There are far fewer lawsuits, lawyers, and accountants. Out of every 10,000 citizens in Japan, for example, only one is trained as a lawyer and only three are trained as accountants. In the U.S., 20 are trained to be lawyers and 40 to be accountants.[3]

SUMMARY

It is a mistake to assume that simply providing more dollars for investment will solve U.S. economic woes. Instead, many companies must revise the process by which they evaluate capital investments. If investments are to yield competitive advantage, companies must also change their definition of investment to include many income statement items. The American business system must come to grips as well with the proliferation of nonproductive speculative investments that often waste resources and direct management attention away from successfully competing in their base businesses.

FOOTNOTES

[1] A. Downs, Brookings Bulletin, October 1980.

[2] Administrative Office of the U.S. Courts; ABA Annual Membership Report, 1979; Office of Management and Budget Appendix to Budget of U.S. Government, 1979.

[3] Japan data derived from Census of Japan, 1975, vol. 5, Part I, Div. I, p. 282; U.N. Statistical Yearbook, 1977, p. 922. U.S. data from Handbook of Labor Statistics, 1978, pp. 82–4.

9

Management of Costs

Another area where U.S. management often lacks a strategic perspective is in managing costs. As has been noted, attaining and sustaining an overall cost advantage are generally the keys to competitive success. There are three significant ways in which many U.S. companies have failed to manage their costs relative to foreign competitors: managing overhead costs, undertaking process engineering, and managing quality control.

MANAGING OVERHEAD COSTS

As surprising as it may seem, many major U.S. companies do not know how much it costs them to produce and distribute most of their goods. They know the total costs of their operation but not the cost of producing one of their products relative to another, or the cost of serving one of their markets relative to another. The reason for this ignorance is the practice of allocating overhead costs both in factories and in distribution organizations.

In most businesses, a large number of different product varieties are manufactured in the same factory or sold and distributed through the same marketing and sales network. The accounting and industrial engineering efforts of most U.S. companies measure the direct labor costs of producing these products precisely: Worker's movements are measured down to seconds, and significant effort is often put into reducing these times. Similarly, much effort goes into negotiating wage contracts to the penny in order to keep direct labor costs low. Yet in most industries, overhead costs associated with manufacturing or marketing and distribution greatly exceed direct labor costs. Manufacturing overheads (or "burden" or "base costs" as they are sometimes called) are usually between 150 to 250 percent of direct labor costs in most plants. These typically include the costs of materials handling, inspection, internal transport, warehousing, setup, changeover of machines, rework, technical service, maintenance, scrap, supervision, machine downtime, and quality control. Most companies allocate these overhead costs proportionally to all products based on direct labor hours.

Similarly, marketing personnel, selling, distribution, warehousing, warranty, field service, and other marketing overheads—often larger than direct labor costs—are typically allocated on some average basis. This "average costing" of overheads can create mistaken impressions of true profitability.

Such average costing by one U.S. company allowed a European competitor in an electrical machinery business to take over a significant share of the U.S. market. Exhibit 45 shows the actual profitability of

EXHIBIT 45
Effects of Correct Reallocation of Machinery Company Overheads on Product Profitability

	Individual Machine		Custom System	
	Reported Profit in Company Accounts	Actual Profit[1]	Reported Profit in Company Accounts	Actual Profit
Price	$100	$100	$700	$700
Direct Labor	10	10	35	35
Raw Materials	35	35	130	130
Manufacturing Overheads	20	14	70	105
Marketing and Selling	20	12	140	190
Custom Engineering	—	—	150	150
Other Overhead	10	10	80	80
Profit before Interest and Tax	$5	$19	$95	$10
PBIT%	5.0	19.0	13.1	1.4

Source: Client study.

---

[1] After reallocation.

two different product lines for the U.S. competitor and the profits reported in the "allocated" cost system. The U.S. firm's cost system measured direct labor time for customizing its products and creating computer-based systems. But it did not show that, as customizing costs rise, a whole series of other overhead costs—such as extra inspection, rework, callibration, supervision, and installation—also rise. By focusing on the equipment end of the business and not participating in the customized systems, a German competitor was able to charge a lower price. The U.S. firm, believing that the customized end of the line was more profitable, gave up the equipment volume. Within the system's sales division, incentives were given to salespeople to sell the large systems, since it was assumed that they were more profitable. As Exhibit 46 shows, this was incorrect. As the degree of customization increased, marketing overheads also increased. It was only after the U.S. firm's mix of business shifted toward the supposedly more profitable customized systems, while its overall profit continued to decline, that the firm began to question its strategy and eventually its cost system.

U.S. companies in a number of industries have tended to overcost the simpler ends of their product line sold to higher-volume customers by "averaging" them with manufacturing overheads from more complex products and extra distribution costs from smaller customers. Meanwhile, Japanese competitors have focused on sales to high-volume customers at the simple end of the product line. Consequently, they have achieved lower costs than the U.S. firms. Believing that these simpler products sold to large customers were less profitable, the U.S. firms have retreated from that end of the market. Blaming low Japanese wages and unfair trade practices, U.S. managers have often spoken of ceding the low, "cheap" end of the business to the Japanese or Koreans and have focused instead on the "higher-value-added," "higher-price-realization," or "higher-quality" end of the line, assuming that the foreigners will not be able to penetrate these products.

History has shown—in such businesses as motorcycles, radios, televisions, watches, cameras, and in various segments of industrial machinery—that once they have established a foothold at the lower end of the line, Japanese competitors have often followed the retreating U.S. firms all the way through the product line.

122

EXHIBIT 46
Overhead Penalties of Product Customization

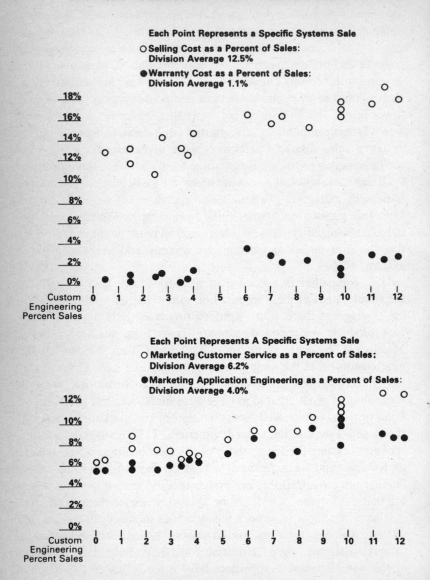

Each Point Represents a Specific Systems Sale
○ Selling Cost as a Percent of Sales:
   Division Average 12.5%
● Warranty Cost as a Percent of Sales:
   Division Average 1.1%

Custom
Engineering
Percent Sales

Each Point Represents A Specific Systems Sale
○ Marketing Customer Service as a Percent of Sales:
   Division Average 6.2%
● Marketing Application Engineering as a Percent of Sales:
   Division Average 4.0%

Custom
Engineering
Percent Sales

Source: Client study.

Exhibit 47 shows an example of this pattern. In this consumer durable, the cost of serving customers varied according to the size of the customer. The U.S. company's pricing did not reflect these differences. Japanese competitors concentrated on large customers who could be served at low cost. These customers received price discounts reflecting their lower service costs. After building a volume base, the Japanese then proceeded to take other customers away from the U.S. competitor, who became less able to compete as its volume shrank.

EXHIBIT 47
Marketing and Selling Cost as a Function of Customer Size

(Manufacturer's Cost to Serve as a Percent of Manufacturer's Sales)

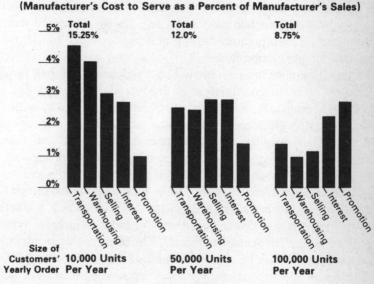

Source: Client study.

UNDERTAKING PROCESS ENGINEERING

A related problem of managing overhead costs is the lack of attention given by many U.S. companies to process engineering. When asked to compare their production costs to those of Japanese, German, or Swedish manufacturers, many U.S. managers contend that all competitors use similar machinery and buy from the same group of machinery suppliers; therefore, production-cost differences are probably minimal. This contention is often incorrect. The overall system costs for foreign competitors are often far lower, despite similar machinery, because of the important role played by process or manufacturing engineering within many foreign companies. Specifically, foreign manufacturers use more in-house design and customization of equipment, better coordination of design and process engineers, and greater care in introducing variations in the product line than do their U.S. counterparts.

In many Japanese, German, and Swedish companies, a high proportion of machinery is either designed in-house or altered or customized considerably after purchase. This allows greater adaption to the total flow of the production process, often reducing material-handling requirements or incorporating testing or scrap-recovery functions directly into the production flow.

Another difference between many U.S. companies and their foreign competitors is in the coordination of product and process design. In many U.S. companies, a tension exists between the two, with the product designers preeminent. In Germany and Japan, it is more common for product designers to coordinate at an early stage with process engineers. Product designers and process engineers work together to achieve reliable, low-cost production processes.

U.S. and foreign companies also differ with regard to the integration of marketing and manufacturing. In many U.S. companies, marketing personnel request new product variations in order to increase volume by appealing to different customer tastes. The result of this proliferation in the product line can be seen in Exhibit 48, an example of product proliferation in electric motors. As new product variations were added to the product line, manufacturing overheads increased dramatically, Japanese, German, and Swedish companies are more cautious about such marketing demands.

It is often possible to achieve considerable product variety without substantially increasing manufacturing overheads if the process is designed in advance to accomodate the variety and if the variations affect only certain parts of the process. This kind of product variety requires foresight, substantial cooperation between marketing and production functions, and a clear understanding of overhead costs. Japanese producers have been particularly adept in this area.

If U.S. companies are to achieve relative cost advantage, they must give greater attention to reducing manufacturing overheads by customizing machinery and to better coordinating process engineering with product design and marketing.

EXHIBIT 48
Electric Equipment Product Proliferation,
1970–1974
(Manufacturing Overhead as a Percent of Direct Labor Cost Per Unit)

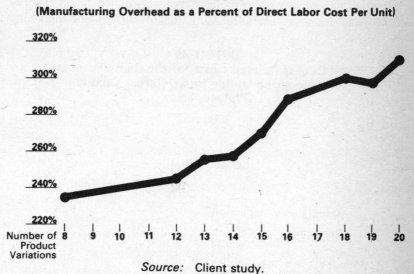

Source: Client study.

MANAGING QUALITY CONTROL

Both industrial customers and consumers have become aware of significant quality differences between many products produced in the United States and those produced in Japan, West Germany, or Sweden. Whether it is Swedish tools, special steels, cars, or heat exchangers; Japanese cars, televisions, or appliances; or German machine tools or specialty chemicals, foreign products have gained reputations for quality that often surpass those of U.S. goods. These reputations often allow foreign products to command price premiums over U.S. goods. But the cost of producing higher-quality goods is often no more than that of producing goods of lower quality.

Exhibit 49 compares the total cost of a U.S. product manufactured with little expenditure for quality control with the same product produced by a European company with substantial quality control. The extra costs associated with the addition of better materials and extra inspections actually led to a lower total cost, because of savings in rework, warranty, and scrappage. In this case. the U.S. company failed to keep track of its total quality-control costs, since different profit centers in the company had responsibility for materials, factory quality control, and warranty. The purchasing, manufacturing, and marketing

EXHIBIT 49
Total Quality Related Costs for the Same Product Manufactured Under Two Different Quality Philosophies

(Cost Per Unit)	American Competitor	European Competitor
Direct Labor Inspection	—	$.25
Inspection of Incoming Components	$.10	.22
Materials Overspecified for Reliability in Design	.45	1.05
Testing During Process	.15	.15
Amortization of Fixed Investment in Testing Equipment Preproduction Test Runs	.25	.70
In-Plant Quality-Control Supervisors	.50	.40
Rework	.85	.20
Scrappage	.75	.30
Warranty	1.05	.25
Total	$4.10	$3.52

Source: Client study.

departments each devised ways to control quality costs, but the firm failed to reap cost advantages associated with a total systems approach to quality.

In addition to their failure to assess the full costs associated with quality, U.S. firms also take a short-term view of quality control, emphasizing fault detection, repair, and warranty rather than fault prevention. Fault prevention usually involves heavy investment in capital equipment and pre-production testing. It may also involve higher materials and direct-labor costs. But fault prevention often results in a lower total systems cost; it is also more effective and provides greater value in the marketplace. Japanese, German, and Swedish companies often favor fault prevention over fault detection. Below are several aspects of a fault-prevention approach.

Overspecification of Materials. Long-term reliability can often be substantially increased through designs that call for slightly higher mechanical specifications on thickness of material or strength of weld than would theoretically be necessary, or for slightly higher tolerances on components. Such designs can also better endure the abuses that occasionally occur in the manufacturing process. In an attempt to save a few pennies on materials, many U.S. companies often specify minimum design levels, and suffer the consequences in rework and warranty calls.

Preproduction Testing of Components. Materials supplied by vendors are often subject to the same types of quality problems that affect final products, even if the vendor is another factory in the same company. Most U.S. factories spot-check a sample of incoming components. By contrast, Japanese and European producers typically conduct tests on all incoming components. For example, Japanese producers might conduct function tests on integrated circuit boards in which they are subjected to a series of different patterns of current flow. Many American companies favor an "on-off" test that determines whether or not current flows through the circuit.

Foreign producers also generally require elaborate testing from the vendor, in some cases purchasing testing machines for the vendor and working with the vendor on the production process. Preproduction testing is often cost effective. The extra cost for equipment and engineering time it entails is often compensated for by reduced rework and warranty costs.

Slower Cycle Times.   Compared to U.S. factories, Japanese and European factories often run at slightly slower cycle times (the amount of time required for one product to complete its passage through an assembly line) for manual assembly operations, thus giving greater discretion to individual workers to vary the speed of the line. They view the slight extra cost in direct labor seconds as more than paid for by savings in fault prevention and subsequent rework and warranty. U.S. companies tend to focus on direct labor seconds, ignoring the systemwide savings.

More Thorough Design Debugging.   The process of designing a new product is complex. Manufacturing-process engineers in many foreign companies enter this effort earlier, and their opinions are given a higher status than in the U.S. This often makes a significant difference in the number of faults introduced into a product in its first year of production. Moreover, thorough testing on prototype products as they come from the initial preintroduction production runs can save a great deal of the cost of retooling, machine downtime, and rework. This testing often requires expensive equipment to perform climate and shock tests. It is often hard to justify this equipment in a U.S. company, since it is auxiliary to the production process and its savings are in overhead.

Higher Levels of Automation.   Automated equipment can reduce the level of faults introduced into a product. Often the greatest savings from such automation derives from reductions in rework, testing, and warranty. This is particularly true for materials handling automation, an area in which U.S. companies often lag significantly behind their foreign competitors.

Greater Investment in Quality Awareness of the Work Force.   European and Japanese companies have placed greater emphasis than U.S. companies on involving shop-floor workers in the quality process. Japanese "quality circles" and European willingness to give workers more authority on the shop floor enhance the commitment of workers to quality. Such systems often require a substantial initial investment in lost production time and changeovers of factory organization, but the investment can pay off for the company by reducing the necessity for inspection and supervision.

By contrast, most U.S. companies tend to depend on elaborate systems of checkers and inspectors. Efforts to involve workers in quality control often tend to be "gimmicks"—special one-time rewards for quality suggestions, or contests of various sorts—that seem disingenuous in the light of management's obvious failure to invest in quality. When some U.S. companies have initiated quality circles, they have expected immediate results. They do not realize that it took eight to ten years for these systems to work effectively in most Japanese factories.

To some extent, higher levels of quality have been forced on Japanese, German, and Swedish companies by the low tolerance of their domestic consumers for poor quality. U.S. companies should take note, for U.S. customers are also beginning to adopt such an attitude.

SUMMARY

U.S. companies are dogged in their attempts to keep wages low, cut direct labor time, and reduce the cost of product materials. They are too often outcompeted by foreign companies, however, in overheads, process engineering, and quality costs. These factors often result in higher costs for U.S. companies than for their foreign competitors, with the result that the U.S. companies lose competitive ground.

10

Pricing Policy

Most companies would like to sell their products at a higher price than their competitors charge. Price premiums reflect the willingness of customers to attach greater worth to one company's product than to its competitors. Price premiums can result from a higher-quality product in terms of reliability, durability, or product capability; from better distribution or service; or from a better brand image (because of superior advertising, promotion, or distribution. But price premiums can be a source of continuing competitive leadership—and therefore of wealth creation—only when they can be sustained without loss of market share.

U.S. companies have often made two mistakes in pricing their products in the face of foreign competition: They have maintained price umbrellas and they have relied on non-sustainable pricing strategies.

PRICING UMBRELLAS

By cutting its price, a company that is willing to earn a low return to penetrate a new market can often gain market share at the expense of the established market leader that insists on maintaining current profitability. If the new entrant can gain volume and share, its cost position can improve to the point that it becomes the cost leader.

Many U.S. companies held significant cost advantages over foreign competitors in the 1950s and 1960s. Foreign competitors trying to catch up to their U.S. counterparts needed to gain market volume in order to gain sufficient experience and scale to amortize their investments, as described earlier. Therefore, they often cut prices in order to gain market share.

The U.S. leaders, accustomed to high profits, often refused to cut their prices to meet the prices of foreign competitors. Instead, they opted for advertising and promotion, stressing the quality, good service, and reputation of their products. This strategy was common in mature business segments with low growth rates, since managers needed to generate high profits in order to satisfy investors. The results of this approach were high profits in the short run, but a serious deterioration of competitive position, followed by losses in the long run.

By contrast, Exhibit 50 shows the steps taken by a major European producer of a mechanical component. This producer refused to hold a price umbrella when its market was invaded by Japanese competitors. The producer told its shareholders not to expect more than minimal profits for a few years while it fought to maintain its market share in

EXHIBIT 50
**Aggressive Defense Through Competitive Pricing
in a European Mechanical Component**

(Percent of Return on Investment Before Tax)

Source: Client study.

Europe. It then succeeded in increasing the cost of entry for the Japanese company. The Japanese company had planned to accept a 2-percent return on sales, compared to the 10-percent return for the industry leader. When the European company dropped its price to meet the Japanese competition, the European company was left with a 4-percent return on sales, but the Japanese company was forced to lose 4 percent on sales in order to gain market share. After a four-year battle, the Japanese company had achieved very little market penetration, and profits were rising again for the European company.

NONSUSTAINABLE PRICING STRATEGIES

Many U.S. marketing managers have sought to achieve higher prices through investing in both brand image and product differentiation. These investments have often been undertaken in response to foreign penetration by lower-priced but simpler versions of the same product. U.S. companies have tried to counter this potential price erosion by differentiating their product from the lower-priced version and creating customer loyalty to the higher-priced version. This strategy has often consisted of adding new product features and charging the customer a considerably higher price than the incremental costs incurred by adding the features.

This strategy has often failed. The only truly defensible way to compete in the long run is to achieve a cost advantage for a comparable product, or to develop a price premium that is supported by strong investment barriers, such as an elaborate distribution or service and spare parts network, product technology leadership, or a well-established brand image. Too many U.S. companies have relied instead on cosmetic changes and superficial features that may sustain their price premium in the short run but that divert resources from more basic quality improvements or cost reductions in the long run.

11

International Strategies

The large U.S. domestic market is the envy of every company in Europe. Without venturing beyond U.S. borders, most U.S. companies can gain a huge market base over which to amortize fixed costs and the costs of research and development. They can build world-scale plants, and gain considerable experience in a business, without having to challenge export markets. This large market has been a mixed blessing, however, for it has made U.S. companies less aggressive abroad. As the U.S. market has matured in many industries, and high-growth markets have simultaneously arisen abroad, foreign competitors (often with U.S. licensed technology) have used their rapidly growing home markets to gain experience and improve their cost positions.

Many U.S. companies sought unsuccessfully to become more international in the late 1950s and 1960s. They found some European markets to be partially protected, and European governments sometimes hostile to their initiatives. In general, these international ventures were less profitable than opportunities in the U.S. At the same time, Japan was well protected. The only way to gain entrance to the Japanese market was through technology licenses or somewhat unequal joint ventures. Licenses were preferred, since they provided short-term profits with little short-term risk, while joint ventures were relatively unprofitable. Finally, developing countries were unpredictable and highly risky markets.

As a result of these problems, by the early 1970s, international divisions of U.S. companies were often viewed as "Siberia" by corporate managers. Horror stories abounded about the failure of international ventures.

Because of this legacy, many U.S. companies today are not particularly adept at competing internationally. This chapter explores some of the reasons why this ineptness continues.

THE MEANING OF INTERNATIONAL BUSINESSES

Companies often mean very different things when they talk about "international businesses." U.S. companies in sheltered businesses may expand to become international by buying similar sheltered businesses in other countries. This has been the case for some wholesale and retail businesses, such as food companies and department stores. In these circumstances, there is little potential synergy among the different international operations of the company.

Alternatively, U.S. companies may export products when high-profit opportunities arise abroad. This has been the case, for example, with exports of large appliances or automobiles to the Middle East. These exports usually require little product modification or other investment, and are viewed as "icing on the cake" rather than as intrinsic parts of a U.S. business.

In still other cases, U.S. companies in sheltered or highly specialized businesses may sell technology licenses or enter short-lived joint ventures abroad, in order to better amortize their research and development activities and add to their cash flow without significant investment.

In none of these cases are the businesses truly "international" in the sense of requiring a worldwide integrated strategy. Truly international businesses are those in which there is a considerable flow of products and investments across borders, and competitive interactions in one part of the world have a direct effect on the business in other parts of the world.

Although U.S. companies that have developed international activities in sheltered businesses or on an opportunistic basis have often been successful, U.S. companies have generally faltered in truly international businesses. This faltering stems from the failure of U.S. companies to manage the business as one international entity, their reluctance to enter and remain in competitors' home markets, their lack of responsiveness to Third-World sales, their over reliance on the low labor costs of developing countries, and their lack of sophistication in licensing of technology.

FAILURE TO MANAGE THE BUSINESS AS ONE INTERNATIONAL ENTITY

U.S. companies often view overseas markets as providing only incremental volume to support the home operation. While the U.S.

market is often the largest market for many products, it is now generally among the slower-growing markets. In many businesses, scale in component manufacture, R&D, or application engineering may be significantly boosted through foreign sales. Many U.S. companies do not recognize this opportunity.

By contrast, Japanese companies with a smaller home market follow an aggressive export strategy. They often begin by exporting to Third-World markets, which are growing quickly but are still small relative to the U.S. market. These markets collectively add significant sales volume, which allows the Japanese company to overcome its smaller home market disadvantage. This penetration is often spearheaded by price reductions.

Typically, managers of U.S. companies in these markets are concerned about their current profitability, and do not look beyond a two- or three-year period, after which they will return to the home office. Accordingly, they are willing to sacrifice market share to the Japanese competitor rather than experience a decline in current profits. Moreover, since the Japanese market share is often taken from market growth, it does not affect the current sales level of the U.S. company. Such short-sighted strategies usually go unnoticed by management in the U.S.; market-share data, especially in Third-World countries, are difficult to track. Subsequently, when the Japanese come to dominate a foreign market and growth turns negative for the U.S. company, these developments are viewed as just another sign that overseas businesses are "losers."

The most crucial problem with this strategy for U.S. companies is not the loss of opportunity in the foreign market nor even the current loss in component volume, R&D, and amortization, though these are also serious. Most importantly, this strategy strengthens the Japanese competitor; by virtue of added scale and experience it is then in a better position to challenge the U.S. company in its domestic market.

U.S. companies must view international businesses as one integrated chessboard on which every move is planned for its strategic effect on the whole game. Seen in this light, it might be appropriate for certain foreign profit centers to lose money for a number of years while they fight a foreign challenge—in order to better protect the base business in the U.S. over the long term. In other cases, individual markets may need to be sacrificed in order to marshall resources for battles in other markets. Volume, profit, and price targets for each market must be seen in relation to the business as a whole, worldwide.

Just as market strategies must be coordinated, so too must product strategies be integrated. It is crucial for U.S. companies to determine which elements of a product are to be internationally uniform and traded, and which are to be tailored to local markets. In some businesses whose end product is too big and bulky to ship, Japanese or European companies have internationalized the supply of key components or capital equipment for automating product manufacture. This helps them achieve competitive cost advantages in key areas of the business and also improves productivity at home.

An international product strategy requires knowledge of which aspects of the cost structure are crucial and where leverage can be gained from broader amortization. The goal is to identify specific components that comprise a significant enough part of total product cost and for which savings from international scale will outweigh transport and customization costs. For example, motors for table saws can be an international business even though the saws themselves may not be. Significant international manufacturing-scale economies can be gained in the motors that more than offset the costs of transportation and of modifying the voltage from one country to another. U.S. companies have been slower than their Japanese and European counterparts to identify these sorts of opportunities. When their final product is not significantly traded in international markets, they do not regard themselves as being in potentially international businesses.

Companies that fail to integrate their domestic and international markets and product strategies will be at an increasing disadvantage relative to those that do.

RELUCTANCE TO ENTER AND REMAIN IN COMPETITORS' HOME MARKETS

Another serious mistake of U.S. companies is their reluctance to enter their competitors' home markets, particularly in France, West Germany, and Japan. To be sure, all three of these markets have been extremely difficult to enter in many product areas. Unfamiliar standards and other nontariff barriers, complex distribution, and nationalistic consumer preferences have made life difficult for would-be U.S. exporters. Despite these obstacles, it is essential that U.S. companies confront their international competitors in the competitors' home markets. Even if these operations do not show a profit, they can have significant competitive value.

A competitor that is challenged in its home market is prevented from using that market as a source of capital with which to make large penetration investments in other markets. The competitor is also prevented from "matrix pricing" in the U.S. market—that is, cutting its price in the U.S., where it has small volume relative to its total world volume, thereby jeopardizing the larger volume of the U.S. company, which will suffer greater proportional losses by meeting the price cut. Finally, by participating in a competitors' home market, the U.S. company can gain valuable information about a competitors' strengths, weaknesses, and plans.

Although U.S. companies have invested in Japan, France, and Germany, they have not often been willing to sustain the necessary losses for a long enough time to reap the full competitive benefits of the investment. There have been notable exceptions—such as IBM, Polaroid, Texas Instruments, Caterpillar, and Omark—who have endured hardships to become significant competitors in the Japanese market. In general, however, the French, German, and Japanese marketplaces are littered with U.S. firms that came, stayed a few years, and left after a few setbacks. By contrast, Japanese firms often expect to lose money for five or more years when entering U.S. or European markets, and will sustain losses for even longer periods if necessary.

LACK OF RESPONSIVENESS TO THIRD-WORLD MARKETING

Many U.S. firms have lost ground to European and Japanese companies by failing to be sufficiently flexible and farsighted in their dealings with developing countries. Flexibility involves willingness to do many things: to give up control of significant parts of the business, to reinvest profits within the host country, to accept local content requirements, to negotiate with government officials, to accept export requirements, and to provide liberal financing. The governments of developing countries with large or growing home markets often insist on technical assistance, local content, and/or export requirements for local investment. Local companies based in these countries often insist on majority or parity share in joint ventures. In addition, the foreign company often must invest considerable time and energy in negotiations and in developing projects. U.S. companies often are unwilling to take these steps.

As governments and companies in the newly industrializing countries become more sophisticated, many U.S. companies, accustomed to being dominant in such relationships and to taking high profits at will from their foreign operations, find themselves displaced by French, German, Japanese, and Italian firms that are willing to be more flexible.

Two recent examples illustrate this shortsightedness. The first involves a bid to build a plant for a commodity plastic in a Latin American country. A German firm agreed to buy part of the output of the plant to sell in Germany and in other countries. The firm also agreed to a very liberal financing plan that was assisted by the German government and to liberal ownership provisions. In return, it negotiated guaranteed contracts for export to the Latin American country of related specialty chemicals and for use of German equipment in the commodity resin operation and certain dowstream plants. The German company received the benefits of a guaranteed fast-growth market, thus allowing increased scale potential at its new specialty chemical plant in Germany. The company also gained the ability to sell and further amortize the development of its process technology in the mature commodity chemical process, plus a lucrative engineering and construction contract for the Latin American plant.

Through its liberal financing assistance, the German government helped support the competitive development of one of its companies and considerably increased exports. The government also helped support the increasing sophistication of its work force by trading some jobs and exports in a mature commodity chemical business for an expansion of the more sophisticated specialty chemical business. Two U.S. competitors, leaders in the field, reviewed the requirements for local content, equity structure for the venture, and financing, and decided not to bid.

The other example involves two U.S. and one French company in a vehicle business competing for a series of orders in developing countries. Local assembly, financing, and, to a lesser extent, purchase price were the keys to a foreign government's decisions to approve a vendor. The French company made offers that would not have returned any profit whatsoever from the equipment orders and that involved the French government in a very liberal financing package. The justification for this decision rested on two basic competitive factors. First, sales of spare parts make up 30 percent of total sales in the business and 50 percent of total profits in any given year. Second, a relatively small number of these pieces of equipment are sold in each product generation. Securing volume in order to amortize the expensive development costs of each generation is crucial to long-term profitability and to the ability of a company to fund the next generation.

The French company had a small base for its previous generation and had difficulty contemplating its next development generation. The two U.S. companies were both much larger. To them, the extra volume and future cash generation from sales of spare parts seemed too long term an issue to be concerned with. As a result, the French company picked up orders in Third-World countries for 15 percent of the world market, allowing it to become a significant force in the business worldwide. Its next generation of the product, developed with the underpinnings of revenues from spare parts gained from these orders years later, has made significant inroads into the U.S. market.

Developing countries offer important growing markets for many products. The larger volume of sales can be critical to the international competitive position of many companies. In becoming more flexible, U.S. companies would not only be enhancing the development of these countries but would also be defending their own competitive positions.

OVERRELIANCE ON LOW LABOR COSTS IN DEVELOPING COUNTRIES

U.S. firms have been among the most aggressive in moving their factories offshore to take advantage of cheap labor in less developed countries. This is particularly true of the clothing, consumer electronics, metal-working, and electrical equipment industries. Although this strategy is often an appropriate means of encouraging development in a country and of improving the cost position of the U.S. company, it can result in inefficiencies that offset any such advantages.

A low-labor-cost offshore manufacturing base increases a company's transport and tariff costs. It may also generate hidden costs, such as increased problems in quality control, a long pipeline of costly in-process inventory, and slow response time for coordination between designers and the factory or the factory and the field. Japanese and

German companies have sought low-cost labor to a much more limited extent than have U.S. firms. Their offshore moves tend to be designed for market penetration rather than strictly for low-cost labor. Moreover, when Japanese or German companies move offshore, they tend to keep a factory in the home country. They automate this factory so they can compare its production costs to those in the low-cost, labor-intensive factory abroad. Eventually, they often automate the factory in the low-labor-cost country as well.

Many U.S. companies, particularly those in the electronics industry, are being challenged by Japanese competitors that have found ways to automate the same processes that the U.S. companies are undertaking with low-wage labor in Mexico, Singapore, and Malaysia. U.S. firms may fail to recognize the hidden costs associated with their dependence on low-wage labor, particularly when they use it as a substitute for new investment in process engineering.

TECHNOLOGY LICENSING

Japan and West Germany, the countries with the most rapid growth in living standard, have maintained negative trade balances in technology for many years. Furthermore, they grant licenses for their technologies more slowly and to a lesser extent than do their U.S. counterparts.

Licensing of technology can be an easy method of amortizing development costs and making quick profits without additional capital investment, which raises ROIs. But licensees can become competitors. Licenses in nonsheltered businesses should only be provided to foreign companies in cases where technology is changing quickly and the U.S. company is confident of its ability to stay in the lead of technological change, or where the U.S. company can maintain significant manufacturing or marketing leadership in the product area.

In short, U.S. companies must become more aware of international competition and the international marketplace. If the U.S. and its companies are to prosper, they can no longer view international business as an adjunct to domestic business or as a source of quick profits. Rather, international business must be integrated into a worldwide competitive strategy.

12

Worker-Management Relations

Workers and union leaders in the U.S. often recoil at talk of cost reductions and productivity improvements. Cost reductions have become identified with plant closings and real reductions in wages. Increased productivity often signals layoffs, work speed-ups, and harsher working conditions. U.S. companies have been far slower than their international counterparts to increase worker security and give workers a greater stake in productivity improvements.

Improvements in productivity and competitive position should ultimately contribute to lower prices for the average consumer and higher real wages and greater job security for workers. These improvements should be in the best interest of workers and their unions. It is common for trade unions in Sweden, Japan, and West Germany to support the introduction of productivity-improving machinery. In the U.S., such moves are often viewed with hostility and suspicion.

An adversarial relationship exists between workers and management in every economy, since each group represents a different function in the workplace. But this relationship takes place within the bounds of different laws and conventions in each society, where there are differing degrees of hostility and differing abilities to reach peaceful agreements without disrupting production. In the U.S., for example, a 60-hour work week without overtime pay is no longer within the range of reasonable business demands. On the other hand, U.S. management is unwilling to share business information with employees. Moreover, it feels free to close a plant for economic reasons with limited notice, and to lay off workers without pay during a recession.

Swedish or Japanese management (by law in Sweden and by convention in Japan) would not withhold information on company investment plans from workers, nor close a plant on short notice, nor lay off workers in a recession. Exhibit 51 presents some differences

EXHIBIT 51 Worker Rights in Large Companies in Selected Countries

	W. Germany	France	Japan	U.K.	Netherlands	Sweden	U.S.
Average Period of Notice for Shutdown	2–6 months by law	1–3 months by law	1 month by law 6 months by custom	3 months by law	2–6 months by law	6 months + by law	None
Worker Representation in Management	1 3–1 2 of Board Members from workers	Consultation with workers' council on decisions affecting work rules	No law, but 2 3 of companies have board members who are active in unions	None	Consultation with workers council on all major management decisions	2 members on board; consultation on all major management decisions	None
Paid Leaves							
Sickness (not including disability insurance)	6 weeks full pay and 4 weeks 75% pay	50% of earnings up to 36 months after brief waiting period	80% of wages indefinitely	Average 50% for 6 months	80% of pay for one year	6 months at full pay	None
Maternity or Paternity	6 months after birth and 6 weeks before birth with monthly allowance and guarantee against dismissal	4 months at 90% pay with monthly nursing allowance and guarantee against dismissal	No law, but 3 months paid leave is widely adhered to	6 weeks at 90% salary	3 months full pay	9 months full pay shared between parents	None
Employee Rights on Employer Insolvency	First priority is 68% average pay for one year to all workers	Guaranteed income maintenance allowances varying by age and seniority	Full wage for 2 years; 80% of 3 months salary guaranteed by the state	Guaranteed one week day for every year of service	80% of wages for 6 months guaranteed, then 75% for additional time to a maximum of 2 years	90% of wages for 6 months to 2 years	None

Sources: U.S. Department of Labor, Country Labor Profiles; Interviews with Labor Counselors of embassies of each country; interview with AMS, the Swedish Labor Market Board.

EXHIBIT 52
Labor Disputes in Selected Countries

(Working Days Lost Per 1,000 Employees 1970–1977)

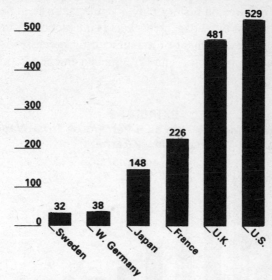

Sources: Assembled from country labor profiles; U.S. Department of Labor, Bureau of International Labor Affairs, 1979.

among countries in the accepted ground rules for labor-management relations. One can see from this exhibit that, relative to companies in other countries, U.S. companies provide considerably less job security, in terms of the ability of a company to dismiss or lay off workers. U.S. companies also provide fewer leaves for vacation or illness. In addition, there is less worker participation, in terms of access to company information, less board representation for workers, and less worker input to shop-floor decisions in U.S. companies.

U.S. companies also have a poor record in bringing negotiations between workers and management to a nondisruptive conclusion. The U.S. experiences over 10 times the number of days lost to industrial disputes per 1,000 employees as does Sweden or Germany. It ranks at the bottom of the list, with 30 to 40 days lost in Germany or Sweden as compared to 529 in the U.S. (Exhibit 52). Many of the countries with the fewest work stoppages, the highest benefits for workers, and better productivity gains (Sweden, Germany, Holland, and Japan) are also among the more highly unionized (Exhibit 53).

It is of course difficult to make crossnational comparisons in this area because culture and history play a significant role in determining appropriate patterns of management-worker interaction. A brief review of the historical development of manufacturing processes is useful in explaining the problems of employee-management relations in the United States.

EXHIBIT 53
Union Membership as a Percent of Total Wage and Salary Earners
(Percent in 1978)

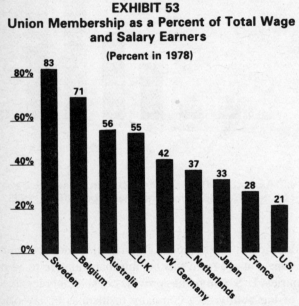

Sources: Report of the President on U.S. Competitiveness, September 1980; Office of Foreign Economic Research, U.S. Department of Labor, Table V 27.

HISTORICAL DEVELOPMENT OF MANUFACTURING PROCESSES IN THE U.S.

Modern American manufacturing technologies began with the standardization promoted by Eli Whitney in assembling identical rifles from identical parts for the U.S. army in the 1800s. With the development of more sophisticated machine tools, a fair degree of standardization was introduced into the production of parts in many industries.

Further standardized assembly of parts can be traced to the slaughterhouses of the 1800s, which instituted a rigid mass production by breaking down the steps of the production process and assigning workers to repeatable tasks within a line of production. Flexible mass production originated with Montgomery Ward's notions of flexible ordering from a long list of standardized products and the flexible process of assembling those orders. The assembly line was developed further in the early 1900s in the auto industry.

The combining of standardization with the assembly line led to a dramatic increase in quality and productivity. It was the advent of "scientific management," however, that signaled the beginning of modern management technologies. In essence, this was a system for analyzing work according to its required motions and the time required to perform each motion. This analysis allowed each productive operation to be factored down into its components and sequenced to ensure the highest level of productivity consistent with reasonable levels of quality and fatigue. Jobs were made "simpler" and more uniform, and subspecialization became the norm. One worker inserted bolts and another screwed down the nuts. Scientific managers became industrial engineers, and industrial engineers became part of management. Accordingly, the design of what was to be done—the process—was officially removed from the workers.

When they lost responsibility for the process, workers became less responsible for the product. The solution to problems of quality control under scientific management was, inevitably, a mechanical one. It called for a system of inspectors, and inspectors over inspectors, combined with random sampling. If the processes were followed, defects would be caught.

This system is still with us. Indeed, it was considered a dramatic step when, in connection with its support of the Chrysler Corporation bail-out, the United Auto Workers demanded that ordinary workers be allowed to assume responsibility for identifying defects and systematically removing defective vehicles from the assembly lines.

The system of the scientifically managed assembly line using standardized parts to produce a standardized product became part of the engine of U.S. productivity growth for most of the first half of the twentieth century. But it has led directly to charges of "dehumanization" and to less flexibility in the use and role of workers.

Once the drive toward scientific management was underway and work was being reduced to simple, fractionated patterns, the question of pay scales arose. When members of different crafts offered particular skills, differential rates of pay were standard. When almost all employees were performing simple, routine tasks, the natural direction would seem to have been in favor of the compression of wage rates for all but the most irreducible minimum of highly skilled workers. This is in fact what *did* happen in Japan and Sweden. Nevertheless, U.S. managers, fearing that work standardization would encourage unionization, introduced individual incentive schemes into the workplace. Though performing the same tasks, workers were given individual bonuses for greater productivity, with pay based on the number of pieces completed in a day of work. Where the flow of production made piecework less relevant, an elaborately stratified job structure with extensive, if minor, wage-rate distinctions was created. Job ladders were established that wended their way through either individual plants or through the entire structure of an industry. Opportunities for mobility were minimal, but they were sufficient to produce a pattern whereby, before the Second World War, there were between 45,000 and 50,000 different job classifications in the U.S. Steel Company alone. Wartime efforts by the government reduced that number, but only to one-third of the earlier figure.

As unions formed, they were forced to respond to the standardized workplace and stratified incentive system in a way which has locked these practices into the American work system. As Robert Cole summarizes it:

> Instead of the individualized incentive payment systems often preferred by management, the unions sought standard job rates. The outcome was a melding of union interest in control over job opportunities and management attempts to systematically rationalize work operations. The convergence contributed to the development of tight and narrowly defined job definitions . . . The emergent unions had two basic options. They could struggle to increase the amount of worker discretion on the job, thereby "enlarging" the job, or even insist on a worker voice in job design. Alternatively the unions could accept the given framework of power and struggle to make quantitative improvements in worker rewards. The first option was clearly a radical one which the unions eventually rejected in the face of management

and government power and lack of worker support. They accepted the more limited solution, whereby collective bargaining came to legitimate the existing extreme division of labor.[1]

One of the goals of unionization was to reduce the uncertainties of employment, and seeking that goal in the system in place legitimized literally thousands of job categories based on "skills" (some of which could be learned in a matter of weeks), with an elaborate seniority structure. The structure was locked in and modified to prevent the laying off of workers or the reassignment of workers of greater seniority from one job category to another, thereby displacing other workers. By granting some degree of job protection, it also meant that senior workers were prepared to share their skills with newer ones in times of high employment.

This process also led to the perpetuation of functionless jobs, such as maintaining firemen on diesel trains or using linotypers to reset advertising copy delivered to a newspaper in stereotype. This elaborate system of functions and the rigidity it introduced into factories have also sapped the time and energy of both managers and workers, thus hindering productivity. Most importantly, they have led to worker alienation and persistent tensions in the workplace.

There are a few general principles of worker-management interaction, not often observed in the U.S., which appear to play an important role in improving the ability of management and workers to collaborate more productively.

JOB SECURITY AND CAREER DEVELOPMENT

It is difficult to gain workers' commitment to a company if they know that the company is not ultimately committed to developing their careers. To be sure, workers, whether management or employee, may be appropriately discharged from a company if they are found to be stealing or embezzling funds or endangering the health of others. On occasion, it is also necessary to dismiss people who simply cannot perform their jobs satisfactorily, regardless of the amount of aid, assistance, and training they are given. However, there is no justification for making workers bear the brunt of productivity improvements, plant closings, or recessions.

Most developed countries have established procedures to guard the worker's job security in these situations. In Sweden and Japan, for example, the government reimburses companies for keeping workers on the payroll (or in training courses) during recessions. Moreover, in both of these countries, and in a number of other European countries, plant closings require significant periods of notification. Arrangements are made to transfer employees to equivalent jobs, to provide retraining, and to compensate both the workers and the communities in which the plants are located. In cases of plant productivity improvements, efforts are made to expand output or to find equivalent jobs in the vicinity for affected employees.

It is in a company's best interest to be concerned about the career development of all employees, not just the few at the top. For many U.S. companies, it would not only be more humane but also less costly to develop the employees they have rather than to bear the substantial costs of employee disaffection and high worker turnover.

U.S. businesses cannot expect loyalty to run in only one direction. They must take more care to provide better job security. Workers must know that improved productivity will not hurt them as it helps the society at large.

WORKER PARTICIPATION IN DESIGNING WORK ENVIRONMENTS

An inexplicable double standard guides many managers and professionals in their own career advancement and job enrichment relative to that of blue-collar or clerical workers. The gap between the average blue-collar wage and the top executive salary compensation is larger in the U.S. than in any developed country. While top management typically seeks to help other managers enrich their jobs, it often seeks only to discipline and control blue-collar or clerical workers.

Even though worker motivation may not play the most significant role in competitive productivity development, it nevertheless does enter the picture. Low turnover rates, good training, positive motivation, and a flexible plant structure for job definitions can all improve productivity. An environment in which workers feel there is scope for real job enrichment, and in which they have a better understanding of the effect of their work on the organization, also constitutes an important aspect of improved living standards.

ALTERNATIVES FROM OTHER COUNTRIES

Other countries have developed patterns of worker-management relations that have produced greater flexibility and cooperation then those in the U.S. There is a tendency in the U.S. to think that the patterns in other countries are different because of ethnic or historical reasons. While the Japanese and Germans do have a number of social and industrial practices that can be traced ultimately to cultural roots, and while some of their practices vary widely from those in the U.S., most of their techniques for securing efficiency and productivity originated in the U.S. They merely adopted U.S. ideas and modified them to suit their needs.

Japan

The Japanese have been able to build on scientific management and on other Western ideas in ways that are very different from U.S. efforts, largely because threats to employment and status have not been viewed by management as appropriate incentives for maintaining high productivity.

In the Japanese system, workers in large industries begin employment immediately after school. Recruiting is done annually and, once a worker is hired, he or she can traditionally count on lifetime employment, that is, until retirement. Managerial workers are recruited from institutions of higher education. For them, too, lifetime employment is guaranteed. At a relatively advanced stage in their careers, certain managers are selected for senior status and may remain with the firm in a major position until a very advanced age. All managers begin by working on the shop floor. Some even move into management after having achieved senior positions in local trade unions.

Wage rates are set largely on the basis of seniority combined with ability. Ability does not mean "skill." While skilled employees are recognized in Japanese industry, most workers are considered in terms of the whole range of skills they might learn. They are hired to work, not to fill a particular job. Merit pay has traditionally been all but unknown, although there is intense peer pressure to produce and a constant evaluation of workers by supervisors.

The Japanese built their system around a basic world view that every worker is ultimately perfectable, and that the purpose of supervision and management is to enable workers to achieve their full potential. It is a world view that not all managers share, but it is something to which more than lip service is rendered.

Wage rates are bargained annually in terms of projected growth in national and industrial productivity, at the so-called "spring offensive" when government, industry, and labor all bargain together. In addition to the base wage rate, across-the-board bonuses based on the individual firm's productivity are given annually. These bonuses are usually in the range of five- to six-months' worth of wages, and the collective incentive these provide is a major impetus in interfirm competition.

There still is a great deal of "family feeling" within large industries, derived in part from a pattern of company-owned dormitories for single workers, company-sponsored recreation and educational programs, company-sponsored retail outlets, and other amenities. This, coupled with lifetime employment practices and an emphasis on group harmony and the virtues of communal activity, has led to a cohesive team-spirit approach among workers and managers.

Even today, interfirm job shifts are much rarer for Japanese than they are for Americans in comparable work situations. It is particularly unusual for a Japanese manager to begin with one established firm and move in midcareer to another, or for a firm to hire any "permanent" employees away from other firms.

Strikes are equally rare, and most that do occur are *pro forma*, lasting only a few hours or days, and designed to bring management back to the "proper" course of decisionmaking in a consultative-consensual framework.

With a tradition of consultative decisionmaking (which is not, of course, the same as a system requiring universal consent to any decision), coupled with a great deal of employment stability, a lack of internal job competition among workers, and a population with similar educational backgrounds, it is not surprising that the Japanese have achieved great flexibility in work assignments. In spite of Japan's high rate of industrial diversification, this factor has made layoffs even less likely than they would have been over the last several decades.

Similarly, the Japanese have pioneered statistically based quality control and quality-control circles comprised of workers and supervisors. These circles determine not merely where quality can be improved but also engage in general shop-floor planning and evaluation, allowing workers a high level of discretion in reorganizing production processes. They have resulted in marked productivity increases.

These breakthroughs are very real, but their reality and success vary substantially from firm to firm. Some Japanese companies, even very successful ones, are much more rigid than others. In some firms, quality-control circles are very limited bodies that function primarily as sounding boards. In others, the circles have a great deal of leeway to change the way things are done in the plant—although, always, management reserves the final, official say. Like statistical quality control, the circles derive from American and European theorists and, in some cases, from American practices, which have been modified in unique and highly useful ways.

Europe

In Western Europe, the pattern of work design and labor utilization is in many ways similar to that in the U.S. There are significant differences, however, between practices in the European continental countries (Germany, Austria, Holland, Belgium, Denmark, Norway, Sweden, and Finland) on the one hand, and those in the U.K. and U.S. on the other. Unions in continental countries tend to be highly aggregated, representing broad industry groups. Jurisdictional disputes are rare. Central wage agreements are negotiated in one form or another, forming guidelines for individual firm negotiations.

In continental countries, there have been moves toward legally mandated worker corepresentation or codetermination at various decision-making levels within companies, from shop floor to board of directors. In some countries, decisions affecting work organization must, by law, receive worker approval. Workers, as a group, have a legal right to receive information; in some cases, the workers must approve various types of management decisions before they can take effect.

Also, most continental countries have laws protecting job security. Provision is made for notice and severance pay in connection with plant closings.

In most large continental companies, unionization is accepted, and attention is given to improving relations between management and unions in order to achieve stability. Smaller firms tend to be unionized in Scandanavia but not in Germany or the Benelux countries. Even where companies are not unionized, a cooperative relationship exists, with ground rules similar to those in unionized companies.

The U.K. exists in sharp contrast. There, fights for pay differentials and jurisdictional disputes among unions aggravate a system of rigid work rules and inflexible business organization.

This brief summary of labor-management relations in the U.S., as compared to the relations of its international competitors, presents a troubling picture. The poor pattern of U.S. labor-management relations contributes not only to the nation's declining competitive productivity but also to the insecurity and lower standard of living of its working population. U.S. managers have lagged behind their Japanese and continental European counterparts in eliciting cooperation from the work force, in encouraging greater commitment to productivity, and in using human resources to the fullest.

In the following chapters, we will show how U.S. management failure has contributed to declining international competitive positions in specific industries.

FOOTNOTE

[1] Cole, Robert E. *Work, Mobility and Participation: A Comparative Study of American and Japanese Industry*. University of California Press, 1979.

13

The Declining Competitive Position of The U.S. Steel Industry

In the 1950s, U.S. steelmakers produced almost 50 percent of the world's steel.* They had the world's largest, most efficient steel-producing facilities. While the U.S. had the world's highest wage rates, it was the world's lowest-cost producer of steel, and the world's largest exporter. The combination of high productivity and access to good, low-cost raw materials gave the U.S. a significant competitive advantage. Today, the U.S. produces only 16 percent of the total world steel output and exports less than one-tenth of the amount exported by the Japanese.[1] Imports took over 18 percent of U.S. consumption of steel in 1978 before barriers were erected to limit them.[2]

Declining productivity in the steel industry has had a wide-ranging impact. U.S. producers of automobiles, appliances, ships, and other steel-using products have been put at a serious disadvantage by having to buy higher-priced American steel. In 1977 and 1978, companies manufacturing cars in the U.S. had to pay 25 to 30 percent more for their steel than did their Japanese counterparts.[3]

U.S. VERSUS JAPANESE STEEL PRODUCTION

The overriding cause of the U.S. steel industry's decline relative to Japan has been its drop in relative productivity. Despite the rise of

* The steel industry is not homogenous but consists of a number of distinct businesses. The business covered in this chapter is basic commodity steel, including products such as high-volume grades of hot- and cold-rolled sheet, hot-rolled bars, welded pipe, seamless pipe, rod and wire, and small structurals. It does not include specialty steels, such as stainless, tool, or reinforcing bars, or specific finishing operations, such as high-tolerance cold-rolled bars.

Japanese wages relative to U.S. wages—from 12 percent in 1960, to 33 percent in 1972, to 58 percent in 1979*—Japanese production costs for a ton of steel have improved relative to U.S. costs since the early 1960s. This results from differential improvements in productivity and the use of raw materials.

Overall, leading Japanese mills have had a 30 to 35 percent operating cost advantage over leading U.S. mills for the production of standard flat-rolled steel products. These lower Japanese costs are attributable in part to lower labor costs, but more significantly to process scale and technology and to raw materials sourcing and technology.

The process of making steel has many steps. Coals are blended and purified to make coke, which is then combined with iron ore in a blast furnace to make a purer form of iron called pig iron. This is then combined with steel scrap and other materials in a steelmaking furnace. The molten steel that emerges then goes through various stages of semifinishing in rolling mills that make round or rectangular shapes called slabs, billets, or blooms. Finally, these shapes are rolled and drawn a varying number of times to produce wire, sheets, bars, rods, pipe, and other finished steel products. Japanese plants are more efficient than their U.S. counterparts in a number of these steps.

Every doubling in size of a blast furnace can result in 30 percent reduction in the cost of pig iron production. In 1977, Japan had 25 blast furnaces capable of producing over 2 million tons of iron annually; the U.S. had none. In fact, most U.S. furnaces were under 1 million tons in capacity.

Differences in steelmaking furnace costs result primarily from the type of technology used. Basic oxygen furnaces (BOF) are more efficient than open hearths; and continuous slab or billet casting is more efficient than the production of ingots and the subsequent rolling of the ingot on slab, bloom, or billet mills. Japanese companies adopted both basic oxygen furnaces and continuous casting technologies faster than did their U.S. counterparts. By 1978, 78 percent of Japanese steel was produced in BOF furnaces, compared to 58 percent of U.S. steel;

---

*These figures are presented by the U.S. Labor Department. The comparisons are misleading, however, since they do not include all the benefits available to Japanese workers but not to U.S. workers. If these added benefits are included, Japanese labor costs are about 70 percent of U.S. rates.

and 51 percent of Japanese steel was continuously cast, compared to 15 percent of U.S. steel.

In addition, rolling mills (hot strip, cold rolling, plate, tar, rod, etc.) have all improved in speed and operating efficiencies. Japanese mills are much newer and have substantially better process-control efficiency than do U.S. mills.[4]

More significant than differences in direct labor productivity are differences in overheads and indirect labor costs—such as materials handling, rework, internal transport costs, maintenance, and setup. The fact that Japanese plants are bigger (Exhibit 54) and newer (Exhibit

EXHIBIT 54
Capacities of Integrated Japanese and U.S. Steel Plants

Capacity	U.S.		Japan	
Millions of Metric Tons	Number of Plants	Percent Production	Number of Plants	Percent Production
Over 8	0	0	7	70
7–8	2	11	1	6
5.5–7	2	9	1	5
4.5–5.5	3	11	1	4
3.6–4.5	4	12	—	—
2.7–3.6	9	22	—	—
1.8–2.7	11	18	5	9
0.9–1.8	15	15	—	—
Under 0.9	11	2	8	6

Source: Client study.

55), and incorporate more sophisticated materials-handling procedures than many American plants makes them more efficient in overheads. Since most U.S. plants have been expanded through incremental investments, they tend to have a much more cumbersome product flow than do Japanese plants. This results in a significant penalty in overhead cost.

The Japanese industry has also invested to overcome its inherent disadvantage in raw materials. Unlike the U.S., Japan possesses neither iron ore nor coking coal resources. By building ships that could carry

EXHIBIT 55
Japanese and U.S. Steel Plants Constructed
Since 1950

	Mill	Year of 1st Operation	Capacity in Thousands of Metric Tons
Japanese			
Nippon	Kimitsu	1965	14
	Yawata	1959	12
	Sakai	1961	4
	Nagoya	1958	7
	Oita	1971	12
NKK	Fukayama	1965	16
Kawasaki	Chiba	1952	6
	Mitsushima	1961	10
Sumitomo	Wakayama	1960	9
	Kashima	1967	15
Kobe	Kagoshima	1968	10
U.S.			
U.S. Steel	Fairless	1952	5
Bethlehem	Burns Harbor	1968	6

Source: Client study.

large quantities of materials, the Japanese have been able to ship high-quality ore from Australia and Brazil and coal from the U.S., Canada, and Australia at lower costs than the U.S. pays to bring lower-quality ore from Minnesota to Ohio or Pennsylvania. Japanese companies have also made investments in these countries to guarantee their sources of supply.

These investments make U.S. access to domestic sources of coal (with the exception of domestic low-volatile coal) or iron a drawback rather than an advantage. Constructed at sites with access to deepwater ports, Japanese mills have been better able to take advantage of newly developed higher-quality and lower-cost sources of raw materials.

Overall, costs of mining iron ore in surface mines in Australia with high iron purity and low overburden ratios are lower than mining costs in Minnesota and Michigan. Similarly, coal mined in Australia and Canada in large open pit mines is lower in cost than that mined in the U.S., by a 3-to-1 margin. Lower mining costs plus reduced transport costs have given the Japanese a significant cost advantage.

In addition to sourcing and shipping factors, Japanese producers have gained a raw material advantage from their coal-blending and blast-furnace technology. The value of different types of coal depends on their strength and fluidity. Some U.S. coals of low and medium volatility are particularly valuable. Japanese companies have developed coal-blending procedures that allow them to use a lower-grade mix of coking coals to attain optimum results. This use of a higher proportion of lower-grade coals has allowed Japanese companies to use less of the expensive U.S. coals. Similarly, Japanese blast-furnace technology allows them to use less coke per ton of pig iron produced (coke rate) than their American counterparts use.[5]

A final competitive advantage for Japanese producers stems from materials recovery. Japanese companies have improved their means of gathering not just bulk steel scrap but also iron and steel "fines," which are given off by most steel processes. Not only has this process reduced pollution and health hazards, but the recycling of these fines has improved overall yields from the raw materials used in the mills.

For comparable steel products, Japanese productivity is now 25 to 30 percent higher than American productivity.[6] For large exporting plants of flat-rolled products, such as Oita, the difference in productivity is even higher. Japanese plants have incurred significantly higher capital costs, interest burdens, pollution-control expenditures, and R&D and process-engineering costs, which lessen the overall cost gap. But these are all investments, rather than continuing operating costs. Even if they are included, the cost gap remains in the 20 to 25 percent range.

HOW THE U.S. LOST ITS COMPETITIVE ADVANTAGE

The Japanese have built the world's most efficient steel industry. The venture required large, well-directed capital investments and aggressive pursuit of export markets to support continued rapid growth, despite decreases in the rate of growth of home consumption.

The massive capital investments that allowed Japan to overtake the U.S. in efficiency occurred primarily between 1966 and 1972, when the Japanese steel industry increased its assets by over 23 percent a year, compared to only 4 percent per year for the U.S. This increase in assets took place despite a lower average rate of return on assets— 1.8 percent for the five big Japanese steel companies as opposed to 3.8 percent for the eight largest U.S. companies. During this period, the Japanese companies replaced outmoded equipment (such as open hearths built in the 1950s and early 1960s) while they expanded capacity. Their major goal was to achieve the lowest possible operating costs rather than to calculate elaborate discounted cash flows on existing open hearths versus new basic oxygen furnaces. Japanese companies incurred a marginal debt-to-equity ratio of almost 11 to 1 during these years, allowing a satisfactory return on equity and guaranteeing the continued improvement of their competitive productivity. U.S. companies increased their debt levels significantly but did not follow as aggressive an investment or financing strategy (Exhibit 56).

EXHIBIT 56
Financing of Steel Investment

	Japanese Big 5 (1966-72)	U.S. Big 8 (1966-73)
Asset Growth Per Year	23.6%	4.2%
Average Return on Assets (After Interest)	1.8%	3.8%
Average Return on Equity	20.0%	6.5%
Marginal Debt-to-Equity Ratio, 1966–72 (1973)[1]	11.6:1	1.7:1
Debt-to-Equity Ratio, 1972	6.3:1	0.82:1
Cash Sources for Financing		
Debt	91%	63%
Retained Earnings	1%	37%
New Equity	8%	—

Source: Client study.

[1] All liabilities included as debt.

While it is correct to say that Japanese companies outspent their American counterparts during the 1960s and 1970s, this is not the primary reason that they overtook U.S. industry in productivity. In fact, even though the Japanese did spend more, U.S. industry was spending at a sizable rate as well. Over the 29 years between 1950 and 1979, U.S. companies invested over $60 billion (in 1978 dollars).

Part of the U.S. industry's problem is attributable to poor investment choices. When large sums of money have been invested in the U.S. steel business, they have tended to be invested in marginal facilities designed to overcome specific production bottlenecks and thereby increase total capacity. Because of relatively low capital cost outlays per additional ton of steel, these "round-out" investments usually showed better discounted cash flow (DCF) rates of return and were less risky than totally new (greenfield) plants.

But this type of investment typically created a number of problems. If the new facility did not fit at the old site, it was often placed somewhere else at the plant, complicating product flows. Also, many round-out investments did not meet their ROI targets because of incorrect estimates of indirect cost savings or penalties. Often a round-out met its direct labor operating cost targets but not its total cost targets. Maintenance, material handling, and setup costs were invariably greater than predicted. Because the new mill was often too large for the older mills that used its output, it was underutilized; this inevitably gave rise to calls for additional round-out investments to overcome the newly formed bottlenecks.

Thus, U.S. steel companies made small, incremental investments to obtain "cheap" capacity rather than make the larger, more aggressive, and riskier investments that could have led to superior productivity overall. In fact, because of its high capital costs, the Bethlehem Steel plant at Burns Harbor, Indiana, was long viewed as unprofitable, even though it is the only fully integrated large-scale greenfield plant built in the U.S. since 1952. Overall, U.S. steel companies have sought to keep the return on investment—ROI—up by keeping the "I" low, but this strategy has left whole plants uncompetitive. In the long run this scheme has been self-defeating.

An additional difference in U.S. and Japanese company strategies has been the attitude toward exports. Japanese home consumption of steel began to slow in the early 1970s. Their response was to increase exports aggressively, from 25 to 45 percent of production in the mid-1970s, thus allowing a continued expansion of domestic production.

This increase in exports did not come easily. Japanese companies made large investments in more than 50 finishing facilities in developing countries in order to establish a market for semifinished goods exports. Penetrating the wary U.S. and European markets required large initial marketing investments as well. The Japanese industry was prepared to make these investments and to await a long-term payback.

U.S. companies have never been aggressive in pursuing export markets. As Exhibit 57 demonstrates, they export three times less tonnage to Latin America and four times less to Europe than do their Japanese counterparts.

Underlying these strategic mistakes is an attitudinal problem, which

EXHIBIT 57
Steel Exports, 1978

	U.S.	Japan
	Millions of Metric Tons	Millions of Metric Tons
Production	127	110
Home Consumption	124	70
Destination		
Canada	0.8	0.5
Latin America	0.9	3.1
East Asia (Incl. China)	0.5	18.3
European Economic Community	0.2	0.8
Other Developed Countries	0.1	1.7
Other Developing Countries (Non-OECD Members)	0.3	8.3
Japan/U.S.	0.1	7.5
	2.9	40.2

Source: "The Steel Market in 1979 and the Outlook for 1980," OECD, Paris, 1980.

has caused American managers to react defensively to the foreign steel threat. Beginning in the 1960s, steel industry officials argued that foreign imports were based on cheap labor, dumping, and unfair trade practices and therefore asked for government protection. They compiled huge amounts of evidence, some of it undoubtedly accurate, which showed penetration pricing in the U.S. market, nontariff barriers in Japan, low wage costs, and government assistance as factors contributing to the advantages enjoyed by foreign steel exporters.

These allegations were combined with ringing defenses of the American industry from steel executives, such as this quotation from the president of Republic Steel in 1968: "The most frequently heard suggestion for solving the steel import problem is that the domestic industry should regain its former commanding lead in steel technology. The suggestion stems in part from the mistaken belief that the industry has been too slow to adopt new technological developments. The fact is that American steel technology is superior to any other country."[7]

Voluntary restraint agreements against foreign imports, first established in 1968 and then renewed in 1971, may have made some sense, given the obstacles to free trade in other countries. But what is not understandable is the lack of initiative on the part of steelmakers to invest aggressively for expansion, productivity improvement, and export under the umbrella of this temporary protection. Instead, the early 1970s saw continued minimum round-outs and an emphasis on diversification investments outside of steel in order to limit exposure in the steel industry. Steel companies made investments in a variety of projects, ranging from downstream uses of steel to housing developments.

The early 1970s also witnessed two erroneous and widespread predictions. The first—promulgated by various industry experts and adopted by the industry—predicted serious world steel shortages, particularly in the U.S., by 1980. Over 1 billion tons of demand was forecast for 1980, an estimate that was more than 200 million tons off.[8]

The second, and perhaps more serious set of errors predicted an end to the Japanese threat in the 1970s because of changes in the yen-dollar relationship and the world energy picture. Both these changes, it was thought, would work to the detriment of the Japanese industry. Thus, in 1971, the president of Bethlehem Steel said "the long-range threat of foreign steel competition seems to be diminishing."[9] In 1973, when the boom in steel demand caused the Japanese to partially withdraw and raise prices in the U.S. market, the president of the American Iron and Steel Institute (AISI) predicted that American buyers would not so easily buy Japanese steel again after the shortages and price increases experienced that year. Finally, in a 1975 *Wall Street Journal* article, the president of Jones and Laughlin Steel Company said

> the steel import situation has changed dramatically and perhaps permanently during the past two years. . . . In this period, both European and Japanese competitors have experienced sharply increasing costs for labor, raw materials and energy, which have in conjunction with the double devaluation of the dollar raised the cost per ton of foreign steel delivered to about the same levels as American steel. . . . The era of cheap foreign steel has gone the way of cheap foreign oil, never to return.[10]

It is interesting to note how mistaken were the U.S. commentators in understanding the effects of currency change on Japanese steel competitiveness. The Japanese industry buys its raw materials (about 32 percent of total cost for the whole industry) from abroad in contracts valued in dollars. A devaluation of the dollar by 25 percent results in about a 4-percent decrease in cost for the Japanese industry (historically, contracts have been renegotiated upward by about 50 percent after devaluations). If exports in dollars represent 20 percent of Japanese production and they suffer a decline of 25 percent in price realization, then this is a 5-percent negative effect. The net effect on Japanese companies as a whole of a 25-percent dollar-to-yen devaluation is thus only 1 percent.

During the early 1970s, this lack of understanding of market development and of competitors was a serious problem in the U.S. steel industry. A reasonably small circle of "industry experts" and company leaders had set up a fairly insulated and mutually reinforcing mythology about the strength of the American steel industry and the vulnerability of the Japanese steel industry, if stripped of its "unfair trade practices." Business leaders spent too much time worrying about unfair trading and the need to diversify investments instead of planning investments to reassert technological and productivity leadership.

By the mid-1970s, the handwriting was on the wall. Even in AISI statistics, Japanese firms had passed U.S. firms in productivity, and imports had risen again. As Exhibit 58 shows, even with optimistic

EXHIBIT 58
Ability of Major U.S. Steelmakers to Finance
Greenfield Plants, 1970–1974

	After-Tax Profit (Per Year Average) In Millions of Dollars	Cash Available[1] In Millions of Dollars	Years to Finance New Greenfield Facility[2]
U.S. Steel	284	568	6.8
Bethlehem	183	366	10.7
National	91	182	21.4
Republic	61	122	32.0
Armco	95	190	20.5
Jones and Laughlin	46	92	42.4
Youngstown	41	82	47.6

Source: Company annual reports.

[1] No dividends and 1:1 debt-to-equity ratio; depreciation used for upkeep and maintenance of existing facilities.

[2] Assumed to be 6 million tons at $650/annual ton ($3.9 billion). In fact, the cost per annual ton is now considerably higher.

assumptions, no individual U.S. firm could build a new greenfield facility. Yet industry leaders continued to rail against unfair trade practices. They also complained about pollution-control requirements.

It is worth noting that the industry's criticism of pollution-control requirements as a major cause of its competitive problems by the mid-1970s is questionable at best. During the 1970s, the Japanese steel industry spent more on pollution control than did the American steel industry, both in absolute terms and as a percentage of total investment (Exhibit 59). Pollution and safety levels and working conditions in Japanese mills today are, on the average, far superior to those in American mills. In general, Japanese companies have taken the less costly and more effective measure of designing new equipment with pollution control and safety in mind rather than retrofitting existing equipment.

In sum, the U.S. steel industry's underlying assumptions about the steel business prevented it from making the aggressive investments in modernization that were needed to match the pace of Japanese investment. From the U.S. company's point of view, the discounted cash flow return from a new low-cost greenfield mill could not justify its construction. Levels of debt as high as these in the Japanese industry

EXHIBIT 59
Pollution-Control Investment at Steel Mills

	U.S.			Japan		
	Total Investment In Millions of Dollars	Absolute Expenditure In Millions of Dollars	Percent of Total Investment	Total Investment In Millions of Dollars	Absolute Expenditure In Millions of Dollars	Percent of Total Investment
1971	1,473	162	11	2,433	219	9
1972	1,188	202	17	2,185	284	13
1973	1,428	100	7	2,165	368	17
1974	2,211	199	9	2,926	556	19
1975	3,236	453	14	3,806	685	18
1976	3,260	489	15	4,381	920	21
1977	2,267	408	18	3,700	555	15
	15,063	1,913	12.7	21,596	3,587	16.6

Source: "Technology and Steel Industry Competitiveness," Office of Technology Assessments, U.S. Congress, Washington, D.C., 1980, p. 351.

were unthinkable. Since no attempts were made to export in large quantities, growth rates were too slow to justify large additions to capacity. The investments the companies did make in round-out modernization left the U.S. less competitive than it was when the modernization started.

THE RECENT PAST IN THE STEEL INDUSTRY

In recent years, the most significant development in the world steel industry has been the rise of certain developing countries as producers and exporters of steel. Developing countries have gone from 7.4 percent of world steel production in 1967, to 9 percent in 1974, and to 13.5 percent in 1979. The percentage is expected to grow to 17 percent by 1984. Korea, Brazil, Venezuela, and others are expanding capacity rapidly, despite the slow growth of steel consumption on a worldwide basis.

Japanese steel companies, sensing a business opportunity, have become major exporters of steel technology, engineering services, and equipment to third-world countries. Again, U.S. steel companies have been less aggressive. Developing countries can buy reasonably sophisticated technology; combined with their low wage costs (and, in the case of OPEC countries, low fuel cost), this technology makes them competitive in exporting steel. With Japanese help, Brazilian and Korean steel mills at key plants can now provide steel at productivity levels about one-half to two-thirds those of American producers. Their wage rates of one-eighth U.S. levels give them a cost advantage.

Many European and most U.S. steel companies have remained uncompetitive and in crisis. A "trigger price" mechanism of protection has been instituted in the U.S. to minimize imports; the EEC has also restricted imports to Europe. Major rationalizations are under way in France, Sweden, the U.K., and Italy to improve the efficiency of their industries.

For the U.S., the major problem of overcoming the technology gap with Japan remains. In the long run, this will be the only way to develop a healthy and self-sustaining steel industry.

FOOTNOTES

[1] In 1979, the U.S. steel industry exported 3 million tons of steel while the Japanese steel industry exported 40 million tons.

[2] See Chapter 17, p. 208, the steel "trigger price" system.

[3] Actual prices paid for comparable grade and quantity of cold-rolled steel coils as revealed in a client's purchasing records:

	Sheet Product $/Ton	Bar Product $/Ton
Japanese Purchaser	231	161
U.S. Purchaser	318	224

Source: Client study.

[4] The following table shows relative average ages of selected Japanese and U.S. steel-rolling mills.

	U.S. Percent Older Than		Japan Percent Older Than	
	25 Years	20 Years	25 Years	20 Years
Plate Mills	45%	54%	5%	20%
Hot-Strip Mills	16	32	—	10
Cold-Strip Mills	29	54	—	15
Wire-Rod Mills	17	18	—	5

Source: Client study.

[5] The following table shows the value of Japanese blast-furnace and coal-blending techniques in making coal use more efficient in steel production. Less coal is used and a less expensive mix of coals is used in Japanese steelmaking.

	Coke Per Ton of Pig Iron Produced (kg.)		Value Mix of Coals Blended (Index of Price)	
	U.S.	Japan	U.S.	Japan
1965	650	507	100	88
1970	636	478	100	82
1975	611	443	100	71
1978	597	429	100	69

Source: Client study.

[6] This figure is obtained from client studies. Estimates made by other sources vary considerably, though almost all show a significant productivity and total cost advantage for Japanese producers. Two of the most thorough studies are "Technology and Steel Industry Competitiveness" by the Office of Technology Assessment, Congress of the United States, Washington, D.C., 1980 and "The United States Steel Industry and its International Rivals: Trends and Factors Determining International Competitiveness" from the Bureau of Economics of the Federal Trade Commission, Washington, D.C., November 1977.

[7] *Business Week*, July 1968, p. 26.

[8] See, for example, "Projection 85," a comprehensive forecast prepared by the International Iron and Steel Institute in 1973, or numerous articles by Father William Hogan of Fordham University, an acknowledged expert associated with the U.S. steel industry, such as "Steel Capacity Warning," *Metal Bulletin Monthly*, June 1973. In general, the industry has long suffered from an inbred group of experts who reinforced an incorrect "common wisdom."

[9] James H. Walker, quoted in *Business Week*, December 18, 1971, p. 20.

[10] "Drop in imports makes steel men wonder if days of cheap foreign steel are over," *Wall Street Journal*, December 30, 1975, p. 22.

14

The Competitive Battle for The Color Television Industry

The color television industry originated in the United States in the mid-1950s. In 1964, U.S. companies produced over 1 million sets. The Japanese industry started later; it was built up on over 400 licenses, primarily from U.S. companies and from Philips, the Dutch producer. In 1964, Japanese companies produced only a few thousand color sets and did not export.

By 1977, 42 percent of all color television sets sold in the world (not including the Communist countries) were manufactured by Japanese companies; less than 10 percent were manufactured by U.S. producers. Japan also had a 37-percent share of the United States market (Exhibit 60). Europe has remained relatively free of Japanese sets, mainly because of the special transmission systems used there and the accompanying licenses, which have temporarily placed legal limits on imports.

An orderly marketing agreement was instituted in the U.S. in July 1977, to limit Japanese imports to just under 1.6 million color units. Partly in response to this agreement, Japanese producers accelerated the building of television assembly plants in the United States (Exhibit 61). Five Japanese producers also established facilities in Europe in anticipation of the expiration of the special transmission systems licenses beginning in 1981. As Japanese producers decreased their exports to the United States, other Far Eastern producers, using Japanese components in many cases, increased theirs. The total share of imports in U.S. consumption has, therefore, declined only slightly. In 1978, exports from Korea made up 5 percent of U.S. color television consumption and those from Taiwan 6 percent.

In 1960, 27 American companies produced television receivers. By 1970, only 17 remained. Currently, there are five American producers,

EXHIBIT 60
Japanese Color Television Industry, 1977

	Market Size	Japanese Products Made in Japan In Millions of Units	Japanese Local Production In Millions of Units	Japanese Total In Millions of Units	Percent of Market Share
Japan	5.3	5.3		5.3	100%
U.S.	9.3	2.0	1.4	3.4	37
Europe	9.0	.6	.3	.9	10
Others	5.4	1.6	1.0	2.6	48
Total	29.0	9.5	2.7	12.2	42

Source: Client study.

EXHIBIT 61
Japanese Color Television Production Facilities in the U.S.

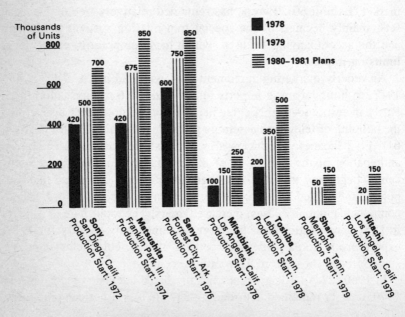

Sources: *Television Digest* and *Consumer Electronics.*

but only three have any significant market position (Exhibit 62). Profits are low to nonexistent. The Americans compete with seven Japanese and one European manufacturer producing in the U.S., plus imports from Korean and Taiwanese companies. While leading U.S. television producers have gone bankrupt, foreign producers have been investing heavily and establishing final assembly plants in the U.S.

How has the U.S. lost its strong initial position? What has happened in the color television industry? Let us first look at the success of the Japanese producers.

The reasons for the success of the Japanese producers relative to their American counterparts can be traced to their cost advantage, the better quality of their product, and their marketing and distribution strategies.

EXHIBIT 62
American Producers of Television Receivers in U.S., 1960–1980

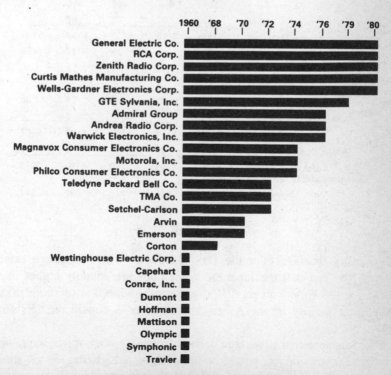

Source: Television Digest.

THE JAPANESE COST ADVANTAGE

Exhibit 63 shows a rough comparison of total production costs for a U.S. producer, a Japanese factory operating in Japan, and a Japanese factory operating in the U.S. The comparison includes both a leading Japanese company and one of the high-cost Japanese producers. The Japanese producers have between a 5-percent and a 20-percent deliv-

EXHIBIT 63
19" Color Television Cost Comparisons, 1979

	U.S. Producer	Japanese Sets Produced in Japan		Japanese Sets Produced in U.S.	
		Low-Cost Producer	High-Cost Producer	Low-Cost Producer	High-Cost Producer
Purchased Materials					
Picture Tube	$62	$57	$58	$66	$66
Other	89	62	71	67	74
Total Materials	$151	$119	$129	$133	$140
Labor and Variable Overhead	32	24	29	23	28
Overheads (Excluding Marketing and Distribution)	41	31	37	29	36
Quality Cost Penalty	—	—	—	3	3
Subtotal	$224	$174	$195	$188	$207
Freight, Duty, Insurance	6	25	25	6	6
Total Cost Before Marketing and Distribution	$230	$199	$220	$194	$213
Advantage	$2	$31	$10	$36	$17

Source: Client study.

ered cost advantage over the U.S. producer. This advantage exists despite the fact that the Japanese wage rates are actually higher than those for the American producer, especially when the offshore manufacturing facility of the American producer is considered (Exhibit 64).

The Japanese cost advantage derives from a number of factors: fewer electrical components, single-board design, a high degree of automation in insertion and in materials handling, sophisticated component

EXHIBIT 64
1979 Labor Rates

		U.S. Producer[1]
Labor Rates (Wages & Benefits) $/hour	Offshore Facility	1.04
	U.S. Facility	8.22
	Weighted Average Labor Rate	4.44
Person/Hours Per Set		2.68
Direct Labor Cost		11.90

		Japanese Low-Cost Producer	Japanese High-Cost Producer
Labor Rates (Wages & Benefits) $/hour	Main Facility	8.50	8.50
	Cottage Subassembly[2]	5.95	5.95
	Weighted Average Labor Rate	8.00	7.40
Person/Hours Per Set		0.85	1.26
Direct Labor Cost		6.80	9.32

Source: Client study.

technology, and integration of the major Japanese producers. The only major problem for Japanese producers selling in the U.S. is the high cost of picture tubes. This results from the 15-percent tariff imposed by the U.S. on the import of tubes. Thus, Japanese producers must purchase tubes from American producers at high prices.

In 1978, the number of electrical components in Japanese color television sets ranged from 380 for Matsushita to 493 for Sanyo, compared to an average of close to 600 for American producers. With

---

[1] U.S. producer performs subassemblies in low-wage country and final assembly in U.S. factory.

[2] Japanese producers use small companies in Japan with low-wage rates for some subassemblies. These are called "cottage industries."

fewer components, the Japanese have saved on the cost of materials and assembly time. The major reasons for the difference in component counts are a higher level of integration within the integrated circuits used by the Japanese, lower power consumption, and less emphasis on circuit isolation and protection.

Until recently, American sets had multiple boards while most Japanese sets had only one main board. American designers chose this approach for ease of serviceability. The Japanese designers, by contrast, felt that a single board was preferable; it increased reliability because of fewer contact points and fewer assembly tasks. Along with a quality-control program, the Japanese sought to minimize the introduction of faults in the set, rather than to facilitate servicing. The single-board chassis reduced assembly steps; it also reduced connectors and wires and board material, and it permitted significant reductions in testing time. This single-board approach has provided significant cost savings to Japanese producers.

Greater insertion automation saves labor, leads to greater potential for automated testing, and improves set reliability. In 1978, only about 40 percent of U.S. components were inserted automatically, compared to Japanese rates of 65 to 80 percent. The Japanese succeeded in automating insertion of radial as well as axial components and, in some cases, even integrated circuits. Because U.S. producers, until recently, could insert only axial components automatically, they tended to design their sets to incorporate a greater number of axials. This type of design resulted in lower board component density, requiring bigger boards and slower insertion cycle times.

The more advanced Japanese plants also use automatic transfer machines for moving the main circuit board from one insertion station to the next. Japanese companies are beginning to use robots in final assembly, in packing lines, and in stock control.

The most significant cost advantage enjoyed by the Japanese television producers is their component scale and integration. The major Japanese producers make their own integrated circuits, and they have close relationships with other large "semi–independent" component suppliers. This helps account for the lower component counts and efficient board design. Japanese companies often sell the circuits they develop to competitors to amortize their own development costs, but only after they have had a six-month to one-year lead in integrating the new circuits into their own chassis.

In addition, the size of the Japanese component industry provides scale advantages. Japanese producers have facilities that are as much as 10 times larger than western competitors for key components, such as fixed resistors, ceramic capacitors, and speakers. Most of the components now used in American television sets are purchased in the Far East, often at prices higher than those paid by Japanese companies. (While U.S. electronic component enterprises are often as large as those of the Japanese, U.S. firms have concentrated more on military and industrial applications rather than consumer ones.)

The savings offered by these factors affect all parts of the cost of producting a set, from materials to overheads. In the early 1970s, Japanese producers operated at a higher cost than their American counterparts, despite lower wage rates. Since then, however, the Japanese have brought out successive generations, each of which is lower in real cost than the previous. American producers have also cut costs with each successive generation, but since the mid-1970s they have tended to be a generation or two behind the Japanese. To date, a significant gap still exists.

THE QUALITY OF JAPANESE TELEVISIONS

In addition to a superior cost position, Japanese success has rested on set reliability. Exhibit 65 shows field service call rates (the number of service calls made per 100 sets in the first year of operation) in the U.S. market for foreign and domestic producers. Although Japanese sets have been requiring more service calls recently, their rates remain considerably below those of American producers. Quasar has gone from worst to best among American-produced brands since it was purchased by Matsushita, the Japanese producer.

To a great extent, the Japanese record is based on the reliability of their components, but this is only part of the story. Japanese success also depends on such factors as the following: Japanese quality-control procedures for television sets follow a fault-prevention strategy; chassis are designed with a slight overspecification on components; preproduction testing procedures are very elaborate for new chassis. In addition, Japanese producers coordinate carefully with component suppliers, and multifunction tests are performed on 100 percent of

EXHIBIT 65
Color Television Service Call Rates

(Percent of Sets Requiring Service Calls)

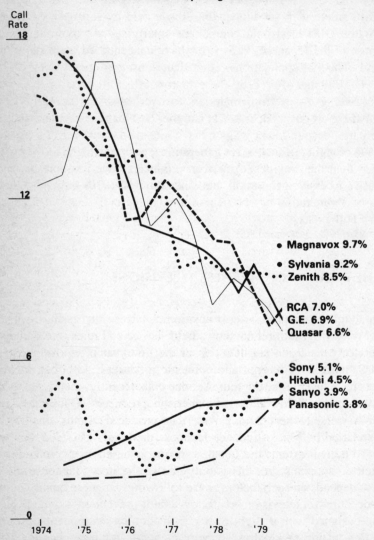

Call
Rate

18

12

• Magnavox 9.7%
• Sylvania 9.2%
• Zenith 8.5%

RCA 7.0%
G.E. 6.9%
Quasar 6.6%

6

Sony 5.1%
Hitachi 4.5%
Sanyo 3.9%
Panasonic 3.8%

0
1974 '75 '76 '77 '78 '79

Source: Trendex.

incoming components. The use of a single-board main chassis simplifies the wiring and reduces the number of connection points in the set, thereby also reducing the chances for defective solder joints. A large portion of the components is inserted automatically; material handling, too, is automated at a significant number of places in the factory. Hand insertion is done in a line, which can be worker controlled; the worker is responsible for removing defective sets from the line. Some final testing of assembled sets is done; this usually involves half an hour to four hours of "burn in" (running the set to see if it works properly).

American companies usually operate under a different system. They rely more heavily on testing within the production process and after. Their design cycles do not include as rigorous a preproduction test and they do not invest as heavily in incoming component testing. While Japanese manufacturers use a "zero defect" goal, American manufacturers work toward an AQL (acceptable quality level) goal, which allows a certain acceptable percentage of defects. AQL specification can result in lower materials costs, but the Japanese believe that it contributes to higher total systems costs. American manufacturers use subassembly and assembly test stations with "doglegs" (lines that run off the production process to rework products that do not pass the tests); there is also a long "burn in" test at the end of the process. Japanese factories used to have in-process testing at many stages but have now cut down on it as superfluous.

While an average Japanese factory has less than 1 percent fall-off rate in production (less than one set in 100 must be removed from the line during its production for rework), for many American factories the figure is over 50 percent. Compared to U.S. companies, the Japanese are able to achieve better quality levels at lower costs; this has allowed them to offer better warranty coverage than is offered by U.S. manufacturers. When Japanese companies initially extended their warranty periods from three months to one year (at an incremental cost of less than 1 percent of sales), a U.S. company that followed suit saw its own warranty costs rise from 3 to 9 percent of sales.

JAPANESE MARKETING AND DISTRIBUTION STRATEGIES

The final factor contributing to the Japanese success has been their marketing and distribution strategies. The major retail outlets for color televisions in the United States have traditionally been small independent dealers. To sell and service these tens of thousands of dealers, manufacturers developed elaborate distribution systems. These distribution systems, combined with brand images bought with advertising, created a significant barrier against new companies trying to enter the business.

Japanese companies (with the exception of Sony) penetrated the U.S. market primarily through private label and large discount and chain stores, which were growing faster than independent dealers in the first half of the 1970s. Thus, they avoided the necessity of building elaborate distribution networks and brand images. They used their lower-cost position to offer a wider margin for the dealer and a lower price for the consumer. More recently, the Japanese have aggressively pursued groups of independent dealers, who have joined together in buying clubs to do joint purchasing. The Japanese offer them better prices and margins than they could obtain from U.S. manufacturers. By focusing in this manner, Japanese producers have been able to penetrate the U.S. market rapidly and relatively cheaply.

COMPETITIVE DYNAMICS IN THE INDUSTRY

These changes in the relative success of the U.S. and Japanese color television industries can also be understood by analyzing different management attitudes and strategies.

With the rapid rise in wage rates and the yen-dollar exchange relationship in the early 1970s, many American managers thought that the Japanese industry would lose its ability to compete. But the major Japanese producers undertook a series of aggressive investments in product design, process automation, and new product development. These steps led to cost and quality advantages in the latter half of the decade in color televisions and to eventual domination of the world market in video cassette recorders. The Japanese responses to increasing labor costs in Japan were to introduce a first generation of automatic component-insertion machines, spend heavily on integrated circuit development, and pioneer elaborate preproduction testing of components.

The Japanese producers also undertook an aggressive export program in order to build the volume necessary to amortize the large investments they were making in new machinery and in research and development. They priced aggressively and designed models specifically for the U.S. and eventually the European markets, overcoming barriers of technology, style, and distribution.

The U.S. producers followed a different strategy. They responded to increased Japanese exports to the U.S. with a series of lawsuits, Congressional demands, and petitions to trade commissions complaining about unfair Japanese competition. At the same time, U.S. producers moved offshore in search of cheap labor for component production and board assembly: Zenith to Mexico and Taiwan; General Electric to Singapore and Ireland; Magnavox to Taiwan; RCA to Mexico. Although the U.S. producers undertook some product investments, most of their effort went into additional styling and minor performance features rather than into basic cost-reducing designs on the set itself. They introduced some early automatic insertion machines, but they did not put in the effort necessary to debug and fully utilize them.

After the recession in 1975, which hit the industry very hard, many U.S. producers drastically reduced their research and development and capital expenditures. The color television business was relegated to a secondary position in several companies with multibusiness portfolios.

Although some of the allegations against the Japanese companies did have merit, the U.S. companies ultimately failed because they invested in lawsuits, offshore production bases, and cosmetic features rather than in basic product design, process improvements, and export market development. Whatever dumping the Japanese may have engaged in was a minor aspect of their competitive success. The real basis was their well-designed investments to cut costs and increase quality and their designs for fundamentally new products.

CURRENT PROSPECTS IN THE COLOR TELEVISION INDUSTRY

The competitive battle for the American color television industry is not over. Significant technological changes will be occurring in the basic receiver itself; new peripheral products and features are still being added to the set; and wholly new products such as VCR, Videodisc and Viewdata are growing rapidly. Imports from Korea and Taiwan are likely to continue to increase in the standard end of the market. In new product areas, although the Japanese will undertake various assembly functions in the U.S., most production-process engineering and product design will be undertaken in Japan. Some jobs and substitution of import value added will occur, but these will not be substantial in comparison to the size of the world business. Aggressive strategies are still possible for the three remaining U.S. companies, if they have learned from these past mistakes.

15

The Competitive Situation of an Electromechanical Capital Good

The electromechanical capital good (ECG) business* is part of the power generation and distribution equipment industry. It is large equipment, crucial to the operation of an electrical network, sold mainly to public utilities and to large industrial plants. Purchasing decisions are subject to very strict engineering standards and testing tolerances. The resources and experience necessary to design, manufacture, market, and service such equipment are available to only a few companies in the world.

In the ECG business, as in many other parts of the power equipment industry, U.S. industry pioneered product innovation from the early 1900s through the 1960s. American technology was introduced in Europe and Japan after the First World War and was used again after the Second World War, when European and Japanese companies began to reconstruct their businesses. Until the late 1960s, the U.S. leader was also the largest ECG company in the world, and U.S. industry accounted for all the world's exports. The industry structure in the U.S. was fairly well stabilized, with one company possessing 40 percent of the market, and three more specialized followers of roughly equal size.

From the end of the Second World War until the late 1960s, the U.S. market grew at about 3 percent per year in real terms. At the end of that period, the U.S. still represented almost half of the world market. The U.S. leader maintained its share of the market, and ex-

---

* Because the situation described in this example is more recent and competitively more sensitive than either the steel or television example, the specific product has been disguised.

ported to South America, South East Asia, and nonproducing developed countries (Canada and Australia). Sales grew at 4 percent per year in real terms, reaching $160 million in 1970. Return on sales (before taxes) fell from its abnormally high postwar period level of 40 percent, stabilizing around 20 percent during the 1960s. Positive cash flows were generated in excess of necessary reinvestments in plant and working capital.

Around 1970, however, the world seemed to change for the U.S. leader, whose financial performance gradually declined. Market share dropped to 30 percent, sales leveled around $120 million, return on sales fell to 5 percent, and net cash flows became negative. Imports have now taken over 15 percent of the U.S. market, and most of the export markets have dried up for U.S. companies.

EUROPEAN COMPETITORS IN THE ECG INDUSTRY

Meanwhile, European competitors—mostly in France and Germany— have emerged as the world leaders. They are fast-growing (10 percent in real terms), increasingly profitable companies that invest agressively. The top three European companies, now two to three times larger than the U.S. leader, have established a worldwide manufacturing and marketing presence as well as a technological lead. They are growing faster and are more profitable than the U.S. leaders.

Some of the success of the European competitors is due to higher growth in electrical load and infrastructure investment in Europe than in the U.S. during the 1970s. European countries have now reached maturity in their electrical network, much as the U.S. did in the mid-1960s. Recent data suggest, however, that European competitors continue to grow, particularly in export markets outside the U.S., Europe, and Japan. These foreign competitors are now engaged in a fierce battle among themselves for new markets. U.S. companies have a very small share of these new markets (Exhibit 66). Two U.S. competitors have already dropped out or been taken over, and imports into the U.S. are increasing. The remaining two U.S. competitors will have to invest heavily to survive.

Why did this dramatic change occur? Three groups of factors can be identified that changed the nature of the industry and competitive positions within it: the role and structure of public utilities in the U.S.

and in Europe, technological substitution, and the emergence of the Third World as a key market.

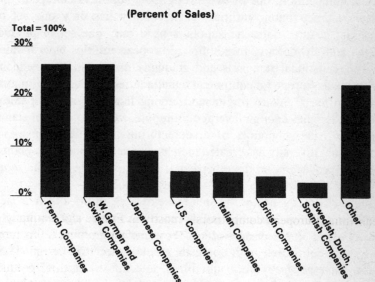

EXHIBIT 66
Market Shares for Producers in Developing Countries, 1975–1978

(Percent of Sales)

Total = 100%

Sources: Manufacturers associations, trade statistics.

ROLE OF PUBLIC UTILITIES AS A CUSTOMER

The U.S. public utilities industry is more fragmented, conservative, and disorganized than public utilities industries in other countries. In most developed countries, a few very large utilities, generally publicly owned, operate the electrical network and specify the type of equipment needed. In France, for example, the government merged all the small private utilities into one public company, EDF, which is now the largest electricity producer in the world. In West Germany, half a dozen very large regional utilities represent more than three-quarters of the country's electricity production. In the U.K., the CEGB, the coordinating body for all utilities, draws up specifications. In Italy, EN EL has been organized on the French model. In small countries like Sweden and Holland, large national utilities assisted domestic ECG suppliers when they were still small and uncompetitive. They were careful not to maintain uneconomic sources of supply for too long, however. Seeking to help the best suppliers to emerge, they split orders only among a limited number of candidates. After a period of internal competition, one or two strong ECG suppliers emerged.

With national public utilities, each country has only one set of standards; in turn, domestic suppliers need only one set of product designs and technology. In addition, European utilities have harmonized their national standards and gradually created a homogeneous market inside Europe for equipment manufacturers. By contrast, public utilities in the U.S. are fragmented among hundreds of companies. None of them has enough leverage to impose one set of design standards. Given the economies of manufacturing in the ECG business, such product diversity has created increasing overheads in U.S. plants. European producers, on the other hand, have been able to build more automated lines around a larger volume per model.

Another consequence of the small size of U.S. utilities is their lack of testing facilities. European utilities each have very large testing labs and high-level engineering staffs to examine new products. In turn, these staffs collaborate with domestic manufacturers on design. U.S. utilities have generally been unwilling to accept the risks of product innovation, even though new network requirements such as higher load characteristics have made innovations necessary. Rather than working with U.S. producers to pioneer new equipment, many U.S. utilities prefer to purchase European equipment, which has already been tested on European networks.

TECHNOLOGICAL SUBSTITUTION

Over the past decade, the ECG business has been revolutionized by a new technology. Ironically, this new technology originated in the U.S. leader's laboratories but was never introduced in the U.S. because of the utilities' conservatism. Instead, the U.S. producer licensed European competitors who spent three to five years in product development and testing with their domestic utilities before introducing the innovations in the late 1960s.

The new technology provides higher performance at lower cost than the old technology. The product is more compact, can work with higher electrical loads, needs less maintenance, is easier to install, and is less dangerous. Moreover, production is totally different. Instead of designing and producing particular equipment for each utility's requirement and each network's characteristics, producers can design the ECG in modules that can be easily assembled into various systems and with various combinations. Economies of scale therefore apply to the whole volume of modules required by the complete market range rather than to a specific volume per model.

This new "modular" technology is penetrating most world markets, and has grown from 20 percent of total sales in 1965 to over 50 percent in 1978. European utilities have converted their whole network, even though this has required new investments before the old technology is physically obsolete. Japanese utilities, followed by Third-World countries, also have adopted the technology. The new technology has been growing at 12 percent a year while the whole world market has been growing at 5 percent.

Whereas a U.S. company with 40 percent of the large U.S. market previously had the largest production scale in the world, the definition of scale has now changed. European competitors with more standardized customer requirements and modular manufacturing can experience greater economies of scale. The definition of scale makes the exploitation of new market opportunities much more important in establishing a long-term cost advantage; hence the critical role played by newly industrialized countries.

THE EMERGENCE OF THIRD-WORLD MARKETS

Newly industrialized countries are not only important in businesses such as clothing, steel, and shipbuilding. They have also become critical in the competition among developed countries, particularly when their market represents the major part of world growth. In the ECG business, Brazil represents a larger market than Germany and one that is almost one-third the size of the U.S. market. Altogether, developing countries represent 40 percent of world market and more than 70 percent of world growth (Exhibit 67).

EXHIBIT 67
Percent of Electrical Capital Goods Sales
in the World Market

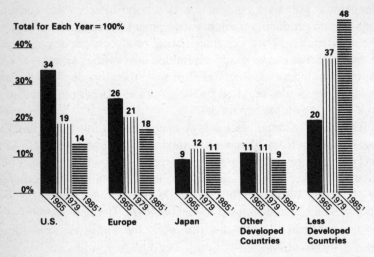

Sources: Manufacturers associations, trade statistics, interviews.

In many businesses, selling and servicing are very different processes in developing countries than they are in developed countries, requiring special organizations, resources, and experience. Because of the lack of qualified staff in developing countries, part of the engineering work that is typically done by the customer has to be carried out by the supplier. Accordingly, ECG's are often included in "packages" or even in "turnkey" plants* (Exhibit 68). Much larger worldwide organization and more field service are therefore required in local markets. European ECG manufacturers, soon followed by the Japanese, were first to develop a specific package and turnkey capability. The Europeans have even developed special companies that handle package and turnkey contracts exclusively. They have also established local civil-engineering capability in cooperation with local contractors. Package and turnkey sales now represent 60 percent of the French competitors' exports and 50 percent of the German.

---

* With turnkey plants, the engineering contractor agrees to provide a complete plant to a customer without any work required of the customer. The supplier just "turns over the key" to the buyer when the plant is completed.

EXHIBIT 68
Worldwide Electrical Capital Goods Sales, 1975–1978

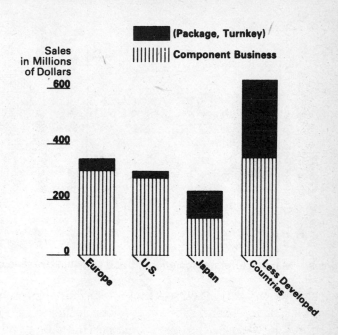

Source: Client study.

By contrast, the U.S. leader can only offer a few technicians, most of whom are unfamiliar with the developing country's network requirements. Exports to developing countries are only 4 percent of the U.S. leader's sales. Its share in these fast-growth markets is less than one-tenth that of its European competitors.

In the coming years, changes in these developing-country markets may make it even more difficult for the U.S. manufacturers to compete. These countries may close their borders to imports and offer a protected base to the first multinationals established in the country. Moreover, several of these countries will become bases for new scale plants in components that are sensitive to wage-rate differentials. Thus, the European and Japanese ECG competitors will not only have "locked in" the largest growth markets but also will have established the lowest cost position for producing various components for re-export.

EXHIBIT 69

Potential Competitors in the ECG World Market

(Percent of Total World Market, 1975–78)

Competitor—	1 W.German	2 French	3 French	4 W.German	5 Japanese	6 U.S.
W. Germany	—	5	5	—	5	5
France	—	—	—	4	4	4
Italy	—	—	—	3	3	3
U.K.	2	2	2	2	2	2
Other European Countries[1]	4	3	5	5	5	4
Brazil	—	—	—	—	7	7
India	—	—	—	—	5	5
Korea	1	1	1	1	1	1
Japan	12	12	12	12	—	12
Total Not Accessible	19%	23%	25%	27%	32%	43%
Total Accessible	81%	77%	75%	73%	68%	57%

Source: Client study.

[1] Sweden, Holland, Spain, Switzerland.

THE U.S. DILEMMA

In sum, U.S. competitors in the ECG business were initially penalized by a fragmented, conservative customer base, whereas European competitors could take advantage of innovative public purchasing attitudes.

The U.S. companies themselves, however, can be faulted on a number of grounds: They failed to change technology early enough, and they did not invest in new modular equipment plants. They did not recognize the tremendous export potential offered by the newly emerging countries nor the new distribution channels that were required. The U.S. companies lacked the necessary package and turnkey capability to pursue these markets successfully. They failed altogether to adopt a worldwide vision for a business that was becoming truly international.

The results of this competitive shortsightedness are illustrated in Exhibit 69, which shows that the U.S. industry has access to only 57 percent of the world market now while European competitors have access to 80 percent because of their strategies in developing countries. As a consequence, the U.S. industry may be vulnerable to a frontal attack by European competitors who are eager to build volume for their new technology and who view the U.S. market as untapped potential for substitution.

16

Summary: Why Don't U.S. Businesses Compete More Successfully?

In the preceding chapters, various reasons for the competitive decline of the U.S. at the firm level have been reviewed. Investment decisions, cost management, pricing policies, approaches to international businesses, and worker-management relations have been explored. Three industries have been examined in order to illustrate that the problems they exemplify are endemic to a wide range of U.S. businesses.

This summary suggests some of the underlying causes of the inability of U.S. businesses to compete more successfully in today's international competitive environment.

ACCOUNTING SYSTEMS

The problems of lack of attention to manufacturing overheads and poor definitions of investment result partly from the organization of company accounting systems. Most financial accounting systems have been developed to provide information for tax authorities and banks. Most cost-accounting systems have been designed to provide managers of different departments with the information they need to control their department costs according to predetermined budgets.

Those uses of accounting systems are necessary. However, the information they provide is ill suited to strategic analysis. Since these accounting systems offer no dynamic model of cost behavior, they obscure the total effect of changes in manufacturing process, product design and variety, and pricing and investment decisions. Because the systems fail to separate the long-term earning power of business investments from ongoing costs, they make it impossible to analyze dynamic projections of changes in earnings potential.

The few strategic decisions that a business makes each year set the basic course for the long term. They determine the success or failure of the business at the most fundamental level. Certainly, accounting information for banks and tax authorities and for departmental control are important to the day-to-day business; these systems, however, relate only to execution and not to basic direction. An ongoing means of accounting to provide strategic information is also necessary.

COMPETITIVE ANALYSIS

The activities of competitors determine one's own growth and profitability. Yet U.S. companies are often less sophisticated than their foreign competitors in monitoring these activities.

U.S. and Japanese firms in many industries often send delegations of technicians to visit each other's plants. Japanese companies then integrate the information from the trip reports into their total planning systems. They analyze in minute detail the specific process steps that the technicians found interesting and for which the company may wish to purchase licenses. Top management incorporates data from these reports into estimates of competitive cost position and the likelihood of competitor expansions. This information is often also integrated into an elaborate system for culling information on competitors from public and semiprivate sources, to produce assessments of plans and of competitors' strengths and weaknesses.

In many U.S. companies, by contrast, competitive information lies scattered around in different departments; trip reports may be read by the curious but they are not systematically analyzed. It is all too common to find top-level U.S. managers who do not even know the volume and product ranges of foreign competitors. Information on competitors is not integrated into strategy formulation in a systematic way.

The reasons for these differences in competitive analysis are partly historical. Japanese and German firms have undertaken careful competitive analyses since the end of the Second World War. They have studied techniques of U.S. companies and have learned from them. They have measured their progress in rebuilding their industries by how fast they were catching up to U.S. companies in product development and manufacturing. The habit and discipline of this vigorous competitive analysis have continued as Japanese and German companies have caught up with—and in many cases surpassed—their U.S. counterparts in productivity and technology.

By contrast, for too many years, U.S. firms have assumed that the only relevant competitors were domestic. U.S. companies have taken foreign competitors too lightly. Competitive analysis is at least as important as market forecasts and cost accounting. Systems must be established in U.S. companies to conduct this analysis systematically and thoroughly.

EVALUATION SYSTEMS

One of the attitudes that pervades U.S. business is the short time frame of U.S. managers. This shortsighted attitude manifests itself in the investment approval system, in the ways in which international businesses are managed, in attitudes toward worker security and job enrichment, and in issues of quality. This attitude is also evident in the propensity of many U.S. managers to spend a significant portion of their time rearranging industrial assets. Finesse in legal and financial manipulation often yields greater short-term rewards than skill in increasing productivity.

The origins of the emphasis on a short-term view lie in the systems of evaluation in many U.S. companies. Perhaps the problem begins with the stock market, the banks, and the business press, all of which respond quarterly or even weekly to earnings and sales figures, and which find it difficult to evaluate short-term sacrifices undertaken for long-term returns.

Whatever the external reason, internal evaluation systems rarely look to long-term results. Managers who raise prices may be valued highly for the improved earnings they provide during their three-year tenure before promotion, but their successors will suffer the consequences—loss of market share and long-term profitability in the long run.

Similarly, bonuses are often tied to yearly volume, cash flow, and/ or profit targets. Managers sometimes engage in activities counterproductive to the long-term interests of the company in order to "meet their numbers." Such activities may include depleting inventories at the end of the year to improve ROI's or cash flows, relaxing quality standards to meet volume of production targets, or delaying needed expense investments to meet profit targets. These managers are not being irresponsible or dishonest; they are only adhering to the priorities set by the internal system of evaluation.

Systems for evaluating workers can also be shortsighted. Greater worker responsibility and participation require investments of time and energy in the short run, though they generally yield higher long-run benefits than systems based on discipline, fear, and distrust.

ATTITUDES

Better strategic thinking and planning can be brought about by improvements in U.S. systems of accounting, competitive analysis, and evaluation. Improved strategic planning also requires changes of attitude and habit on the part of those inside companies who make strategy and those outside companies who evaluate the firms' progress.

U.S. companies must acquire more of an international perspective on business affairs; it is necessary to take more risks, to lengthen time horizons on investment returns, to develop a keen awareness about the movements of competitors, and to elevate the status of manufacturing in company hierarchies. It is also important to take a more constructive view towards the work force, whose concerns are often invisible to top management even though the workers are the heart of the organization.

SUMMARY

Basic decisions that affect U.S. productivity developments, both absolute and relative to those in other countries, are made in individual firms. A framework for considering various groups of businesses according to their competitive economic characteristics has been presented, dividing businesses into sheltered, raw-material based, low-wage, and complex-factor cost groupings. The categories provide bases for business management and policy direction.

In sheltered businesses, managers should aim for market-share leadership within appropriate geographical regions, putting together what one European business manager called "a string of pearls," a series of individually leading plants. For the policymaker, traditional antitrust enforcement to ensure domestic competition is probably the main policy mechanism to encourage productivity improvements.

In order to gain a competitive productivity advantage, the company leader in raw materials businesses must seek control of, or access to the best deposits wherever they exist. The policymaker should inventory and monitor potential domestic resources since they form the basis of the country's export and import needs. Policies must be developed to manage limited or depletable resources in order to ensure long-term benefit for the country.

For low-wage businesses, managers must either secure positions in low-wage countries or slowly phase out of the domestic business. Policymakers must foresee and plan for the eventual phasing-out of these businesses from our economy. The key challenges to policymakers are the ability to anticipate changes in the structure of the industry and to ease the social disruption associated with them, without impeding their progress.

Success in complex-factor cost businesses, which make up the majority of U.S. production and exports, will be crucial to the future success of the U.S. economy. U.S. companies must identify the key competitive elements in their various businesses and devise and implement strategies to gain leadership through sustainable cost advantage or price premium.

The failure of many of our companies to accomplish this goal over the past decade has been a major cause of our economic problems. The result of these failures of competitive strategy has been the loss of employment, foreign exchange, and ultimately of real wealth for Americans. U.S. competitive positions have repeatedly been lost to foreign competitors. Some losses—such as in automobiles, small refrigerators, and motorcycles—are quite visible to the average American. Other, far more numerous losses—such as in numerically controlled machine tools, plastic moulding machines, and electronic discrete components—are less visible but equally important to the American economy.

One should not infer from this that all U.S. companies in complex-factor cost businesses have been losing competitive productivity to foreign competitors. Many U.S. companies are still strong competitors; they are growing and producing positive trade balance in thousands of businesses, from computers to power tools to sheets and towels. The problem is that the U.S. has lost competitiveness in too many areas; and unless business practices are improved, the U.S. faces the threat of further erosion in areas where it is currently the leader.

III

THE ROLE OF GOVERNMENT

As the preceding chapters have shown, some American firms are failing in international competition because they have not developed strategies for achieving and maintaining competitive advantage in key areas of their businesses. But their competitive decline is also due to another factor over which individual firms have less control: the failure of government industrial strategy.

Without government support, American business will find it increasingly difficult to achieve competitive leadership in today's international environment. This does not mean that government can effectively supplant or second-guess the strategic decisions of business. Nor does it mean that all firms are or should be dependent on the government. It simply means that the competitive strength of the economy as a whole requires a coherent set of public policies for improving competitive productivity in industry.

Government policies expressly formulated to stimulate economic development are not new to the United States. The U.S. has a strong tradition of government subsidies and tariffs designed to stimulate and protect new industries. Alexander Hamilton's "Report on Manufacturers"[1] is a classic formation of such industrial policies, shades of which can also be seen in the "American System" proposed by Henry Clay and John C. Calhoun. Throughout the early nineteenth century, government—particularly at the state level—was viewed as an agent of economic development. Rather than seek to limit its power or intrusiveness in private transactions, citizens saw government (and the legal order it imposed) as a primary vehicle for mobilizing the resources of the community toward greater productivity.[2] Government was a partner in enterprise. While the initiative rested with the private entrepreneur, government shared in the risk by providing direct subsidies and supplying a legal framework that indirectly subsidized risk-taking.

Indeed, in 1854, when the British Ordinance Department sent a commission to America to discover why its exhibits at the Crystal Palace had included so many ingenious products, the commission found that the "American system of manufacturing" was based not only on plentiful resources—wood, water power, and cheap land—but also on large government contracts, funds, and facilities.[3]

Nevertheless, except for the tariffs and quotas that protected our "infant" industries against foreign competitors through most of the nineteenth and early twentieth centuries, few, if any, of these development policies were focused expressly on international competition. Nor did the U.S. government concern itself directly with the adjustments of capital and labor markets to structural changes in the world economy. With abundant resources and an ever-increasing domestic market, adjustment was no problem.

During the past 10 to 15 years, however, the U.S. has become irrevocably dependent on international trade. Any change in world market conditions has a profound effect on the domestic economy. Today, the U.S. and every other advanced industrial country must deal with two key issues of economic adjustment. First, each country must cope with businesses that face long-term competitive declines because of the increasing cost of raw materials, the cost advantages of low-wage countries, and the easy migration of capital and technology abroad. Second, each country must concern itself with existing and potential businesses that are growing rapidly and are capable of gaining long-term competitive leadership in world markets.

DECLINING BUSINESSES

Theoretically, a nation has three strategic choices with regard to declining businesses. As a practical matter, however, it has only two. A nation can ease the adjustment of capital and labor out of these businesses by assisting workers with retraining and relocating, by subsidizing the development of new businesses within the same region or community, and by helping firms to salvage those portions of declining businesses that are capable of becoming competitive on their own. A second choice is for a nation to protect declining businesses from foreign competition by erecting tariffs, quotas, or "voluntary" export agreements and by subsidizing the cost of maintaining those businesses in the face of more competitive imports. The third alternative—doing nothing and allowing the market to work on its own, with resulting bankruptcies, unemployment, and community or regional decline—is generally politically unacceptable and causes serious human hardship, and is, practically speaking, no alternative at all.

As the following chapters show, the U.S. has chosen to rely primarily on the second alternative, while its more successful trading partners have increasingly strived to achieve the first. At great expense to consumers and to the rest of the economy, the U.S. has chosen to maintain businesses whose overall competitive position is declining. The U.S. has thereby increased the cost to other domestic businesses of obtaining goods and services that are protected from international competition, thus jeopardizing the international competitiveness of these other businesses as well. In short, rather than accelerating the adjustment of capital and labor to changing conditions and world markets, the U.S. has retarded these adjustments.

By contrast, other advanced industrial countries have devised a variety of measures for accelerating the movement of capital and labor out of declining businesses, although on occasion they have also resorted to various forms of protection. In recent years, other industrialized nations have grown increasingly sophisticated in their policies for retraining and relocating workers, for developing new industry in depressed regions, and for restructuring declining industries in ways that boost their most competitive businesses.

GROWING BUSINESSES

A nation also has two practical choices with regard to businesses that are capable of gaining long-term competitive leadership in world markets. First, it can explicitly hasten their development by reducing their short-term capital and labor cost. In the short term, a nation can reduce the cost of capital by helping the businesses to fund research, by subsidizing certain high-risk investments, and by sharing the cost of developing foreign markets. It can reduce the cost of labor by subsidizing education and training. Alternatively, a nation can forego a consciously constructed policy and allow its promotional policies to be shaped by politically powerful businesses and geographic regions and by the necessities of its defense programs. This second alternative results in a hodgepodge of subsidies, loan guarantees, tax expenditures, and procurement contracts. Some of these measures inadvertently promote businesses capable of gaining long-term competitiveness, but many of them are simply wasted.

The following chapters show how the U.S. has chosen to rely primarily on the second alternative, while its major successful trading partners have chosen to rely on the first. While U.S. defense procurement and defense-related research and development programs have spawned some highly competitive industries, these programs have been undertaken without regard to their effects on the commercial development of civilian markets. Accordingly, these positive effects have been inadvertent, and there is no reason to suppose they will continue in the future. Other subsidies, meanwhile, have been dictated more by political expedience than by industrial strategy. In contrast, other advanced industrial nations encourage their potentially most competitive businesses through measures that directly complement the strategies employed by the businesses themselves.

The contrast between the *de facto* industrial policies of the U.S. and the more directed policies of its trading partners is stark. For reasons of ideology or politics, or both, the U.S. has failed to acknowledge the practical choices confronting it. Instead, it has clung tenaciously to the notion that government can and should be "neutral" with regard to market adjustments. The vast array of U.S. tariffs, quotas, "voluntary" export agreements, and bail-outs for declining businesses are viewed as isolated exceptions to this rule of neutrality; its defense-related expenditures, tax breaks, and assorted subsidies for other industries are seen as being somehow unrelated to industrial development or to market dynamics. Consequently, the U.S. has neither neutrality nor rationality. Meanwhile, its trading partners are becoming ever more efficient in designing and administering policies to aid their industries in adapting to market changes. As a result, the competitive strategies employed by their individual firms have been substantially enhanced.

The directness with which trading partners of the U.S. have embraced positive adjustment policies has enabled them to design these policies more rationally and use them more efficiently than the U.S. does. More importantly, such explicitness has also better enabled them to fashion a consensus around these policies, so that the labor, financial, and industrial communities are in general agreement about the overall direction of economic development and any sacrifices it entails. By refusing to make explicit policy choices, the U.S. has obscured these choices from public view, rendering them more susceptible to political manipulation by special interests. Simultaneously, it is more difficult for the government to achieve a consensus in favor of any overall strategy for regaining competitiveness—short of simply throwing public money and tax breaks indiscriminately in the direction of wealthy individuals and business.

This section first describes recent U.S. policies that deal with the twin issues of declining and growing businesses. Then the focus shifts to Europe and Japan, with a survey of their explicit industrial policies and a discussion of how they compare with one another and with the U.S. in coping with these two problems.

General policies—laws governing antitrust, environmental protection, consumer protection, worker safety, and general working conditions—inevitably affect industries and businesses differently. If they are designed and implemented correctly, these general measures effectively "tax" industries in proportion to the cost the industries impose upon society as a whole.

In contrast, selective policies directly and positively affect the allocation of capital and labor in the economy. Therefore, they have far greater potential for either accelerating or retarding economic adjustment. Thus, we will focus mainly on selective government policies that are targeted to specific industries, businesses, or regions, rather than on general policies that affect the entire economy in the aggregate.

FOOTNOTES

[1] In his "Report on the Subject of Manufacturers," Alexander Hamilton argued that government support to industry would strengthen agriculture, create many opportunities for enterprise and investment, and generate employment. Indeed, he distinguished between ongoing subsidies and measures specifically targeted to growing industries:

> The continuance of bounties on manufacturers long established must always be of questionable policy; because a presumption would arise, in every such case, that there were natural and inherent impediments to

success. But, in new undertakings, they are so justifiable as they are oftentimes necessary. There is no purpose to which public money can be more beneficially applied than to the acquisition of a new and useful branch of industry; no consideration more valuable than a permanent addition to the general stock of productive labor. *Source:* Alexander Hamilton, "Report on the Subject of Manufacturers," in *The Works of Hamilton,* III. New York: John F. Trow, 1850, pp. 248–49.

[2] See Hurst, James Willard. "The Release of Energy," in his *Law and the Conditions of Freedom in the Nineteenth Century United States.* Madison: University of Wisconsin Press, 1956.

[3] For a discussion of nineteenth century industrial policy, see, e.g., Taylor, George. *The Transportation Revolution, 1815 to 1860, The Economic History of the United States,* Vol. 4. New York: Rinehart, 1951; Handlin, Oscar. *Commonwealth: A Study of the Role of Government in the American Economy, Massachusetts 1774–1861.* New York: New York University Press, 1947; Heath, Milton. "Laissez-Faire in Georgia, 1732 to 1861," *Journal of Economic History,* 3 (1943), pp. 78–100; Hartz, Louis. *Economic Policy and Democratic Thought: Pennsylvania, 1776–1860.* Cambridge: Harvard University Press, 1948; Pierce, Harry. *Railroads of New York.* Cambridge: Harvard University Press, 1953; Goodrich, Carter and Segal, Harvey H. "Baltimore's Aid to Railroads," *Journal of Economic History,* 13 (1953), p. 2; Callender, G.S. "The Early Transportation and Banking Enterprises of the States in Relation to the Growth of Corporations," *Quarterly Journal of Economics,* 17 (1902), pp. 111–162; Handlin, Oscar. "Origins of the American Business Corporation," *Journal of Economic History,* 5 (1945), pp. 1–23; Horwitz, Morton J. *The Transformation of American Law, 1780–1860.* Cambridge: Harvard University Press, 1977.

17

U.S. Policies for Declining Businesses

Since 1965, the U.S. has suffered competitive declines in textiles, apparel, footwear, steel, automobiles, shipbuilding, color television receivers, and several other major industries. In some businesses within these industries, this decline is the inevitable result of low-wage competition. However, as the case studies of the steel, television, and ECG industries showed, not all declines reflect irreversible long-term cost disadvantages; some are attributable to poor strategy at the firm level. Certain businesses within these industries are salvageable, capable of being restored to competitive health.

The main point is that government policy has done little to reverse these declines; indeed, in some respects, it has exacerbated them. Rather than facilitating adaptation—that is, easing the flow of capital and labor to the most competitive businesses within the industry or to related and highly competitive businesses outside the industry—government policy has tended toward the opposite direction, both retarding capital and labor adjustments and often jeopardizing the positions of the most competitive businesses.

The U.S. has dealt with competitive declines primarily by seeking to protect declining businesses from imports. Increasingly, this has come to mean "voluntary" agreements with foreign countries to limit exports to the U.S. Meanwhile, programs for retraining and relocating workers and for developing new industries in affected regions have been underfunded and are currently being phased out. In addition, the U.S. has had no systematic programs for helping industries to restructure themselves and salvage their most competitive parts, short of the draconian measures mandated by U.S. bankruptcy laws.

PROTECTION FROM IMPORTS

Tariff rate levels among industrialized countries are lower today than they have been at any time during this century (Exhibit 70). Industries that can demonstrate injury from import competition may obtain temporary tariff protection or assistance from the government. If industries can show that imports are being "dumped" on the U.S. market at prices below their sales price in their domestic markets they can also obtain the imposition of duties on imports.[1] U.S. industries have actively sought both forms of special relief. By and large, however, unilateral tariff increases have become a thing of the past. Governments in all advanced industrial countries now understand that unilateral increases typically generate retaliatory increases by other countries, and that the net result is harmful to everyone.

EXHIBIT 70
Ratio of Duties Collected to Value of U.S. Imports, 1930–1974.

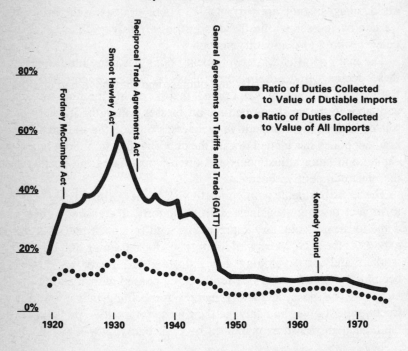

Source: Dobson, John M. *Two Centuries of Tariffs: The Background and Emergence of the International Trade Commission.* Washington, D.C.: U.S. Government Printing Office, 1976, p. 34.

Despite the overall trend toward reduced tariffs, in recent years, a wide variety of products has been subject to import quotas that have been "voluntarily" negotiated between the U.S. and particular foreign companies or governments. These restrictions have been voluntary only in the sense that foreign companies and countries have acceded to the request of the U.S. government to limit their exports, under possible threat of a unilateral tariff, the withdrawal of military aid, or some other more objectionable alternative. Notable among these voluntary restrictions have been those governing textiles, apparel, color television receivers, footwear, steel, and automobiles.

These voluntary restrictions have been politically convenient because they have allowed the U.S. President to avoid the necessity of asking Congress to enact unilateral tariffs or quotas, or to rescind any aspect of U.S. multilateral tariff agreements. They also have permitted administrations to maintain a theoretical commitment to free trade, since they avoid the high visibility of a formal tariff or quota. Finally, these voluntary restrictions have enabled the U.S. to avoid the negative effects on foreign policy that are associated with an across-the-board tariff or quota. But these restrictions have shared many of the disadvantages of unilateral tariffs and quotas, and they have had additional drawbacks of their own.

First, like tariffs, quotas, and other devices that artificially maintain the price of domestic goods, these voluntary restrictions have multiplier effects upon the rest of the economy, thus undermining the competitiveness of other domestic industries that depend upon the imported goods. Within an economy increasingly subject to foreign trade, any restriction on imports is apt to jeopardize the competitiveness of other related industries.

The experience of the U.S. textile and apparel industries illustrates this multiplier effect. The competitiveness of much of the U.S. textile industry seriously declined during the past several decades, in part because of the historic protection accorded to wool and cotton fiber producers. Price supports for cotton, first imposed in 1932, coupled with quotas that were imposed on raw cotton imports, made domestic cotton more expensive than cotton sold in the world market. To make matters worse, between 1956 and 1964, U.S. raw cotton exports were subsidized by the federal government, thereby allowing foreign textile manufacturers to purchase U.S. cotton at a world price that was 25 percent below its domestic price. Similarly, U.S. sheep growers were protected from foreign imports by a duty of 25 percent per pound on imported raw wool. Since the supply of domestic wool was insufficient to meet the needs of U.S. wool textile manufacturers, the textile manufacturers were forced to pay the higher price for imported wool.

As a result of these restrictions, by the mid-1950s, U.S. textile manufacturers found themselves at a severe cost disadvantage relative to manufacturers in other countries, particularly in Japan, where textile machinery was as modern and productive as that in the U.S. By 1957, textile imports had reached such a high level that U.S. manufacturers obtained the government's commitment to seek an agreement with Japan limiting its export of cotton textiles. But this agreement merely shifted the foreign production of cotton textiles from Japan to Hong Kong and encouraged Japanese textile manufacturers to shift their production from cotton to wool and manufactured fibers. The flow of cheap foreign textiles into the U.S. was unabated. Several other agreements were negotiated to cover specific fibers and countries. When these had also failed to stem the flow, in 1973 the U.S. entered into the Multi-Fiber Agreement with 18 textile-manufacturing countries, including Hong Kong, Korea, and Taiwan. This agreement limited exports to the U.S. of a broad range of textiles, including those based on wool and manufactured fibers.

As the domestic price of textiles gradually increased because of these series of agreements, U.S. apparel manufacturers, the primary industrial users of textiles, soon found themselves at a cost disadvantage relative to foreign apparel manufacturers. The cost disadvantage was compounded by the fact that the restraints on foreign textiles had encouraged foreign textile producers to shift to the manufacture of apparel for export, thereby channeling their relatively cheap textiles into the U.S. markets in the form of finished goods. Accordingly, by the mid-1960s, Hong Kong, Korea, and Taiwan were all flooding the U.S. market with relatively cheap apparel. The U.S. apparel manufacturers then obtained protection against these imports.

Another disadvantage of voluntary import restrictions is that they encourage foreign manufacturers to upgrade their products in order to maintain their earnings. Thus the restrictions often push foreign producers into the more expensive or specially tailored end of the U.S. market, where domestic manufacturers would otherwise have the best chance of maintaining competitiveness.

When foreign imports of steel seriously threatened domestic sales of U.S. steel companies in 1969, the U.S. manufacturers obtained a voluntary restraint agreement for the imports, based on a maximum tonnage limit of steel. In addition to harming the competitiveness of all U.S. manufacturers dependent on steel (including manufacturers of autos, drilling equipment, and appliances), the agreement encouraged foreign manufacturers to shift their production to specialty steel products, such as stainless, alloy, and tool steels. U.S. producers of specialty steel had been the most competitive businesses in the domestic steel industry and were relatively immune to foreign imports. But, as a result of this shift in foreign production, they found themselves directly challenged by foreign producers sooner than might have otherwise occurred.

Ironically, despite their substantial costs to the economy at large, voluntary export restrictions have not provided complete protection for U.S. industries. Often this is because exporters from countries that are not subject to the agreements have rushed in to take advantage of the newly created marketing opportunities. Indeed, even manufacturers from restricted countries have circumvented the agreements by exporting from nonrestricted countries.

Foreign manufacturers have also simply altered their products in such a way that they fall outside the agreements. For example, in response to a dramatic increase of imported shoes from Korea and Taiwan, the U.S. negotiated voluntary export agreements with these countries in 1977. One year later, footwear imports from Hong Kong, Italy, and Brazil had more than filled the gap. Moreover, since the 1977 agreements did not cover rubber footwear, Korean and Taiwanese manufacturers merely changed the composition of their products, substituting rubber for leather in certain parts of the shoe. The U.S. was again flooded with imports from Korea and Taiwan of rubber footwear that fell outside the agreements.

The same pattern followed in the wake of a 1977 agreement that limited Japan's export of color television receivers. By 1978, color television receivers were streaming into the United States from Taiwan and Korea. When these countries agreed to restrictions on receivers, color televisions began entering the U.S. in the form of subassemblies and components, which were not covered by any agreements. By this time, most U.S. television manufacturers had already established foreign operations abroad to produce their own subassemblies and components. As a result, it was hardly in their interest to seek another round of agreements restricting these types of imports as well.

At best, voluntary restrictions have merely postponed the competitive decline of the industries they were designed to protect. They have not aided or encouraged these industries to restructure in order to improve their long-term competitive positions. As we saw in Chapter 13, the U.S. steel industry failed to take advantage of the "breathing space" it enjoyed in the wake of the first round of voluntary restrictions that went into effect in 1968. Indeed, the industry's capital expenditures for each of the six subsequent years were below their 1968 level. In 1977, when imports of foreign steel seriously threatened sales of domestic steel companies, U.S. companies obtained a "trigger price" for the imports, based on the costs of producing and transporting Japanese steel; any imported steel that is sold below this price triggers an antidumping investigation. Since the trigger-price system was initiated, the steel industry still has not undertaken any major restructuring. The same failure to retool during periods of protection has characterized most of the textile, apparel, footwear, and color television industries.

Industrial Restructuring

Part of the problem of import protection has been that the U.S. government has never made protection contingent upon an industry's willingness to restructure itself. Another part of the problem is that the industries have had difficulty raising the capital necessary for restructuring. Banks and investors are understandably reluctant to sink money into enterprises that show little promise of profitability in the short run. The U.S. government could have stepped in to fund restructuring, but it did not.

The Trade Act of 1974 authorized the government to provide loans and loan guarantees for the purpose of industry restructuring, but it limited eligibility to companies that had already experienced an absolute decrease in sales or production. As a result, funds for restructuring have come too late, after serious decline has already set in. Moreover, only the weakest companies have been eligible for funding, rather than those within the industry that still have a good chance of regaining market share. Worse still, the funding has been too small. In the apparel industry, for example, the average grant has been approximately $1 million, far too little to permit major retooling.

There has been one notable exception to the governmental failure to aid industry restructuring: the Commerce Department's Footwear Revitalization Program, established in 1977 and funded for three years at a level of $56 million. The program was explicitly aimed at restoring the competitiveness of the footwear industry. It provided loans, loan guarantees, and technical assistance to help companies achieve timely deliveries, improve servicing, and enhance their quality control. It also launched an aggressive export drive to locate European markets for U.S. footwear, and a joint research effort with the industry to improve manufacturing technology. Preliminary evidence suggested that, although poorly funded, the program did improve the performance of major parts of the industry and was far more cost effective than mere protection.

By and large, however, the only industry restructuring in which the government has directly participated has entailed rolling back various health, safety, and environmental regulations. Both the U.S. auto and steel industries have consistently argued that such rollbacks are necessary preconditions for their competitive survival. As a result, both the Carter and Reagan administrations have trimmed, rescinded, or extended the timetables for compliance with certain regulations. But investments mandated by health, safety, or environmental regulations have had only a marginal impact on the competitiveness of these industries.

During the 1970s, for example, the steel industry spent an average of $365 million annually to reduce pollution and improve worker safety; this figure was approximately 17 percent of its total capital investment during the decade. Japanese steel manufacturers, meanwhile, invested more than twice that amount in pollution control and worker safety. West German manufacturers spent about the same amount as U.S. manufacturers. Moreover, 48 percent of the cost of pollution abatement required of U.S. manufacturers was underwritten by state and local governments through industrial development bonds. In short, the competitive decline of U.S. industry is not attributable to these requirements, and regulatory rollbacks are unlikely to result in industrial revitalization.

As a practical matter, was some kind of protection from imports politically inevitable? The answer is no. These competitive problems did not arise overnight. The signs of difficulty could be clearly seen many years in advance. Had the U.S. government worked closely with

the declining businesses and their unions at an early stage, in anticipation of more serious competitive decline, it could have developed
a strategy for salvaging the most competitive parts of the industry
through carefully targeted rationalizations; new investments in plants,
machinery, and research and development; and funds to help develop
foreign markets.

Indeed, the most competitive firms in these declining industries often
did not seek protection. This was the case for much of the textile
industry in the face of the protection accorded to raw-fiber producers.
This was also the case for a significant portion of the apparel industry
with regard to protection given to textile manufacturers. Part of the
footwear industry, did not seek protection, nor did specialty steel
producers in light of the protection given to carbon-steel manufacturers.
Similarly, it was no accident that General Motors opposed protection
against Japanese imports while Ford favored such protection in 1979.
Now, seeing its own profits threatened from abroad, a less confident
General Motors has joined the pro-protection chorus.

Instead of easing the transition of capital and labor to the more
competitive businesses within an industry, the U.S. government has
repeatedly watched industry after industry lose market share to foreign
producers until the least competitive businesses are able to form a
strong political coalition, often with the support of organized labor,
to demand and obtain protection. The only change in tactic has been
a gradual movement on the part of the U.S. government to support
voluntary export agreements that are less and less formal, that rest
upon even more subtle suggestions and threats. This shift toward in-
formality has permitted governments both in the U.S. and abroad to
claim fealty to principles of free trade while subtly restricting their
exports and imports. As a result, the citizens involved are less able
to hold their leaders accountable for the substantial costs these restrictions impose upon them.

LABOR ADJUSTMENT

The U.S. government has not only failed to promote industry restructuring but it has also failed to ease the transition of the labor force out

of businesses whose long-term competitive position is in decline. To be sure, during the past decade, several programs have been undertaken with the ostensible aim of aiding labor adjustment out of declining industries. For the most part, these programs have been poorly funded and conceived. More importantly, they have not been coordinated with other government programs that promote new, growing industries. As a result, in order to obtain protection, workers who are threatened by plant closings and layoffs that are attributable to imports have joined in political alliance with businesses that are also threatened by foreign competition. Meanwhile, the U.S. government has continued to develop new job opportunities—primarily in the aerospace industries of the Sunbelt—that provide no relief for the newly unemployed.

Since 1974, workers who can demonstrate that they have suffered directly from an increase in imports have been eligible for unemployment benefits that pay up to 70 percent of their lost wages for up to one year. They have also been eligible for retraining and relocation assistance. But this "trade adjustment assistance" has not been extended to workers and industries that supply or support those directly injured. Thus, while many automobile workers have been eligible, factory workers who make specific components for cars have not. Moreover, rather than ease their adjustment out of declining industries, the assistance has served primarily to keep workers where they are. This is because the program has offered generous unemployment benefits but only relatively meager job-search and relocation assistance.

Unemployment benefits have been generous both because workers are eligible to receive them for twice as long as regular unemployment insurance and because the majority of eligible workers have not been permanently laid off. Of workers eligible for trade adjustment benefits through the end of 1977, 67 percent later returned to work for the firm that had originally laid them off.[2] These rehirings were most common in steel, automobile, and other primary industries, suggesting that the layoffs had been cyclical rather than prompted by imports. In industries such as much of the textile and leather goods industries where the decline has been due to long-term changes in competitive position, the percentage of permanently laid-off workers who received adjustment assistance has been much higher.

As of September 1979, only 18,000 workers had taken advantage of the retraining assistance provided by the program. In part, this was because the Labor Department, which administers retraining programs, had not specifically tailored the program for import-impacted workers. The retraining programs were designed primarily to help unskilled workers develop basic job skills rather than to help older, more highly paid, skilled, or semiskilled employees retrain for new jobs. A major part of the problem has been the difficulty of determining what new jobs these skilled or semiskilled workers should be trained for. The government has not systematically sought to determine or forecast job shortages in the economy at large, nor to link industries currently experiencing shortages of skilled workers with the workers available in declining industries.

In addition, many workers have not participated in the retraining programs because they were not adequately informed about them. Other workers, who were aware of the training, believed—sometimes correctly—that they had not been permanently displaced by imports but would soon be rehired at the same job.

Job-search and relocation allowances, meanwhile, have been limited to a maximum of $1,000 per person, an inadequate sum in many cases. Through September 1979, only 27,000 workers had used job-search allowances, and only about 17,000 had taken advantage of job-relocation funding.

Regional Assistance

Government can help communities and regions that are plagued by declining industries by providing subsidies designed to attract new and growing industries. Such subsidies can provide competitively priced land; aid the upgrading of infrastructure such as streets, roads, bridges, water and sewer systems, and waste treatment plants; and support local efforts to attract foreign investment. As we shall see, major U.S. trading partners have already developed sophisticated programs to accomplish regional development goals.

U.S. regional assistance programs have been largely ineffective. This stems, in part, from the fact that they have been poorly funded and are spread so widely and thinly as to have little impact where they are most needed (Exhibit 71). For example, the U.S. Department of

Agriculture has spent approximately $10 million a year on a grant program to encourage industries to locate in rural areas. In 1981, over 150 firms received grants averaging roughly $59,000 each, hardly enough to attract major new industries.[3]

The Economic Development Administration of the U.S. Department of Commerce has also provided assistance to distressed areas, but program eligibility standards have been drawn so loosely that 80 percent of the communities in the U.S. are eligible. Only a small percentage of these funds have been targeted to communities that lost their industries because of foreign imports. For example, in 1978, only 15 import-affected communities received grants, totaling only $6.3 million.

Even the most popular form of economic development assistance—the Urban Development Action Grant program, initiated in 1977 and administered by the U.S. Department of Housing and Urban Development—has been too indiscriminate to have had much effect. Over half of the nation's localities have been deemed eligible for these funds. Through the first three months of 1981, the U.S. government approved 963 grants totaling $1.8 billion. A few of these grants have been well targeted. For example, with a $1.5-million grant, the city of Philadelphia enticed the Budd Company, maker of railroad cars, to remain in the city and spend $20 million of its own funds for retooling rather than cede its rail business to the Kawasaki Company of Japan. However, many of these grants have been poorly targeted, going to businesses that would have invested in the designated area anyway.

State-sponsored assistance efforts have been equally ineffective. They have encouraged states and localities to bid against one another in seeking to attract new industry rather than to develop a coordinated strategy for regional economic growth. States and localities have sought to lure industries by promising them special tax abatements and low-interest loans backed by government-issued industrial development bonds. But there is little evidence to suggest that these financing packages have justified their costs by successfully attracting industries that otherwise would not have been drawn to the areas. At best, one region's gain has been another's loss, with no overall improvement in matching workers to jobs. At worst, such schemes have eroded local tax bases, leading to the deterioration of the very infrastructure—streets, roads, bridges, sewer systems, and disposal sites—necessary to sustain long-term industrial development. Indeed, investment by all levels of government in such infrastructure has been declining, from $38.6 billion in 1965 to less than $31 billion in 1977, a drop of 21 percent measured in constant 1972 dollars. As a percentage of GNP, infrastructure investment has declined from 4.1 percent in 1965 to 2.3 percent in 1977, a 44-percent drop.[4]

Finally, regional development efforts have been dwarfed by federal expenditures on defense and energy, which have served to channel capital and new jobs to the West and South at the expense of other regions with greater needs for new industrial development. For example, the U.S. aerospace industry, located primarily in the Sunbelt and the Pacific Northwest, is already suffering from a shortage of skilled technicians, engineers, and semiskilled machinists. The anticipated rise in defense spending over the next few years will further exacerbate this shortage, while doing nothing to facilitate the movement of appropriate workers into these jobs from declining industries. Similarly, government-subsidized energy projects have long spurred industrial development in the South and West. The Tennessee Valley Authority, the Bonneville Power Administration in the Pacific Northwest, the Southeastern Power Administration, and the Southwestern Power Administration have all provided low-cost power to new industry.

Forty years ago, there was some logic to fostering economic development in the South and West through military and hydroelectric projects. These areas of the country were underdeveloped, relative to the industrial Midwest and Northeast. But now that the industrial Midwest is in sharp decline, these policies are far less compelling. It is strangely anomalous for the government to spend paltry sums on regional development while simultaneously pouring billions of federal dollars into programs that inadvertently spur even greater economic development in more prosperous regions.

SUMMARY

The reactive approach to the problems of declining businesses was perhaps tolerable 15 years ago, when a much smaller proportion of the U.S. economy was subject to international trade and when rapid economic growth made it comparatively easy for capital and labor to shift into new enterprises. But the U.S. has now become irrevocably dependent on imports and on the exports needed to pay for them. In addition, U.S. growth has slowed to the point that capital is in short supply and newly unemployed workers find it difficult to locate new jobs. Under these circumstances, it is essential that the United States seek to ease the transition of capital and labor out of declining businesses rather than simply postpone such shifts through "voluntary" restrictions on trade and regulatory rollbacks.

The problem of declining businesses will not disappear. Indeed, it will accelerate in the coming years as the pace of international competition picks up. Yesterday it was textiles, apparel, footwear, televisions, and steel. Today it is autos. Tomorrow it will be other industries. The U.S. needs an affirmative policy for industries in distress, a policy that helps them regain competitiveness when possible and simultaneously aids workers and regions to adjust to change. Anything less is not a strategy for economic development but a recipe for slow but sure economic decay.

FOOTNOTES

[1] Under Article XIX of General Agreement on Tariffs and Trade (GATT), a country is allowed relief from the GATT obligations where imports cause or threaten to cause injury to domestic industry. This escape clause, (19 U.S.C. 2251 *et seq.*) is designed to provide temporary import relief in order to facilitate an industry's orderly adjustment to import competition. Petitions for relief are filed with the International Trade Commission. A petitioner may be a trade association, firm, union, or a group of workers who are representative of industry. Once a petition is filed, the Commission is required to determine "whether an article is being imported into the United States in such increased quantities as to be a substantial cause of serious injury, or the threat thereof, to the domestic industry producing an article like or directly competitive with the imported article." (19 U.S.C. 2251 (b) (1).)

After a public hearing, the Commission reports its findings to the President. If the Commission finds that increased imports have been a substantial cause of injury to the domestic industry, it must recommend to the President the imposition of a duty or import restriction or recommend adjustment assistance to affected workers, firms, and communities. (19 U.S.C. 2251 (d) (1).) The

President then determines what import relief is in the "national economic interest of the United States." (19 U.S.C. 2252.) Import relief may consist of new or increased duties; tariff rate quotas; quantitative restrictions; orderly marketing agreements; or a combination of methods. (19 U.S.C. 2253 (a).) The President is then required to inform Congress of his decision to provide import relief. If this action differs from the recommended policy of the Commission, Congress may override the President and uphold the Commission's recommendation. (19 U.S.C. 2253 (b), (c).)

Dumping. Dumping is a trade practice involving price discrimination between national markets. Put more specifically, dumping occurs when an exported article is sold at "less than fair value." (Myerson, Toby S. "A Review of Current Antidumping Procedures," *Columbia Journal of Transnational Law,* 15, 1976, p. 167.) Less than fair value may mean that an article is sold at a price in the export market that is lower than the price in the domestic market. It may also mean that the exported article is being sold at less than its total cost.

The Revenue Act of 1916 marked the first attempt by Congress to deal with the problem of dumped goods. The provision was passed in the fear that European cartels would attempt to destroy small American manufacturing companies that had developed during the First World War. The 1916 Act was poorly drafted, however, and its vagueness led to a second legislative attempt to deal with the practice of dumping. The Antidumping Act of 1921 was enacted in response to claims by manufacturers of predatory price cutting by foreign exporters.

The statutory scheme established by the 1921 Act requires an initial determination by the Treasury Department of whether an imported article is being sold at less than fair value. If the Treasury Department makes such a finding, the case is referred to the International Trade Commission to determine whether there is or is likely to be "injury" to an American "industry." If the Commission makes an affirmative finding, the case is returned to the Treasury Department for an assessment of duty on the goods equal to the "dumping margin."

Despite efforts at refinement, the Antidumping Act remains a vague statute. For example, there is no statutory standard to determine what constitutes an "industry" or an "injury." The Trade Act of 1974 failed to address these two issues. (Campbell, Robert M. "The Foreign Trade Aspects of the Trade Act of 1974," *Washington and Lee Law Review,* 33, 1976, pp. 639, 657.)

In recent years, there has been a dramatic increase in the number of dumping petitions filed with the Treasury Department. Most of these cases have been directed toward Japanese companies. Between 1921 and 1975, the Treasury Department referred 152 cases to the Commission. Seventy of these cases—46 percent of that total—occurred between 1972 and 1975. Between 1960 and 1970, there were six cases of dumping involving Japan that were referred to the Commission. In the five-year period from 1971 to 1975, 32 cases involving Japanese companies were referred to the Commission. In short, American companies appear to be using the Antidumping Act increasingly as a strategic deterrent to the Japanese.

Countervailing Duties. The countervailing duty law of the United States originated in the Tariff Acts of 1890 and 1894. Additional duties on sugar imports were imposed to compensate for direct or indirect bounties paid to exporters. In 1897, Congress expanded this provision to cover all dutiable imports. As originally conceived, the countervailing duty law was essentially protectionist in nature, designed to ensure that our tariff laws were not circumvented by our trading partners through their provision of subsidies for exporters. As a result, the imposition of a countervailing duty required no showing of injury by the domestic firm. ("United States Countervailing Duty Law," *Boston College Industrial and Commercial Law Review,* 17, 1976, pp. 832, 833–34.)

In 1922, the countervailing duty law was expanded to apply to any foreign bounty or grant regardless of whether the subsidy was intended to encourage exports. The statute remained essentially the same until the Trade Act of 1974.

Under the 1974 Act, countervailing duties may be assessed on nondutiable imports to the United States. However, they may only be assessed on these goods if injury to U.S. industry is established. This change alters the original justification of the statute, which was to prevent circumvention of our tariff laws. The purpose of the statute now has shifted to the protection of domestic manufacturers from unfair competition.

The President is given authority to suspend countervailing duties in particular cases if the imposition of duties would prejudice international negotiations regarding the use of subsidies and the application of countervailing duties.

[2] General Accounting Office, *Restricting Trade Act Benefits to Import-Affected Workers Who Cannot Find a Job Can Save Millions,* Washington, D.C.: GAO, 1980, p. 10.

[3] Farmers Home Association, *Status of Loan and Grant Obligation Allotment or Distribution,* Report Code 205-C, St. Louis: U.S. Government Finance Office, 1981, pp. 1–5.

Industrial development grants totalled $4.083 million in 1981, which were distributed to 91 communities.

[4] Council of State Planning Agencies, *America in Ruins,* Washington, D.C.: National Governors Association, 1981.

EXHIBIT 71
Federal Outlays for Regional Development Programs (in millions of dollars, adjusted)

	1978	1979	1980
Tennessee Valley Authority[1]	$1,412	$1,884	$1,965
Regional Development Program, Department of Commerce[2]	60	61	62
Appalachian Regional Commission[3]	261	303	300
Farmers Home Administration, Department of Agriculture[4]	N/A	830	993
Economic Development Administration, Department of Commerce[5]	318	436	483
Bureau of Indian Affairs, Department of Interior[6]	131	135	147
Power Marketing Administration, Department of Energy[7]	159	161	31
Rural Electrification Administration, Department of Agriculture[8]	2,093	2,320	3,188
Total Outlays	$4,434	$6,130	$7,169

Source: The Budget of the United States Government, Appendix for Fiscal Years 1978–81, Washington, D.C.: U.S. Government Printing Office.

FOOTNOTES TO EXHIBIT 71

[1] The Tennessee Valley Authority was created in 1933 and operates under the authority of the Tennessee Valley Authority Act of 1933, as amended, 16 U.S.C.A. § 831 *et. seq.* The TVA was created as a government corporation to promote the development of the Tennessee River Basin, which comprises parts of seven states. The activities of the corporation can be divided into two broad categories. Its power program provides electric power to 80,000 square miles in the river basin. TVA's nonpower activities include promoting the development of natural resources in the region, providing community development assistance, administering a fertilizer development program, and managing a national energy demonstration program. The TVA's activities

are financed by appropriations from Congress and proceeds from its activities. The figures presented represent outlays for TVA's power and nonpower programs.

[2] Title V of the Public Works and Economic Development Act of 1965, 42 U.S.C.A. §§ 3181–3196, authorizes the activities of eight regional commissions covering 34 states. The commissions have the broad objectives of encouraging economic development within a multistate area. These regional commissions cover all or part of the following states:

Four Corners Regional Commission:
Arizona, Colorado, New Mexico, Nevada, and Utah
Coastal Plains Regional Commission:
North Carolina, South Carolina, Georgia, Florida, and Virginia
New England Regional Commission:
Connecticut, Maine, Massachusetts, New Hampshire, Rhode Island, and Vermont
Old West Regional Commission:
Montana, Nebraska, North Dakota, South Dakota, and Wyoming
Pacific Northwest Regional Commission:
Idaho, Oregon, and Washington
Upper Great Lakes Regional Commission:
Michigan, Minnesota, and Wisconsin
Southwest Border Regional Commission:
Arizona, New Mexico, Texas, and California

These commissions are administered through the Department of Commerce. The figures presented represent the combined outlays for development programs and administrative expenses for the eight commissions.

[3] The Appalachian Regional Commission was established under the Appalachian Regional Development Act of 1965, 79 Stat. 5 (1965). The Commission consists of the governors of the 13 states within the region and is funded as an independent agency of the federal government. The Act authorizes a number of economic development programs, including the construction of highways, the operation of health projects, and the establishment of vocational education facilities. The Commission contracts with public and private organizations to conduct these activities.

[4] The Farmers Home Administration, administered through the Department of Agriculture, operates a number of programs to encourage economic development in rural areas. This activity supplements the agency's primary objective of encouraging the development of rural housing. The agency's housing programs are not included in this table. Those activities that are included are the following:

Outlays for the Rural Development Activities of the Farmers
Home Administration (in millions of dollars, unadjusted)

	1980 (est)	1979	1978	1977
Rural Water and Waste Disposal Grants	$301	$287	$180	—
Rural Development Grants	12	11	10	—
Rural Development Planning Grants	7	4	—	—
TOTAL	$320	$302	$190	$122

The rural development grants are designed to stimulate business investment in rural areas. Note that the total for fiscal year 1977 is not allocated
among separate budget accounts. Additional outlays represent agency financ-
ings through the Federal Financing Bank.

[5] The Economic Development Administration operates as an agency of the
Department of Commerce and administers a series of programs authorized
under the Public Works and Economic Development Act of 1965, as
amended, 42 U.S.C.A. § 3121 *et. seq.* These programs are designed to
reduce unemployment in economically distressed areas. These outlays are
allocated among various activities as follows:

Outlays for Economic Development Assistance of the Economic
Development Administration (in millions of dollars, unadjusted)

	1980 (est)	1979	1978	1977
Economic Development Assistant Programs	$473	$423	$307	$242
Development Facilities	10	12	7	47
Industrial Development Loans and Guarantees	—	—	2	6
Planning, Technical Assistance, and Research	—	—	—	1
Development Facilities Grants	—	—	2	1
TOTAL	$483	$436	$318	$297

Note that totals may not compute properly because of rounding. In addition, the budget documents for fiscal year 1980, which outline actual
expenditures for fiscal year 1978, appear to contain a discrepancy of about
$12 million between total outlays and outlays by account. The lower figure
is presented here.

[6] The Bureau of Indian Affairs in the Department of the Interior operates
several programs to encourage economic development among Indian people.

Because information on outlays is not separately presented, the data included in this table for the Bureau of Indian Affairs represents obligations incurred during the fiscal year. The following totals include both direct and reimbursable programs.

Obligations of the Bureau of Indian Affairs for Economic Development Activity (in millions of dollars, unadjusted)

	1980 (est)	1979	1978	1977
Economic Development Programs				
1. Employment development	$ 52	$ 43	$ 46	$ 49
2. Business enterprise development	9	7	8	12
3. Road Maintenance	18	13	11	11
Natural Resources Development				
1. Forestry and agriculture	55	59	56	40
2. Minerals, mining, irrigation, and power	13	13	10	4
TOTAL OBLIGATIONS	$147	$135	$131	$116

[7] The Department of Energy operates a number of separate hydroelectric projects to market electric power to selected regions of the country. The following outlays include both direct and reimbursable programs. In addition, the outlays account for both operating and construction costs.

Outlays of Power Marketing Administrations (in millions of dollars, unadjusted)

	1980 (est)	1979	1978	1977
Alaska Power Administration	$ 3	$ 2	$ 2	$ 2
Bonneville Power Administration	(128)	59	53	(8)
Southeastern Power Administration	1	1	1	1
Southwestern Power Administration	32	20	12	19
Western Area Power Administration	123	79	91	89
TOTAL OUTLAYS	$ 31	$161	$159	$103

The wide variance in outlays for the Bonneville Power Administration represents the effects of financing its programs. See *The Budget of the United States Government, Fiscal Year 1981, Appendix* at 415–417.

[8] The Rural Electrification Administration, an agency of the Department of Agriculture, provides loans and loan guarantees to improve electric and telephone service in rural areas. The Administration operates under authority of the Rural Electrification Act of 1936, as amended, 7 U.S.C. §§ 901-950 (b). In fiscal year 1980, there was an estimated $4.3 million in direct loans outstanding and $8.8 million in outstanding loan guarantees. See *The Budget of the United States Government, Fiscal Year 1981, Appendix* at 149. The table includes outlays of the REA for both its direct and reimbursable programs.

18

U.S. Policies for Growing Businesses

Just as the U.S. has had no systematic programs for coping with the inevitable problems of industrial decline, neither has it had any explicit policies for responding to the special needs of companies in fast-growing but risky businesses that could provide future growth for the economy. To be sure, the U.S. government has channeled billions of dollars and thousands of trained workers into certain industries whose companies have become leading international competitors. But these competitive successes have been largely inadvertent side effects of other government objectives, mainly national defense. In short, U.S. policies affect growing businesses by default rather than by direction.

U.S. policies for aiding growing businesses have largely been by-products of the concern for national security. Some defense-related expenditures have helped accelerate the development of businesses that are highly competitive in world markets, enabling these businesses to move rapidly down their "experience curves" and gain leadership through scale and know-how. For several decades, for example, the agriculture and automobile industries were the keystones of the U.S. economy and leaders in international trade. Government expenditures for both industries, under the broad justification of national security and self-sufficiency, were crucial to their successes. Agricultural price supports, federally funded irrigation projects, funds for agricultural research, and the operation of the Agricultural Extension Service fueled extraordinary gains in output per man-hour and per farm acre. Similarly, the Eisenhower administration's interstate highway legislation in 1956, and the state and local road building it stimulated, contributed directly to the growth and prosperity of the auto industry through the 1960s. The world leadership enjoyed by U.S. aircraft and electronic industries is attributable in part to huge government expenditures undertaken during the 1950s and 1960s for defense, aerospace research, and the education of highly specialized personnel.

In the following sections, the key programs that have inadvertently fostered industrial growth in this country are reviewed.

GOVERNMENT PROCUREMENT

The federal government is the largest single consumer of goods and services in the United States. It is not a single consumer, of course, but rather a group of separate agencies, each with a different purpose. In 1979, these various agencies awarded over $94 billion in contracts. About 75 percent of the total was spent by the Department of Defense, another 4 percent by the National Aeronautics and Space Administration for the U.S. space program, and 6 percent by the Department of Energy.[1]

The size of the budget alone is not as important as the impact federal procurement actions have had on the development of commercial markets. Through its purchases, the government has shaped the development of emerging products and markets. Its impact has been most pronounced in the electronics and aerospace industries. In 1977, government purchases accounted for 56 percent of total aircrafts shipments; government market shares for other products included 57 percent of radio and television communications equipment, 12 percent of engineering and scientific instruments, 33 percent of transmitting electron tubes, and 12 percent of optical instruments and valves.[2]

The impact of federal procurement on the evolution of individual markets is even more striking. For instance, in 1950, government purchases accounted for 92 percent of aerospace sales; in 1972, the government's share stood at 80 percent. In 1980, government purchases had fallen below 50 percent of the market for the first time. A similar pattern emerges in semiconductors. Government purchases of semiconductors accounted for over one-third of the market in 1955 but had declined to 12 percent by 1977 (Exhibit 72). The government was the only purchaser of computers in 1954; in 1962, the government market still represented almost one-half the total sales (Exhibit 73).

Government procurement has provided the stimulus of large demand in the early stages of several new products. Government procurement has also had the effect of promoting U.S. civilian industries because

EXHIBIT 72
Federal Semiconductor Purchases as a Percent of Total Sales

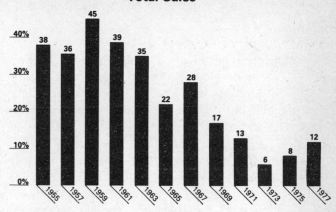

Sources: 1955–1961: Ginzberg, E. *et al. Economic Impact of Large Public Programs,* Salt Lake City, Olympus Publishing Co., 1976; 1963–1973: Bureau of Economics, Federal Trade Commission, *Staff Report on the Semiconductor Industry,* Washington, D.C.: U.S. Government Printing Office, 1977, p. 69; 1975–1977: *Shipments to Federal Government Agencies,* U.S. Bureau of the Census, Washington, D.C.: U.S. Government Printing Office, 1978, MA-175, Table 3.

EXHIBIT 73
Federal Computer Purchases as Percent of Total Sales

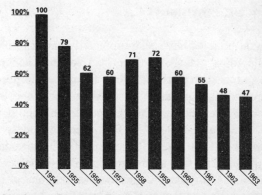

Source: Ginzberg, E. *et al. Economic Impact of Large Public Programs,* Salt Lake City, Olympus Publishing Co., 1976.

of price premiums paid for new technology, "Buy American" provisions, government-owned plant and equipment, and interest-free loans.

Price Premiums

The government has been willing to pay a premium over actual costs in order to subsidize development of products of high quality and new technology. For products that have a commercial application—helicopters or scientific instruments, for example—the government's willingness to pay a premium so early in the product's life has accelerated cost reductions and commercialization. Moreover, the government's demand for pioneering technology has enabled new industries to gain experience and scale efficiencies rapidly, thereby speeding the acceptability of the new technology in more cost-conscious commercial markets. Such "spin-offs" have been a notable development of the U.S. space programs.[3] For example, the Black and Decker Manufacturing Company developed a product line of cordless power tools from work initially done for the space program. The Chrysler Corporation developed new, more reliable electronic clocks and ignition systems that are used in its own cars and sold to other manufacturers. Sentry Products, Inc. developed a silent alarm system for the government and later refined it into a commercial product for correctional facilities, schools, hospitals, and residential buildings.

"Buy American" Provisions

Procurement policies have also protected American producers from foreign competitors. The Buy American Act of 1933 required U.S. agencies to purchase American goods for domestic use if the goods were available at a reasonable cost. Since then, the preference for American goods has been defined by price differentials, establishing the limits of reasonable added cost for buying American goods. Since 1963, differentials have been 50 percent for Department of Defense purchases, 12 percent for goods from small businesses and firms in labor surplus areas, and 6 percent for other purchases.

In addition to updated versions of the Buy American Act, other legislative acts also favor domestic producers. For example, since 1955, the Forest Service has been required to buy domestic twine. In

1968, Congress required the Defense Department to buy American-made buses, and in 1969 the Berry Amendment to a defense appropriations bill mandated procurement of domestic food, clothing, and textile products. In 1970, the Navy was prohibited from using foreign shipyards for construction of its vessels.

The Trade Agreements Act of 1979 sought to reduce protectionism in government procurement, largely on the initiative of U.S. high-technology firms, which sought to penetrate the Japanese and European government markets. However, some of the largest procuring agencies—including the Defense, Energy, and Transportation Departments—were exempted from the Act.

Government-Owned Plant and Equipment

It is difficult to estimate private use of government-owned plant and equipment. The use of government-owned industrial facilities has been in decline since its peak during the Second World War when expansion for war production was largely government financed. However, the GOCOS (government-owned, company-operated facilities) remain important resources for government contractors. Most of these facilities are laboratories for nuclear weapons and space exploration. However, they also include significant production capability.

The Defense Department has built fewer new facilities since the Second World War than has NASA or the Department of Energy, but it has continued to supply plant and equipment to contractors. In 1971, Defense-furnished plant equipment was worth $4.1 billion, over half of which was manufacturing equipment. For example, annual reports filed with the Securities and Exchange Commission show that over half of Rockwell International's aerospace production facilities are government owned and represent 15 percent of the production area for the entire company. Lockheed's second-largest production facility is government property.

Interest-Free Loans

In contrast to commercial manufacturers who recoup their costs only by selling completed products, Defense contractors receive periodic reimbursements of cost. Although the length and scope of the weapons' development process probably make such periodic payments necessary, these payments in effect provide the firms with an interest-free source of working capital. In many aircraft, computer, and instrument businesses, working capital is a large part of total investment. Thus, financing by the Defense Department has great value. For example, one government supplier showed a 6-percent return on sales in its civilian business and a 5.5-percent return on sales for its military business. However, because of progress payments, the military business showed a return on investment of 48 percent compared to 19 percent for the civilian business.

GOVERNMENT FUNDING OF RESEARCH AND DEVELOPMENT

About 50 percent of the research and development undertaken in the U.S. is funded by the federal government. The government actually employs approximately 30 percent of all the nation's scientists and engineers. While the overwhelming bulk of this effort is related to defense, government R&D funding is critical to many industries. For example, in 1977, government provided 70 percent of the development funding for the aircraft industry and 48 percent for the communication equipment industry. During the same year, the government funded only 1 percent of R&D in the pharmaceuticals industry (Exhibit 74). While such differentials no doubt reflect military needs, they also have an important bearing on the relative commercial development of these industries.

Most federal funding of industrial research and development is directly provided to companies on a project basis. In addition, some government laboratories, particularly those in the energy area, are run by private corporations. The government also funds general overheads associated with research and development for companies under contract for specific projects.

Many companies use government funds to support risky ventures or basic areas of research they could not afford to undertake on their own. Government funds also help maintain large research centers that otherwise would be too expensive for the companies to maintain. A

EXHIBIT 74
Federal Expenditures for Applied Research and
Development for Selected Industries, 1977

(In Millions of Dollars)

	Total R&D Expenditure	Federally Funded R&D	Federal Expenditure as a Percent of Total
Guided Missiles and Spacecraft	$3,035	$2,731	90%
Ordnance	288	231	80
Aircraft	3,125	2,150	69
Transportation Equipment (excluding cars and trucks)	201	111	55
Fabricated Metal Products	1,157	608	53
Communication Equipment and Electronic Components	5,038	2,451	48
Electrical Transmission and Distribution Equipment	225	97	43
Electrical Industrial Equipment	299	86	29
Professional and Scientific Instruments	1,280	274	22
Office Computing and Accounting Machines	1,856	140	8
Engines and Turbines	531	51	10
Industrial Machinery	458	34	7
Chemicals	2,024	40	2
Pharmaceuticals	959	12	1
Other	8,521	1,315	15
Total	$28,997	$10,331	36%

Source: National Science Foundation, cited in National Science
Board, *Science Indicators,* 1978 (1979), p. 214.

number of multiproduct contractors funded by the Defense Department
have divisions that are responsible for disseminating the new advances
of their aerospace and defense operations. Civilian-oriented divisions
within the corporation adapt new technologies to commercial products.

EFFECTS OF GOVERNMENT PROGRAMS

What have been the effects of defense-related expenditures on the
international competitive position of the United States? In several industries—notably the semiconductor and aircraft industries—govern-

ment procurement and R&D programs have helped to accelerate new product development, thereby giving U.S. manufacturers a lead over foreign competitors.

The Semiconductor Industry

During the 1950s and the 1960s, the formative years of the semiconductor industry, the Department of Defense and NASA were major purchasers of semiconductors. Government purchasers provided a relatively stable demand for the devices and were therefore important in reducing the risk for new entrants to the industry during this period. In addition, because of its high precision and reliability requirements for military and space equipment, the government was willing to pay a premium for high-quality products that required state-of-the-art technology.

Government R&D funding, all of which came from the Defense Department and NASA, generated basic knowledge and sped up development and production in the industry. In addition to subsidizing research and thus reducing the risk to private industry, this government funding helped pinpoint the areas that were next on the agenda for development and for possible military procurement. The large government commitment thus altered the private perception of the risks of such projects. It gave private investors confidence that the many technical problems associated with new areas of semiconductor technology could be solved, and thereby stimulated private investment in these same areas.

Government-funded R&D also introduced many electrical engineers to the problems of the semiconductor industry. By providing these individuals with experience, that they later used in solving problems for the commercial sector, government R&D substantially increased experience levels in the semiconductor industry.

As a result of government-funded R&D, the U.S. semiconductor industry gained rapid ground. In 1962, an integrated circuit cost $50; by 1968, its cost had dropped to $2.33, making it commercially attractive for installation in many civilian products. Over the same time period, the semiconductor market burgeoned from $4 million to $31 million.

More recently, government R&D funds have been channeled into a program for the development of Very High Speed Integrated Circuits (VHSIC). Its goals are to increase throughput in integrated circuits by a factor of 100 and to have these circuits in pilot-line production within six to seven years. The focus of the project is primarily on military needs, including reliability in severe environments.

While the program is designed partly as an answer to similar R&D efforts by foreign governments, some industry members have criticized it for diverting resources from industrial and consumer areas that are more critical to the commercial future of the integrated circuit industry. The entire six-year program, expected to cost approximately $200 million, may have commercial application only in satellite communications and weather forecasting systems.

The Aircraft Industry

The production of air transport carriers is one of the most successful of all U.S. manufacturing industries. With about a 90-percent share of the world market in recent years, the industry has been a leading contributor to the U.S. trade balance, providing an estimated $9.9 billion in trade surplus in 1979.

The industry's dominance can be attributed in part to the superior product, service, and marketing of U.S. firms. A huge home market has allowed firms to exploit economies of scale and has provided the opportunity of spreading the cost of the learning process. But a key element of the industry's success has been a combination of government policies that nurtured the industry in its early stages and provided R&D support. These policies have also provided a steady market for military sales since the Second World War and have generally promoted the development of air travel, thus stimulating the demand for newer and larger aircraft.

Through the research and development of military aircraft, major technological advances have been made in both design and production processes for civilian aircraft. Even during the period before 1940, there were many significant technology transfers from the military to the civilian sector, including the development of radial air-cooled engines, retractable landing gear, two-way radio communications, the turbo supercharger, and high-octane fuels. With the increased pace of development brought about by the Second World War, such transfers became even more commonplace in the 1940s and 1950s and included the turbojet engine, swept-back wings, adhesive bonding, titanium alloys, and heavy press and numerically controlled machine process technology.

Even more striking has been the wholesale adaptation of military planes to civilian airline use. For example, the Boeing 707 can be traced directly to the B-47 and B-52 bombers; the DC-8 uses many of the designs and systems developed by Douglas in its A-3D, A-4D, and B-66 military aircraft; and Boeing's 747 jumbo jet is based on the design used for its unsuccessful bid for the C-5 cargo plane.

Government support for R&D has taken place not only indirectly by way of military procurement but also through direct government-supported research. This involvement dates back to 1915 when Congress created the National Advisory Committee for Aeronautics (NACA) to supervise and direct the scientific study of the problems of flight, with a view to their practical solution. NACA responsibilities were transferred to NASA upon its establishment in 1958, and that agency continues to oversee aeronautical research programs.

In 1972, a government study was conducted to assess the extent of technology transfer from military programs to civilian aviation. It concluded that since the Second World War, military sponsorship and first use have characterized most of the significant technological advances that have been made in the industry. Furthermore, military research, development, test, and evaluation usually have provided the basis for the acceptance and use by civil aviation of the technological advancements. Of the technological advances made in aviation since 1925, 70 percent were the result of military sponsorship, and an additional 18 percent were sponsored by civil agencies of the government. Because the government has paid such a large proportion of R&D costs, and because the same manufacturers have produced both military and civilian aircraft, U.S. producers have enjoyed a significant advantage in new product and process developments in an industry characterized by rapid and costly technological change.

The military market provides aircraft producers with other advantages besides subsidized R&D. It enables U.S. firms to enjoy advantages of economies of scale for processes that can be used for both civilian and military production. It provides a cushion of production of known length and stable profits. This cushion can be crucial for firms that are competing in a volatile airline market in which development time can now exceed 10 years at costs of more than a billion dollars. It also provides a source of working capital.

The healthy state of this U.S. industry stems in large measure from government policies that have enhanced the advantage of a potentially large home market and that have created conditions enabling U.S. manufacturers to remain in the forefront of aircraft technology. The result is an industry that remains an American success story.

SUMMARY

In sharp contrast to government policies that deal with declining industries by protecting them from imports, U.S. procurement and R&D programs have succeeded in stimulating industrial development, despite the fact that they were not designed expressly to improve international competitiveness.

Defense-related programs have been successful for two reasons. First, they have directly encouraged innovation. Businesses that fail to innovate cease to receive contracts for procurement or R&D. By contrast, the tariffs, quotas, and agreements that have traditionally protected U.S. businesses from imports have enabled firms to avoid the necessity of innovating. Second, these defense-related programs have required the government to work closely with the businesses. Rather than merely react to industry-wide pressures, government has been affirmatively engaged with business in designing programs for procurement and research and development, often years in advance.

But there is no reason to suppose that the nation's interest in industrial development is necessarily consistent with its defense needs. As defense requirements grow more specialized, there may be fewer spin-offs of defense products and technology to the commercial markets. Further, for industries unrelated to aerospace or defense, defense-related procurement has had the perverse effect of draining off skilled engineers and scientists from the commercial sector. This is not to suggest that national security should be subordinated to industrial development, but only that the U.S. should understand the trade-offs implied in seeking to achieve the two goals simultaneously, and should make them explicit. At present, the U.S. does not have the decisionmaking capacity to do this.

FOOTNOTES

[1] *Quarterly Report of Federal Contract Awards, Fiscal Year 1979,* Washington, D.C.: Federal Procurement Data Center, 1979, pp. 2–5. This budget total includes money spent for both products and services. About 53 percent of the budget went to purchase supplies and equipment; 33 percent went to services and construction; and 14 percent went to research and development. Also *Special Analysis 2, Federal Contract Awards Over $10,000 by Product and Service, Fiscal Year 1979,* Washington, D.C.: Federal Procurement Data Center, 1979, p. 3.

[2] Bureau of the Census, Statistical Series MA-175, Table 3, Washington, D.C.: U.S. Department of Commerce, 1977.

[3] Denver University, *Space Benefits: The Secondary Benefits of Aerospace Technology in Other Sectors of the Economy,* Washington, D.C.: NASA, 1980. The examples in this paragraph are drawn from this publication. See also, Haggerty, J.J. *Spinoff 1980: An Annual Report,* Washington, D.C.: NASA, 1980. U.S. Army Material Development and Readiness Command, *Darcom Spinoffs,* Alexandria, Virginia: U.S. Army Publications, n.d.

19

The Network of Government Subsidies

Some U.S. policies have been fashioned in response to declining industries; others have inadvertently promoted the development of new industries. The U.S. government has also promoted certain industries through a bewilderingly wide array of grants, tax breaks, loans and loan guarantees, subsidized insurance, and subsidized purchases and sales programs. Most of these programs have grown randomly over the years in response to the political demands of particular industries or geographic regions.

These policies are important for two quite separate reasons. First, if properly funded and executed, some of these policies could foster the growth of competitive businesses, despite the fact that in their present form they have had little positive effect.

Second, and perhaps more important, this confusing network of government subsidies has served to channel vast quantities of capital to certain industries and thereby away from other industries that might otherwise have become strong international competitors. Since there is only a limited amount of capital for new investment, policies that make investment in certain industries more attractive simultaneously increase the cost of capital for other industries.

This chapter first reviews two sets of policies—those designed to promote exports and those designed to develop small businesses—that have the potential to improve U.S. competitiveness. However, neither set of policies has been properly funded or focused. We then turn to other, more diffuse policies that have served to channel capital rather haphazardly to certain industries.

EXPORT PROMOTION

A variety of federal subsidy programs has been designed expressly to promote exports. Among these programs are the Export-Import Bank, the Commodity Credit Corporation, the Overseas Private Investment Corporation, the Domestic International Sales Corporation provisions of the Internal Revenue Code, and trade promotion activities of the Departments of Commerce and Agriculture. Unfortunately, for the most part, these export promotion programs have been uncoordinated, misdirected, and underfunded.

Let us more closely examine the Export-Import Bank and the Commodity Credit Corporation. Both of these programs help foreign buyers finance their purchases of U.S. exports through a variety of tools, including direct lending, loan guarantees, and subsidized insurance.

Established in 1934, the Ex-Im Bank has assisted in the export of agricultural products, communications equipment, electric power plants, and mining and manufacturing equipment. In recent years, the Bank has focused its efforts on the sale of commercial aircraft. In 1979, aircraft sales represented over 25 percent of all exports assisted by the Bank, a total of $3.4 billion in sales.[1] In 1980, Ex-Im Bank loans helped support $3 billion of the $5 billion jetliner export sales of the Boeing Company, the nation's leading aircraft exporter.[2]

The Bank's emphasis on aircraft sales has, on occasion, left other industries without adequate financing, thus placing U.S. manufacturers at a competitive disadvantage in world markets. For example, a machine-tool manufacturer with plants in Michigan and Great Britain recently received an order from an automaker in Mexico for $20 million worth of equipment. The machine-tool manufacturer would have found it cheaper to make the equipment in its Michigan plant. But the British government offered to finance the project at 7 3/4 percent annual interest if the work were done there. Unable to obtain an Ex-Im Bank loan to finance the work in Michigan, the machine-tool manufacturer will be producing the equipment in Great Britain.

With functions that parallel those of the Export-Import Bank, the Commodity Credit Corporation finances foreign sales of U.S. agricultural commodities, principally wheat, cotton, rice, and feed grains. But this program has been hampered by a highly inefficient scheme for subsidizing U.S. shipping at the same time. At least 50 percent of the commodities financed by the CCC and shipped under this program must be transported in U.S. flag vessels. When U.S. flag vessels are used, the CCC finances the difference in shipping charges between the rates of foreign flag vessels and U.S. flag rates. In 1979, payments to the U.S. maritime industry under this provision exceeded $70 million.

Established as an independent agency by the Foreign Assistance Act of 1969, the Overseas Private Investment Corporation (OPIC) was intended to expand direct investment in developing countries. OPIC encourages the export of capital by providing U.S. investors with insurance against political risks in foreign countries, including losses due to expropriation, inconvertibility, and war damage. Insurance issued under this program for fiscal year 1981 was estimated to be $8.6 billion.

Financial assistance under OPIC has ranged from $4,000 to $100 million, averaging about $2.5 million. In 1979, 43 percent of OPIC's assistance went to manufacturing industries, 12 percent to banking and financial institutions, and 7 percent to agribusiness firms. Though valuable, insurance available under this program is limited when compared with that provided by many other countries.

Under the Domestic International Sales Corporation (DISC) provisions of the Internal Revenue Code, certain domestic corporations that sell products in foreign markets are treated for tax purposes as if they were foreign corporations. The effect of these provisions is to allow deferral of federal income tax on the corporations' current income. Although deferral is normally limited to one-half of the profit attributable to the DISC, liberal pricing and costing regulations have enabled these corporations to defer tax on more than 50 percent of their profits from foreign sales. By 1980, these tax deferrals were costing the federal government approximately $1.4 billion each year. However, there is little evidence to suggest that the DISC program has served to increase exports. Because it is a general measure, it does not distinguish cases in which exports would have occurred anyway. In many cases, firms have found it more advantageous to retain the additional funds provided by DISC rather than to expand exports.[3]

Several other export promotional programs are spread almost randomly throughout the government. For example, the International Trade Administration of the Department of Commerce spends over $50 million a year in its trade development program. The Department conducts market research, sponsors overseas trade shows, and provides U.S. businesses with names of prospective foreign buyers. The Foreign Agricultural Service of the Department of Agriculture performs similar services for farmers. The Service maintains agricultural advisors in 74 locations overseas to identify foreign buyers for U.S. commodities and to provide timely information on shifts in world commodity markets. In addition, the service conducts an extensive export incentive program

EXHIBIT 75
U.S. Export Promotion Programs

(In Millions of 1980 Dollars)

	1976	1977	1978	1979	1980*
Direct Assistance					
Grade Development Programs, Department of Commerce[1]	29	24	21	34	54
Agricultural Export Promotion, Department of Agriculture	45	36	43	49	54
Total Direct Assistance	**$74**	**$60**	**$64**	**$83**	**$108**
Loans, Guarantees, and Insurance					
Export-Import Bank					
Outstanding Loans					
Direct[2]	10,726	11,440	11,435	11,587	12,774
Discount[3]	236	98	115	272	260
Total Loans	10,962	11,538	11,550	11,859	13,034
Outstanding Guarantees and Insurance	10,368	10,044	9,406	9,548	11,732
Total Export-Import Bank Loans, Guarantees, and Insurance	21,330	21,582	20,956	21,407	24,766
Overseas Private Investment Corporation					
Outstanding Loans	0[4]	0[4]	0[4]	23	30
Outstanding Loan Guarantees	200	165	134	92	200
Outstanding Insurance	9,688	9,114	8,905	4,605	8,425
Total OPIC Loans, Guarantees, and Insurance	9,888	9,279	9,039	4,720	8,655
Commodity Credit Corporation, Department of Agriculture					
Outstanding direct loans of the foreign assistance programs	4,877	5,333	5,973	6,451	6,923
Total Loans, Guarantees, and Insurance	**$36,095**	**$36,194**	**$35,868**	**$32,578**	**$40,344**
Tax Expenditures					
Domestic International Sales Corporation	**$1,360**	**$1,560**	**$1,000**	**$1,210**	**$1,400**

*estimated

Source: Appendix to the Budget of the U.S. Government, Fiscal Year 1981, Washington, D.C.: U.S. Government Printing Office, pp. 123–128.

[1] The Department of Commerce has undergone two major reorganizations in recent years. The estimates presented represent obligations incurred under

to develop new market opportunities for agriculture. This program uses product exhibits, trade teams, trade services, market information programs, and trade referral services to expand overseas markets for the U.S. farm sector.

The export promotion programs of the federal government are summarized in Exhibit 75. Comparatively little assistance has come in the form of direct subsidies; most is in the form of subsidized loans, loan guarantees, or insurance (totaling $40.3 billion for 1980), and in tax reductions ($1.4 billion for 1980). Despite their cost, these programs have done little to improve the long-term competitiveness of U.S. industry. To be sure, they have made U.S. exports marginally more attractive and have aided U.S. manufacturers in conducting business abroad. But apart from their focus on commercial aircraft businesses, these programs have not been carefully targeted in businesses for which such funding could be critical for developing a competitive lead in world markets. Nor have these programs been integrated into a coherent export strategy; instead, they have been administered by different bureaucracies, often with different purposes in mind.

SMALL BUSINESS PROMOTION

Another, smaller category of subsidies is designed to aid small business. Direct subsidies to small business amounted to $99 million in

---

programs to encourage U.S. exports. Prior to 1979, no separate estimate is available for obligations incurred by the Department of State to promote U.S. exports abroad. These functions have been transferred to the Department of Commerce and are included in the estimates for 1979 and 1980.

[2] Exim extends long-term financing to foreign purchasers of U.S. exports. In addition, through the cooperative financing facility, Exim extends dollar lines of credit to foreign financial institutions. The estimates represent outstanding loans at the end of the fiscal year.

[3] The discount loan program of the Bank allows U.S. commercial banks to borrow against outstanding export notes.

[4] The loan activity of the Corporation is not separately stated in the budget documents of the U.S. government for these years.

240

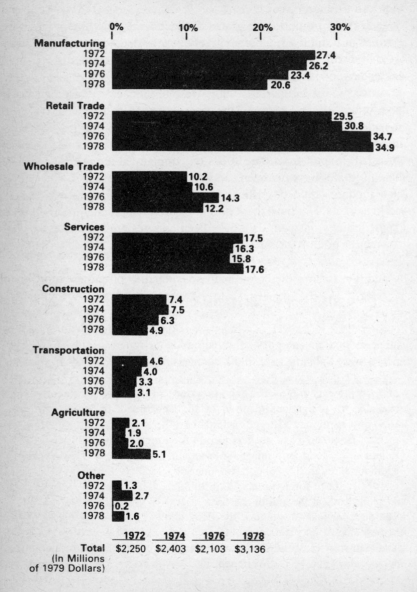

EXHIBIT 76
Small Business Administration Loans and
Loan Guarantees

	1972	1974	1976	1978
Manufacturing	27.4	26.2	23.4	20.6
Retail Trade	29.5	30.8	34.7	34.9
Wholesale Trade	10.2	10.6	14.3	12.2
Services	17.5	16.3	15.8	17.6
Construction	7.4	7.5	6.3	4.9
Transportation	4.6	4.0	3.3	3.1
Agriculture	2.1	1.9	2.0	5.1
Other	1.3	2.7	0.2	1.6
Total (In Millions of 1979 Dollars)	$2,250	$2,403	$2,103	$3,136

Source: SBA.

1980; accumulated loans and loan guarantees totaled $17.9 billion.

For the most part, small business subsidies have been directed at businesses sheltered from international trade. The share of total aid going to manufacturing companies was only 21 percent in 1978, and it has been decreasing steadily (Exhibit 76). Even within manufacturing companies, aid is often concentrated on businesses that serve only local markets. There have been no coordinated efforts to promote small business exports, to identify small businesses that have the greatest potential for success in international markets, or to provide small businesses with information and expertise relevant to their entry into international trade. Overall, the government has not developed any systematic means of identifying small businesses that could make the best use of the assistance; nor has the government developed a means of monitoring their performance.

SUBSIDIES TARGETED TO SPECIFIC INDUSTRIES

In addition to subsidies specifically designed to promote export or to aid small business, the federal government promotes other industries through a host of unrelated programs, including tax laws and rulings, loan guarantees and subsidies, public lands management, and publicly financed insurance.

Selective industry promotion has been growing at a rapid rate. As Exhibit 77 shows, targeted promotional programs in 1920 totaled $6.2 billion (in 1978 dollars) and represented 3.4 percent of the GNP. By 1950, the total had reached $77.1 billion, representing 9.2 percent of the GNP. In 1980, the total was $303.7 billion, representing 13.9 percent of the GNP. Between 1950 and 1980, both procurement and tax expenditures almost tripled as a percentage of the GNP.

Unfortunately, none of these programs has been viewed through the lens of international competitiveness, nor have any been seen as an aspect of a coherent industrial policy. Instead, each program has been formulated by the agencies and Congressional subcommittees that are closest to well-established industries and are therefore most susceptible to special pleading. The result is a political hodgepodge of subsidies. As we see in Exhibit 78, the government now spends five times more money on R&D for commercial fisheries than on R&D for steel; $455 million in tax breaks for the timber industry, but none for the semi-

EXHIBIT 77
Industrial Development Programs, 1920–1980

	1920		1950		1980	
	In Billions of 1978 Dollars	Percent of GNP	In Billions of 1978 Dollars	Percent of GNP	In Billions of 1978 Dollars	Percent of GNP
State and Federal Expenditures on Infrastructure	$5.2	2.8%	$47.7	5.9%	$162.0	5.9%
Federal Government Procurement	1.0	0.6%	10.2	1.3%	94.4	3.8%
Federal Government Expenditures on Research and Promotion	—	—	8.2	1.0%	25.1	1.1%
Tax Expenditures	—	—	7.9	1.0%	62.4	2.9%
Cost of Outstanding Loans and Loan Guarantees	—	—	0.3	—	3.6	0.2%
Total	$6.2	3.4%	$77.1	9.2%	$303.7	13.9%

Sources: Estimates based on budget documents and congressional reports for relevant years.

conductor industry; over $6 billion in loans and loan guarantees to the shipbuilding industry and $940 million in loans to the auto industry. Special tax and credit provisions have channeled one-third of gross domestic investment into residential construction. (See page 248).

Most of these subsidies are hidden from public view. The public costs of loan guarantees, tax expenditures, and insurance are not revealed in the federal budget since they are not direct government expenses. On the other hand, direct subsidies to particular industries are often buried in large program budgets. Following are some examples of such programs.

Direct Grants

There are a number of programs through which the federal government provides funds directly to business in order to encourage economic development, but it is difficult to discern any long-term policy objective or overall strategy for these programs. The only attribute that industry beneficiaries seem to share is political clout, rather than a capacity for international competitiveness. For example, the Maritime Administration within the Department of Commerce provides an operating subsidy to U.S. flag vessels. The purpose of the program is to maintain the U.S. Merchant Marine by equalizing the costs of operating a U.S. flagship and a foreign flagship. In fiscal year 1981, about 20 operators with 173 ships were subsidized. The estimated cost of the program was $348 million.

Similarly, under authority of the Federal Aviation Act, the Civil Aeronautics Board provides subsidy payments to qualified air carriers to cover their operating losses. These payments went to 12 different companies in fiscal year 1980. The average assistance for each carrier was about $6 million, for a total of $72 million.

The U.S. federal government also spends about $13 million a year to provide up to 75 percent of the costs of improving timber stands and about $9 million to train mining and mineral engineers. The remainder of these direct grants goes to support particular agricultural crops or to commercial fishing.

Although the number of programs is relatively large, their total funding—not more than $1 billion in 1981—is small compared to other forms of targeted subsidy. Of far greater monetary importance are targeted tax expenditures, loan guarantees, and insurance.

Targeted Tax Expenditures

Through tax expenditures, the government selectively reduces taxes for business. For example, while the income of most corporations is subject to a standard corporate tax rate, timber companies can grow a stand of timber, cut it, sell it, and be taxed on the proceeds at a lower capital gains rate. Similarly, petroleum companies can claim a percentage of their revenue from a producing well as a deduction from their gross income. This depletion allowance represents an extraordinary form of capital recovery that is unavailable to manufacturing or service firms. The housing industry also benefits from an extensive set of tax expenditures, chiefly one that allows homeowners to deduct interest and property tax payments.

Even general tax expenditures, such as simplified depreciation schedules for different categories of investment, have important patterning effects. Recent tax law changes which divide depreciation into simplified categories enhance the attractiveness of any investment with a useful life that is longer than the depreciation category into which it is placed, but render less attractive an investment with a useful life more closely approximating the category into which it is placed.

Across-the-board policies of accelerated depreciation or investment tax credits seldom aid directly the two categories of business that need them most—declining businesses that need funds to restructure themselves, and emerging businesses that need infusions of capital for new investment. Neither category of business is likely to have current profits against which these deductions can be taken. Notwithstanding the leasing provisions of the new tax code, generalized policies of accelerated depreciation or tax credits seldom facilitate the sort of industrial adjustments that are critical to a healthy economy.

Tax expenditures have been popular means of granting political favors largely because they do not appear as expenditures in the federal budget, although their effect is the same as a direct subsidy. Not surprisingly therefore, tax expenditures have been granted indiscriminately, without regard to their impact on the overall pattern of investment or the development of defensible competitive positions in international trade.

Targeted Loans and Loan Guarantees

The flow of capital funds through the U.S. economy is a continuous process, representing the trading of financial assets and liabilities among individuals who supply funds and those who demand funds. Government loan and loan guarantee programs promote the flow of capital into uses not dictated by market forces. Assisted borrowers are given preferred access to funds. Since the supply of funds in the financial markets is finite, unassisted borrowers are either unable to obtain the funds they require or they must pay a higher rate for them.

Historically, the federal government has intervened in the financial markets to support selected sectors of the economy, most notably housing and agriculture. Consequently, more Americans now own more expensive houses than they would otherwise, and U.S. farms are larger than they would have been otherwise. But, as a result of this diversion, other sectors may be less capital intensive than they would have been had no loan subsidies been provided.

Within the last few years, loans and loan guarantees have been targeted both to particular large firms in economic distress and to specific business segments. For example, loan guarantees of $250 million were provided to the Lockheed Corporation after cost overruns on the C-5A military transport plane and production problems with its L-1011 Tristar airplane threatened the company with bankruptcy. A plan to aid the financially troubled Chrysler Corporation established a loan guarantee board to administer $1.5 billion in loan guarantees. The loan guarantee also required Chrysler to arrange another $2 billion in assistance from workers, dealers, and creditors. In 1980, Congress authorized a sweeping program of loan guarantees and other financial assistance to encourage synthetic fuels development. Legislation has been enacted to authorize loan guarantees for the development of geo-thermal resources, new underground coal mines, electric powered vehicles, and alternative fuel demonstration facilities.

Loans and loan guarantees have become major vehicles for government aid to industry. Despite the expansion of credit market activities in the 1930s, the overall impact of federally assisted borrowing on business remained small. By the early 1950s, direct loans and loan guarantees of the federal government accounted for less than 3 percent of new business debt.* But over the last two decades, loans and loan guarantees have exploded. By 1980, targeted federal loans outstanding totaled $47.3 billion. Targeted loan guarantees outstanding totaled $221.6 billion. Between 1950 and 1980, the direct cost of these outstanding loans and loan guarantees—in terms of subsidized interest rates and defaults—rose from $300 million (in 1978 dollars) to $3.6 billion.

Like tax expenditures, loans and loan guarantees are relatively invisible since they do not appear as expenses in the federal budget. This makes them highly attractive vehicles for political logrolling.

Insurance, Price Guarantees, and Purchase Agreements

These mechanisms reduce the risk of certain investments more directly than do loans and loan guarantees by focusing on the specific source of business risk. For example, the 1954 Atomic Energy Act permitted private ownership and operation of nuclear power plants. However, concerns about financial liability for nuclear accidents made private investors generally unwilling to invest in the emerging industry. More specifically, the insurance industry was unwilling to fully insure these power plants without any experience on the likelihood of financial loss. Accordingly, in 1957, Congress passed the Price-Anderson Act, which provided financial protection to nuclear power plant contractors and operators. The legislation limited liability for any nuclear accident to $560 million. Of that total, $500 million would be assumed by government; private insurers would assume up to $60 million. In a similar way, the government has attempted to induce foreign investments by offering expropriation insurance through the Overseas Private Investment Corporation.

More recently, Congress has been concerned about accelerating the development of synthetic fuels. With the passage of the Energy Security Act of 1980, Congress authorized purchase agreements and price guarantees to encourage private capital to flow into the development of synfuel technology. Such agreements and guarantees were designed to reduce the risk that future oil prices would decline precipitously and eliminate any market for synthetic fuels. In addition, price guarantees protect against other project risks, such as cost overruns.

The government has also established several programs to protect farmers from financial losses caused by fluctuations in the business cycle or by natural disasters. These programs are administered by the Federal Crop Insurance Corporation, the Agricultural Stabilization and Conservation Service of the Department of Agriculture, the Farmers Home Administration, and the Small Business Administration. For fiscal 1981, $2.7 billion of insurance is covered by these programs.

Finally, the government administers a series of narrowly drawn programs designed to protect particular industries from unexpected economic disruptions. For example, the commercial fishing industry has four separate programs of reimbursement for losses, including the foreign seizure of vessels and damage to vessels and equipment from offshore oil drilling. The dairy industry is the beneficiary of a dairy indemnity program that makes payments to farmers who are directed to remove their milk from commercial markets because of chemical contamination. A similar program compensates beekeepers who suffer losses of bees from pesticides. And the operators of both merchant vessels and commercial aircraft benefit from war risk insurance administered by the government.

Literally hundreds of special grants, tax expenditures, loans, loan and price guarantees, insurance, and purchase agreement schemes exist under U.S. law to assist selected producers. U.S. industrial policy may not be coherent or explicit, but it is quite active.

FOOTNOTES

[1] Export-Import Bank of the United States, *1977 Annual Report,* Washington, D.C.: Export-Import Bank, 1980, p. 7.

[2] *Loan and Export-Import Aircraft Financing Policies,* hearing before the Committee on Banking, Housing and Urban Affairs, U.S. Senate, 96th Congress, 2d Session, Washington, D.C.: U.S. Government Printing Office, 1980; W. Stephen Piper, "Unique Sectoral Agreement Establishes Free Trade Framework," *Law and Policy in International Business* 12 (1980), p. 221.

[3] *Congressional Record,* 117 November 20, 1971, 42486-7 (remarks of Senator Nelson).

[4] Saulnier, Raymond Joseph, *et al. Federal Programs of Lending Loan Insurance and Loan Guarantees,* New York: National Bureau of Economic Research, 1956.

EXHIBIT 78
Government Investment in Selected Industries (in Millions of Dollars)

	Research and Development	Other Direct Expenditures	Tax Expenditures	Procurement	Outstanding Loans and Loan Guarantees
Coal [1]	$942	$120	$530	—	—
Forest Products [2]	14	130	455	49	—
Dairy [3]	11	347	—	448	—
Nuclear [4]	5,010	113	—	1,628	—
Cotton [5]	8	232	—	—	—
Petroleum [6]	273	174	3,350	3,733	—
Commercial Fisheries [7]	24	3	—	—	103
Maritime [8]	16	585	70	4,075	6,342
Railroad [9]	55	2,491	—	3	2,064
Housing [10]	53	6,760	23,225	3,044	157,708
Automobiles and Highways [11]	108	1,394	—	1,217	940
Aviation [12]	1,393	2,994	—	7,159	558
Steel [13]	5	45	50	229	393
Semiconductors [14]	55	—	—	4,600	—
Textiles [15]	—	60	—	428	—

FOOTNOTES TO EXHIBIT 78

[1] The estimate on coal research and development is from 1981 Department of Energy Authorization, hearings before the Committee on Science and Technology, U.S. House of Representatives, 96th Congress, 1st Session, Washington, D.C.: U.S. Government Printing Office, 1980, pp. 1099–1199. Other direct promotional expenditures include the abandoned mine reclamation fund, administered by the Department of the Interior, and the abandoned mine program, administered by the Department of Agriculture. These expenditures also include the budgets of the Office of Surface Mining Reclamation and Enforcement in the Department of the Interior; the Mine Safety and Health Review Administration of the Department of Labor; and the Federal Mine Safety and Health Review Commission. The budget of the Mine Safety and Health Review Administration was adjusted to reflect the fact that 65 percent of the Administration's enforcement activities are directed at coal mining. The tax expenditure data are estimates provided by the Joint Committee on Internal Revenue Taxation, U.S. Congress. Of the

total, $520 million represents percentage depletion on coal production; the balance is from the capital gains treatment of royalties.

[2] The data on research and development and other direct expenditures are from the Office of Management and Budget, Washington, D.C., 1980. The tax expenditures are attributable to capital gains treatment for certain timber income. Government expenditures for lumber, millwork, plywood, and veneer are included in the procurement total. Excluded from the table are timber sales from national forests at below fair market value. Recently, the National Resources Defense Council estimated that timber sales below market values represented $50 million annually in foregone revenue. See National Resources Defense Council, "Giving Away the National Forests" (1980).

[3] The data on research and development programs and other direct expenditures are taken from *Agriculture, Rural Development and Related Agencies Appropriations for 1981,* hearings before the Subcommittee on Agriculture, Rural Development and Related Agencies, Committee on Appropriations, U.S. House of Representatives, 96th Congress, 2d Session, Washington, D.C.: U.S. Government Printing Office, 1980. Data are for fiscal year 1980. The research expenditure for the dairy industry is conservatively estimated from the budget of the Annual Health and Plant Inspection Service. In fiscal year 1980, the Service spent $169.2 million on animal disease and pest control. A portion of this budget was spent researching the control of tuberculosis and Brucellosis, two diseases of special concern to dairy farmers. Other direct promotional expenditures include net expenditures on price supports for the dairy industry incurred by the Commodity Credit Corporation. The estimates included in the table represent the activity of the corporation during fiscal year 1979. The estimates in the table do not include any sums expended by the Foreign Agriculture Service to develop foreign markets for U.S. dairy products. See House Appropriations hearings, *supra,* Part 2 at 541.

[4] For data on research and development and for both civilian and military applications of nuclear energy, see *1981 Department of Energy Authorization,* Committee on Science and Technology, House of Representatives, 96th Congress, 1st Session, 1980. The category of other direct promotional expenditures includes the subsidy arising from the operation of uranium enrichment plants. See, General Accounting Office, *Fair Value Pricing: Is it Fair?,* April 18, 1978. The regulatory expenditures are also included and represent the budget for regulatory activities of the Nuclear Regulatory Commission. The table does not include, however, subsidy estimates attributable to the indemnification provisions of the Price-Anderson Act. That Act limits the liability of nuclear plant operators in the event of a nuclear accident. The Act is gradually being phased out (although not for nuclear

reactors operated by nonprofit educational institutions). In 1975, before the phase-out of the Price-Anderson Act was adopted by Congress, the General Accounting Office estimated that the annual indemnity subsidy for a utility with one 1,000 megawatt reactor was about $145,000. See "Selected Aspects of Nuclear Power Plant Reliability and Economics," U.S. General Accounting Office, August 15, 1975. See also "Nuclear Power Costs and Subsidies," U.S. General Accounting Office, June 13, 1979 and "An Analysis of Federal Incentives to Stimulate Energy Production," Batelle Northwest Laboratories, March, 1978 at 127–128.

[5] The majority of funds expended for cotton research are spent to eradicate the boll weevil. The research expenditure combines the sums spent by the Science and Education Administration and the Plant Health Inspection service of the Department of Agriculture. See *Agriculture, Rural Development and Related Agencies Appropriations for 1981,* hearings before the Subcommittee on Agriculture, Rural Development and Related Agencies, Committee on Appropriations, U.S. House of Representatives, 96th Congress, 2d Session, 1980. Other direct promotional expenditures include information services provided by the Agricultural Marketing Service but do not include information services provided to cotton farmers by the Foreign Agricultural Service. Other direct promotional expenditures also include losses realized by the Commodity Credit Corporation for disaster and diversion payments to cotton producers in fiscal year 1979. This payment level will vary from year to year as market conditions change. However, from 1933—when price support programs for cotton were first implemented—to 1979, net losses to the CCC from the U.S. cotton program have exceeded $11 billion in nominal dollars. In addition to price supports, there are four major programs to provide disaster assistance to cotton farmers: federal crop insurance provided by the Federal Crop Insurance Corporation, disaster payments of the Agricultural Stabilization and Conservation Service, emergency production loss loans issued by the Farmers Home Administration, and emergency loans for production losses administered by the Small Business Administration. Other direct expenditures include only an estimate of the losses on the cotton program of the Federal Crop Insurance Corporation. This program covers 8 percent of the total insurable acreage of cotton. From 1948 to 1978, indemnities exceeded premiums by $49.9 million, or about $1.6 million per year. In 1979, the Department of Agriculture estimated that indemnities exceeded premiums by $3.9 million. Other direct promotional expenditures also include sums spent by the Department of Agriculture on inspection and grading of cotton, as well as the administrative costs of the cotton price support program by the Agricultural Stabilization and Conservation Service. Note that the category of other direct promotional expenditures do not include sums expended by the Department of Agriculture to develop overseas mar-

kets for cotton or to finance (through the Commodity Credit Corporation) the purchase of U.S. cotton by foreign buyers. This accounting also does not provide directly for the oversight activities conducted by the Secretary of Agriculture under provisions of the Cotton Research and Promotion Act of 1966, P.L. 89-502. The purpose of that Act was to enable cotton producers to establish a coordinated program of research and promotion to develop markets for cotton. To finance this program, an assessment of $1 per bale was authorized. Administration of the program occurs through a 20-member Cotton Board, appointed by the Secretary of Agriculture from nominations made by producer associations in the Cotton Belt, and a private industry corporation, Cotton, Inc. See "Cotton Research and Promotion Program," Subcommittee on Cotton, Committee on Agriculture, U.S. House of Representatives, 96th Congress, 2d Session, 1980.

[6] For research and development expenditures, see "1981 Department of Energy Authorization," Committee on Science and Technology, U.S. House of Representatives, 96th Congress, 2d Session, 1980 at 1200–1272. Other direct expenditures include demonstration and production projects and the dissemination of energy information. See *Id.* at 1231, 1398–1434. Other direct promotional expenditures include regulatory expenditures that are attributable to the Economic Regulatory Administration and the Federal Energy Regulatory Commission. Not included in the total are sums spent by the Bureau of Land Management, the Geological Survey, and the Coast Guard to manage onshore and offshore petroleum production on federal lands. Also excluded are sums expended by the Department of Energy to explore and develop the naval petroleum reserves. Tax expenditures include the excess of percentage over cost depletion and the expensing of intangible drilling expenses.

[7] Research and development for the commercial fishing industry, are authorized primarily under the Saltonstall-Kennedy Act, 15 U.S.C. 713c-3. That Act provides that a portion of the import duties on fish products be applied directly to research and development programs for fisheries. An estimate of funds spent on research and development can be found in "American Fisheries Protection Act," House Rept. 96-1138, part 1, 96th Congress, 2d Session, 1980 at 20. See also 126 *Congressional Record* at H9395, September 23, 1980 (remarks of Representative Breaux during consideration of H.R. 7039, American Fisheries Promotion Act). Other direct promotional expenditures consist primarily of various insurance programs to protect the U.S. commercial fishing industry from specific risks. These insurance programs include the Fishing Vessel and Gear Damage Compensation Fund and the Fisherman's Contingency Fund. Also included in other direct promotional expenditures are inspection and certification services the government provides for fishery products. No allocation of tax expenditures is made to

the fishing industry, although under the Merchant Marine Act of 1936, commercial fisherman can defer tax liabilities by depositing funds in a Capital Construction Fund. Loans and loan guarantees are from two major programs: the Fisheries Loan Fund and the Federal Ship Financing Fund. Note that this accounting does not reflect changes in policy toward the commercial fishery industry that are reflected in the American Fisheries Protection Act. This legislation passed the House of Representatives on September 23, 1980.

[8] Research and development expenditures represent funds spent by the Maritime Administration of the Department of Commerce. Other direct expenditures include sums spent by the Maritime Administration on two major subsidy programs: the construction differential subsidy and the operating differential subsidy. The category also includes operations and training activities. The tax expenditure estimate is attributable to a tax deferral provision given to certain shipping companies.

[9] The following are 1980 federal outlays for rail transportation as estimated by the Economics Division, Congressional Research Service (in thousands of dollars):

Federal outlays for rail transportation, 1980

Amtrak	$634,000
Non-Amtrak	
Rail Safety	22,886
Research and Development	50,675
Rail Service Assistance	136,000
Northeast Corridor Improvement Program	380,700
Railroad Rehabilitation	78,000
Alaska Railroad	6,500
Total	$1,308,761

[10] The research and development estimate represents activities of the Department of Housing and Urban Development. Other direct expenditures consist of housing assistance programs and are estimated in "Federal Housing Policy: Current Programs and Recurring Issues," Congressional Budget Office, U.S. Congress, June 1978. The study provides estimates for 1980. Tax expenditures for housing are detailed in the same study. Estimates of outstanding loans and loan guarantees are provided in "Federal Credit Activities: An Analysis of the President's Credit Budget for 1981," Congressional Budget Office, February, 1980 at 65–82. Estimates of outstanding loans and loan guarantees have been adjusted to eliminate the "double counting" arising from the guarantee by the Government National Mortgage Association of loan pools guaranteed by the Federal Housing Administration and the Veterans Administration.

[11] Expenditures on automotive research and development by the federal government are outlined in "National Automotive Research Act," hearings before the Committee on Interstate and Foreign Commerce, U.S. House of Representatives, 96th Congress, 2d Session, 1980. Other direct promotional expenditures include funds spent to promote highway safety. Procurement includes passenger cars, trucks, and tractor trailers.

[12] This category actually represents a broad grouping of related industries, including aircraft manufacturers, aircraft component manufacturers, and airline companies. The research and development estimate includes both defense and civilian applications. The category of other direct promotional expenditures includes the federal funds budget of the Federal Aviation Administration, the budget of the Civil Aeronautics Board, and a portion of the budget of the National Transportation Safety Board. Procurement consists of both the acquisition and modification of aircraft and components as well as the acquisition of airline services. Outstanding loans and loan guarantees are outlined in "Federal Credit Activities: An Analysis of the President's Credit Bureau for 1981," Congressional Budget Office, U.S. Congress (1980) at 88–89.

[13] The research and development estimate for the steel industry is for 1978. See "Technology and Steel Industry Competitiveness," Office of Technology Assessment, U.S. Congress at 273. Note that the government is not expanding its research and development program for steel; the Office of Management and Budget has curtailed the activities of the Bureau of Mines in this area. See "An Overall Framework is Needed for Evaluating Steel Industry Related Government Initiatives," U.S. General Accounting Office (forthcoming). The category of other direct expenditures includes trade adjustment assistance to workers administered by the Labor Department. In the four years from April 1975 to May 1979, $179 million was provided to workers in the steel industry, or about $45 million per year. See "Problems in the U.S. Steel Market," hearings before the Subcommittee on Trade, Committee on Ways and Means, U.S. House of Representatives (1980) at 199. The Economic Development Administration focuses its assistance to the steel industry on loans and loan guarantees. Because of the restrictive conditions on trade adjustment assistance to firms, most large steel companies do not file for these benefits. Tax expenditures include the capital gains treatment of loan or royalties and an acceleration in depreciation schedules for steel companies. See GAO report, *supra*. Procurement data include only metal bars, sheets, and shapes. The estimate of outstanding loan and loan guarantees is provided by the Economic Development Administration and includes loan guarantees issued by the EDA in response to the so-called Solomon Report in 1977. See "A Report to the President: A Comprehensive Program for the Steel Industry," U.S. Department of Treasury, December 6, 1977.

[14] The research and development estimate was derived from a variety of sources. The major federal research and development program in semiconductors is the Very High Speed Integrated Circuits (VHSIC) program in the Department of Defense. This program was funded at a level of $30.4 million in fiscal year 1980. Aside from the VHSIC program, industry representatives estimate that the federal government accounts for about 5 percent of total industry spending on research and development. See "Innovation, Competition, and Government Policy in the Semiconductor Industry," Charles River Associates, Inc., 1980 at 6–29. The industry spends about $500 million a year in research and development. See "Competitive Factors Influencing World Trade in Integrated Circuits," U.S. International Trade Commission (1979) at 72. Procurement data are for 1977 and are presented in Charles River Associates, *op. cit.* at 5–10.

[15] Federal funding of research and development for the apparel and textile industries is probably less than $1 million. This total is rarely identified in compilations of the federal research and development budget. See "Research and Development in Industry," National Science Foundation (1977) at 24. The other direct promotional expenditures consist of an estimate of trade adjustment assistance to both firms and workers in the textile and apparel industries. These data were supplied by the Economic Development Administration and the Office of Trade Adjustment Assistance in the Department of Labor. Procurement data include both textiles and clothing.

20

Organization of U.S. Industrial Policy

The United States has an irrational and uncoordinated industrial policy that is comprised of "voluntary" restrictions on imports, occasional bail-outs for major companies near bankruptcy, small sums spent for job training and job relocation, a huge and growing program of defense procurement and defense-related research, and a wide array of subsidies, loan guarantees, and special tax benefits for particular firms or industries. It is an industrial policy by default, in which government and business are inextricably intertwined but in which the goal of international competitiveness has not figured.

Rather than easing the transition from declining to growing businesses, these programs have often had the opposite effect, retarding economic adjustment or siphoning resources away from more competitive enterprises.

The haphazard nature of U.S. industrial policy is partly attributable to the haphazard means by which policies are generated. Virtually the entire federal government and many individual state governments undertake programs that affect the pattern of economic development. For example, the Department of Commerce administers various economic development programs, including public works grants and loans, economic adjustment assistance, business loans for industrial and commercial facilities, guarantees of leases for private industry and of private loans for industrial and commercial facilities, and technical, planning, and research assistance for redevelopment areas. Still other developmental programs are administered by the Community Development Administration of the Department of Housing and Urban Development. In Congress, economic development legislation falls under the jurisdiction of the House Public Works and Transportation Committee; the Senate Environmental and Public Works Committee; the House Banking, Finance, and Urban Affairs Committee; and the Senate Banking, Housing, and Urban Affairs Committee.

Several state governments also have their own economic development programs. Within the past two years, California has undertaken a $22-million program of subsidies aimed at invigorating the state's high-technology businesses. Both Minnesota and North Carolina are financing large microelectronics research centers. Ohio has established a $5-million fund to aid high-technology companies.

Aid to small business as well is channeled through several agencies. The Small Business Administration provides loans, loan guarantees, and management assistance and counseling; it also conducts economic and statistical research into matters affecting small business. Federal insurance programs designed primarily for small businesses are administered by the Federal Emergency Management Agency in the Department of Housing and Urban Development. The Department of Energy's Office of Small Business helps develop appropriate conservation programs. And the House and Senate each have small business committees.

Programs to promote or regulate international trade are implemented in part through the Commerce Department's International Trade Administration. The Export-Import Bank, an independent agency, aids in financing U.S. exports. The State Department's Bureau of Economic and Business Affairs implements programs relating to international business practices, finance, and resources; the Department's Under Secretary for Economic Affairs coordinates a variety of foreign economic policies. The Treasury Department's Office of International Affairs has authority over certain international monetary and investment activities. The Agriculture Department's Foreign Agriculture Service assists in agricultural trade negotiations, coordinates the activities of U.S. representatives who report on crop and market conditions abroad, and establishes overseas trade shows to promote sales of U.S. products. Meanwhile, the Commerce Department's International Trade Commission monitors adherence to international trade agreements, and the Treasury Department's Customs Service assesses countervailing or antidumping duties. In Congress, international trade issues are overseen by no less than 12 separate committees.

Foreign investment in the U.S. is promoted and regulated by another collection of bureaus: The Commerce Department's Office of Foreign Investment, the State Department's Bureau of Economic and Business Affairs, and the Treasury Department's Foreign Assets Control Office.

Foreign investment by U.S. companies is promoted by the Overseas Private Investment Corporation, an independent agency. Economic aid to less-developed countries is administered by the Agency for International Development and Cooperation.

At the same time, the Labor Department's Bureau of International Labor Affairs researches and assists in the development of U.S. foreign economic policy as it affects the income and job opportunities of American workers. The Department's Office of Trade Adjustment Assistance provides funds to American workers who are unemployed because of increased imports, while job-training programs are administered by the Department's Employment and Training Administration. Employment policies in general fall under the jurisdiction of the House Education and Labor Committee and the Senate Labor and Human Resources Committee.

Responsibility for other economic policies is spread willy-nilly throughout the government departments. Antitrust policy is divided between the Antitrust Division of the Department of Justice and the Federal Trade Commission, an independent agency. The Senate and House Judiciary Committees both oversee antitrust activities. Tax policy emanates from the Treasury Department's Internal Revenue Service and its Office of Tax Policy, as well as from the House Ways and Means Committee, the Senate Finance Committee, and the Joint Committee on Taxation. The U.S. Tax Court, the U.S. Court of Claims, and various federal district courts have responsibility for controversies arising under the tax laws. Loans and loan guarantees issue from 40 separate departments or agencies.

Procurement and research and development are undertaken by almost every government agency and department. The General Service Administration's Office of Acquisition Policy administers federal procurement regulations. The Defense Department's Office of the Under Secretary for Research and Engineering coordinates defense procurement policies. Approximately nine Congressional committees oversee government procurement policies. The Defense Department's Advanced Research Projects Agency administers defense-related research programs, while its Defense Logistics Agency serves as a central repository for Defense Department R & D studies in science and technology. The Department of Energy administers R & D programs in solar and wind energy, offshore coal, gasification, and other areas.

In recent years, the President has sought to coordinate this hodge-podge of programs through high-level councils and boards established within the White House. For example, an Office of the Special Trade Representative has been established to negotiate international trade agreements and an Office of Federal Procurement Policy is now co-ordinating government contracting. Economic policy councils have been established to oversee broad economic policies; domestic policy councils coordinate more discrete sets of economic policies. A Regulatory Council was briefly established in the Carter administration to coordinate and oversee government regulation of business. In the waning days of the Carter administration, various "tripartite" boards—comprised of representatives from government, labor, and business—were convened to coordinate government programs affecting particular industries, such as autos, steel, and coal. The Office of Management and Budget has recently taken responsibility for coordinating loans, loan guarantees, and regulatory policy.

Similar coordinating mechanisms have been created in Congress. Budget committees in the House and Senate now set overall spending targets, and the Congressional Budget Office advises Congress on spending and on economic policy. The Office of Technology Assessment provides Congress with information and analysis on the political, economic, and social consequences of technological change. The Joint Economic Committee undertakes various studies of the U.S. economy.

Despite these centralized groups, the process of economic policy formation remains decentralized and chaotic. Because these groups are merely advisory in nature, they cannot directly override the decisions of the various agencies, offices, or committees they seek to coordinate. Indeed, the only governmental bodies with authority to harmonize inconsistent policies are the 94 federal district courts and the 10 federal courts of appeal that review government programs within the context of individual cases and controversies.

Perhaps the most striking feature of the U.S. industrial policy apparatus is the absence of any single agency or office with overall responsibility for monitoring changes in world markets or in the competitiveness of American industry, or for easing the adjustment of the domestic economy to these changes. Despite the awesome number of agencies concerned with U.S. economic performance, competitiveness and adjustment are nowhere regarded as basic goals. Instead, each part of the bureaucracy has tended to view its own specific mandate as paramount, while the larger issues have been consigned to the various coordinating groups.

The failure of U.S. industrial policy is not simply a failure of organization, of course. It is a failure of substantive strategy. The industrial policies of Japan, West Germany, and France have been more successful than U.S. policies because they have explicitly and consciously aimed at improving the international competitiveness of their businesses. They have sought to ease the adjustment of capital and labor out of less competitive businesses and into emerging businesses with the highest potential for growth in world markets.

As the following chapters show, businesses and governments in France, West Germany, and Japan have developed a wide range of tools for working collaboratively toward the common end of international competitiveness. They have not always been successful, but their record over the past decade has been impressive, and there is every reason to suspect that they will be even more successful in the decade ahead.

21

An Introduction to Foreign Industrial Policies

The need for a conscious industrial strategy has been a central tenet of economic policy in most European and Far Eastern countries for well over a decade. Until recently, U.S. policymakers have been largely unaware of these policies, often regarding those it could discern as unfair trade practices or unpredictable government meddling in the free market. Even today, when the existence of explicit industrial policies in these countries is an active subject for political discussion and a common topic for editorial writers, the details of these remain obscure in the U.S.

U.S. PERCEPTIONS OF FOREIGN ECONOMIES

The economic experiences of Germany, France, Great Britain, Sweden, and Japan are not well understood in the United States. This is partly because there has often been a large gap between rhetoric and practice in these nations, and partly because the U.S. tries to fit their experiences into its own economic framework, distorting them in the process. For example, West Germany is commonly considered to be a more liberal, free-market-oriented economy than either Great Britain or France; German officials often characterize themselves as such. Yet a much larger percentage of Germany's GNP is accounted for by the government than in either Great Britain or France. In comparing French and German governments, it is also common to view the Germans as not meddling in the marketplace. Yet the German government's aids to industry have been slightly greater than those provided by the French government (Exhibit 79).

EXHIBIT 79
Selective Government Aids to Industry in France and Germany

			France
	1972–77	1978 In Millions of FF Current	1979 In Millions of FF Current
Total Aids[1]		23,650	31,450
Investments & R&D in Industry		96,200	106,060
Percent	24%	24.6%	29.7%

			W. Germany
	1972–77	1978 In Millions of DM Current	1979 In Millions of DM Current
Total Aids[1]		18,540	20,050
Investments & R&D in Industry		69,260	74,900
Percent	26%	27%	27%

Sources: France: Rapport au Parlement sur les aides publiques l'industrie; Enquetes Dgrst; annual reports of FDES, CUCEP, CEA, and CNES; West Germany: Subventionbericht, BMFT Programs, Fachenbericht, annual reports of ERP, DEG, and HFW.

Similarly, if one speaks with Japanese officials and industry leaders today, one hears the view that Japan is rapidly moving away from the "Japan Inc." concept of the economy and toward a "liberal, free market" approach. In one sense, this is true. In the 1950s and 1960s, while Japan was rebuilding its economy, credit was strictly allocated, high tariffs and quotas were the rule, export subsidies abounded, and the government played a significant role in allocating economic resources. However, when Japanese commentators speak of "liberalizing" their economy, this does not mean that they are adopting laissez-faire attitudes toward industry. The Japanese government continues to play a significant role in industrial development, though this role has evolved relative to changes in Japan's industrial strength and structure.

---

[1] Includes R&D, sectoral and regional policies, promotion of exports, and investments abroad. All forms of aid (grants, special loans, and tax reductions) are included.

For example, there is less overt protection, with more emphasis on R&D assistance in knowledge-intensive industries and on assistance to purchasers of prototype capital equipment. The Japanese government, anxious to avoid trade restrictions in the West, has emphasized its liberalizing trend. However, it would be a mistake to assume that this means the end of its successful industrial policy.

Another common perception in the U.S. is that the selective government intervention in European economies has been the result of "creeping socialism." Yet political labels do not reveal a great deal about the extent of government industrial policy. Sweden, long viewed in the U.S. as the archtype socialist state because of its 46 years of Social Democratic rule (until 1977), had fewer nationalized industries and a less comprehensive industrial policy than did conservatively controlled Japan, Italy, or France. It was the right-of-center coalition that came to power in 1977 that nationalized many Swedish industries and increased selective government aids to industry (Exhibit 80).

It is also important to distinguish short-term from long-term developments and to put trends into international perspective. It was common in 1974 to read apocalyptic articles in Japanese newspapers about how worldwide shortages of raw materials would mean the end of prosperity for the Japanese economy. A 30-percent inflation rate during 1974 confirmed this diagnosis. Many American commentators who picked up these articles took them at face value, and predicted the demise of Japan's export prowess. The U.S. now knows these problems were short-lived. Similarly, it is common in West Germany to proclaim the end of the "German economic miracle" because inflation and unemployment are soaring and growth is stagnating. While the German economy is no doubt suffering the effects of the world recession, its inflation rate is only 5 percent (up from 3 percent) and its unemployment rate is only 5 percent (up from 2 percent), compared to rates of 12 percent inflation and 8 percent unemployment in the U.S.

To understand economic and industrial policies in Europe and Japan, one must go deeper than comparisons of government spending levels, assertions about government intervention versus the free market, discussions of the proportions of industry owned by governments, and the daily economic pronouncements in the newspapers.

In this and the following chapters, we examine the major threads of industrial policy in Germany, France, Great Britain, and Japan. Historical antecedents of industrial policy are reviewed, along with the activities of foreign governments to assist depressed industries and their policies to assist growing industries. The organization of policy agencies is also discussed.

EXHIBIT 80
Selective Government Aids to Industry in Sweden

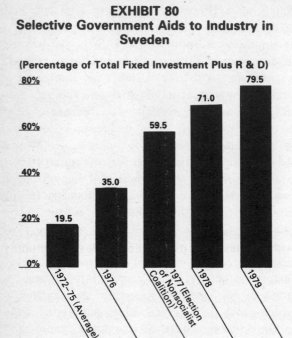

(Percentage of Total Fixed Investment Plus R & D)

Source: "The Engineering Industries and Swedish Industrial Policy," *Telesis,* October 1980, pp. 116–119.

HISTORICAL ANTECEDENTS OF FOREIGN INDUSTRIAL POLICIES

Although debates about the government's role in industrial affairs are as common in Europe and Japan as they are in the United States, these other countries begin from different premises. England and France both have a long tradition, dating back hundreds of years, of an elite economic bureaucracy. In both Japan and Germany, similar admin-

---

[1] Within one year of the election, the ailing steel and shipbuilding industries were nationalized.

istrations were created in the late 1800s under the Mejii restoration and Bismark's unification. Strong national identities were forged in all of these countries, and governments were seen as the agents for developing national unity.

In addition, governments in each of these countries have long played key roles in promoting industrial development. In Germany and Japan, the governments were directly responsible for industrialization in the late 1800s and early 1900s. Although the governments chose to work through private banking systems and private corporations, they gave legitimacy to these private efforts at capital formation. France has a long tradition of government coordination that dates back to before Napoleonic times. By contrast, England was greatly influenced by the laissez-faire teachings of the early nineteenth century. Because industrialization occurred early, England developed a private sector that was less dependent on government. Even here, however, there was a reliance on the government to ensure foreign markets and raw materials sources.

Discussions of government's legitimate role in industry are often confused with debates about ownership of industry. Certainly the issues are interrelated, but the rejection of total state ownership of the means of production in these countries has not meant that the governments have adopted a neutral role in industrial affairs. There are many intermediate stages between laissez-faire and state socialism.

England, France, Germany, and Japan all possess a competent, highly respected bureaucracy that derives authority from a strong national identity and a government with the acknowledged right and responsibility to concern itself directly with industrial development. This is the background against which we must view these nations' recent economic history.

Postwar Reconstruction: 1945–1955

Germany, France, and Japan faced similar problems after the Second World War. Their economies were in ruin, capital and managerial resources were depleted, and many industrialists and companies were discredited for their roles in collaborating with Fascist authorities.

The governments in all three countries led their recoveries by reforming basic industries such as steel, coal, and cement, and by reorganizing the banking systems with a priority on financing industrial development. Some nationalizations also occurred in basic industries or in companies whose owners were viewed as politically unsuited to run businesses because of their collaboration with the German and Japanese war efforts. Price controls, credit rationing, and trade barriers were erected to keep a tight grip on the rebuilding process.

In addition, several public institutions were created to channel funds to basic industries and to develop infrastructure. These included the Japan Development Bank; the F.D.E.S. (Economic and Social Fund), administered by the Ministry of Finance in France; and the E.R.P., created to administer the Marshall Plan funds in Germany.

In all three of these countries, the tradition of "universal banks"— banks heavily involved in the ownership and development of private industrial enterprises—provided a convenient mechanism for government-directed funding of industrial redevelopment. The ministries of finance in each country controlled banking (in France, the three largest banks were nationalized), credit, foreign exchange, and stock markets. The ministries also influenced the allocation of funds by financial institutions, which were used in Germany to dispense and help guide the direction of government funds.

Mechanisms were also developed in these countries for consensus-forming among the major economic constituencies—managers and owners of industrial enterprises, trade unions, banks, and the government. The French formal planning systems, the Japanese MITI advisory councils, and the regular German round tables all provided forums in which various industrial constituencies could meet. These forums were facilitated (particularly in Germany and Japan) by long traditions of well-organized and centralized industrial management associations and, in all three countries, by strong trade unions. These institutional arrangements, combined with government-led efforts at reconstruction, helped further establish the legitimacy of a direct government role in industrial affairs.

Great Britain followed a different pattern. Although some nationalizations were carried out, the bulk of the private sector continued as before the war, with little government assistance.

Consolidation: 1955–1965

After the period of initial reconstruction, the German government gradually abdicated its direction of the industrial system. It eased credit restrictions, protection from trade, foreign exchange laws, and price controls. It also embarked on a path of private allocation of industrial investment combined with collective social programs, using broad Keynesian policies to guide general economic development. German industrial policy thus came to resemble that of Great Britain.

By contrast, the French and the Japanese governments maintained tight restrictions on credit, currency, and trade until the mid-1970s. They also continued to play a selective role in industrial development, guiding the initial growth of various industrial sectors and attempting to manage the evolution of the industrial structure in a more direct way. These governments shared the view that reliance on macroeconomic demand stabilization and on the workings of imperfect markets were insufficient to produce economic growth and security at a socially acceptable pace. Postwar programs in all four countries were established to promote industrial development. These measures included various means of stimulating fixed capital investment, job-training and -placement programs for workers displaced by industrial restructuring, and regional incentive policies to assist slow-developing areas.

The European Common Market was formed during this period. Policies were formulated to coordinate agricultural programs, and the coal and steel programs started a few years earlier were consolidated.

Post-1965: Industrial Restructuring and Technological Innovation

Since the late 1960s, emphasis on industrial policies has intensified in all four of these countries. Like the U.S., these economies have faced problems of unemployment and have seen the need to pioneer new industries. No longer was the focus on problems of reconstruction or employment shortages. Reformulation of industrial policy to confront these new challenges was spurred by changes in the world economy. The development of industry in low-wage countries and the concommitant export of their goods to the developed world caused serious strains for a number of industries, particularly clothing, shoes, textiles, electronic assembly, toys, and metal-working. These strains were exacerbated by the slowing down of world economic growth after the oil crisis in 1974, combined with the further movement of low-wage countries into certain areas of the shipbuilding, steel, and fiber industries. Finally, the opening of new raw material deposits in Australia, Canada, and the newly industrializing countries accelerated the competitive decline of European and Japanese raw materials.

Because all four of these governments were committed to full employment, they felt a responsibility to confront the industrial dislocations caused by these events with new industrial policies and institutions. While looking for solutions to these industrial problems, many officials and business leaders concluded that programs to accelerate the development of new technologies might be an important means of overcoming employment declines in traditional industries. It was also acknowledged that a wide gap had opened between American technology and technology in their countries, because of heavy aerospace and defense spending by the U.S. government. Closing this gap was seen as a necessary precondition to competitiveness and more rapid industrial growth.

As a result of the declining competitive positions of some traditional industries, these four governments developed a series of explicit policies for depressed industries. These included direct subsidies to bankrupt companies, nationalizations of bankrupt companies, government-coordinated industry rationalization, European Economic Community cartels, import restrictions, and enhanced regional and labor market policies. To address the perceived gap in technology, the governments developed programs to assist new high-technology projects through direct R&D funding, investment banks for large or risky projects, and general aid programs for growth industries.

Germany's renewed industrial policy culminated in the creation of the Ministry of Technology in 1972. The British created Economic Development Councils in the early 1960s, then the Industrial Reorganization Commission in the mid-1960s, and finally the Department of Industry and the National Enterprise Board in the mid-1970s. The Japanese and the French maintained their apparatus for conducting industrial policies, though these changed in focus and style.

Japan and all major countries in Europe now have conscious and active policies to promote competitiveness and industrial restructuring. The following chapters outline these policies and the organizations designed to implement them.

22

Foreign Policies for Declining Businesses

RETARDING ADJUSTMENT

As in the United States, foreign governments have often employed subsidies and import restrictions to protect troubled industries. These policies have retarded economic adjustment. What may be the most pervasive defensive subsidy in the industrialized world is accorded by the EEC to certain European agricultural goods. The Common Agricultural Policy (CAP) is a support system of guaranteed prices for major agricultural commodities. Each year the EEC sets intervention prices at which it will buy butter, skim milk powder, beef, and grains, regardless of quantities. Price levels are the same throughout the Community, and tariffs are levied on imports from outside the EEC to bring them to parity with internal prices. The object of the program is to guarantee the Community's self-sufficiency in major agricultural products. Through stable prices for unlimited output, it also aims to shelter farmers from traditional agricultural cycles. Overall, the CAP acts as an instrument of income redistribution, from consumers and taxpayers to farmers. Because of the CAP, EEC prices for agricultural goods are considerably higher than world prices (Exhibit 81).

Since the mid-1970s, the EEC has also significantly increased protective measures against outside manufactured goods. A recent estimate indicates that in 1978, 89 separate actions were undertaken in the EEC to restrict imports, compared to an average of only six per year between 1971 and 1974.[1] As in the United States, many of these measures are negotiated agreements between European countries and the Japanese or less developed countries in the textile, fiber, clothing, steel, automotive, and consumer electronics industries.

EXHIBIT 81
EEC Prices vs. World Prices, 1978–1979

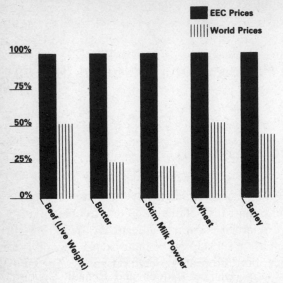

Source: Eurostat.

The Japanese government has also instituted import restrictions to protect uncompetitive industries, mainly in beef and agricultural products, though these have been less widespread than in the U.S. or Europe. Protectionist measures in Japan have been most often used for new, infant industries.

Foreign governments have also provided financial subsidies to troubled companies. The British government has been the most active subsidizer, providing billions of dollars every year in a wide variety of industries, and nationalizing companies to keep them alive. These subsidies have rarely been accompanied by plans to rationalize the declining industries to make them more competitive. Repeatedly, since 1972, the British government has provided grants, loans, and guarantees to companies with the understanding that the funding was only temporary. Repeatedly, funds committed have been insufficient, and more funds have been sought. More recently, the labor force has been cut in these industries, but their competitive positions remain weak.

The French government has also supplied significant subsidies to various distressed companies in textiles, shipbuilding, steel, and other industries. The reactive nature of much of British and French policy is evident in France's policy toward the steel industry.

French industrialists and policymakers failed to see the problems ahead and continued to invest heavily in steel through the early 1970s. Government assistance began with an "industry plan" that called for over $1 billion in government loans to the industry for expansion and rationalization between 1966 and 1971. Between 1970 and 1975, government lending to the steel industry increased by $160 million. In addition, the government made grants of $375 million in support of a steel complex begun in 1971 at Fos on the Mediterranean.

In 1975, declines in world demand made it clear that the French steel industry was still uncompetitive. An additional $300 million was granted to subsidize steel losses in that year. In February 1977, a planning agreement was signed between the steel companies and the government, calling for an additional loan of $370 million.[2]

The government and the steel companies also jointly agreed to spend an additional $50 million to encourage new investments in the Lorraine region, where older steel mills are concentrated. The two major French car manufacturers (Peugeot-Citroën and Renault-Saviem) were encouraged to locate their major capacity additions in this region, thus creating 4,000 jobs each before 1984.

Finally, in September 1978, the government announced that its loans to the steel companies would be converted into some form of equity interest, a move that gives it effective control over the industry. This plan has been partially implemented. However, the amount of continuing subsidy required has been greater than originally anticipated.

ASSISTING ADJUSTMENT

These defensive measures stand in marked contrast to more farsighted policies that have been adopted in Germany and Japan and that are gaining greater acceptance in other countries. These policies are premised on the belief that the only long-term solution to job losses in many uncompetitive businesses is an acceleration of adjustment for affected companies' workers and regions. This means instituting early warning systems for potentially troubled industries, maintaining active regional and labor market policies to assist local communities and workers affected by industrial decay, and assisting company rationalizations.

Both the German and Japanese governments actively examine their national industrial structures and attempt to suggest potential areas of growth and decline. These efforts are not "master plans" for industry, but rather educated attempts to anticipate transitions. These efforts form a basis for ongoing discussions with industry and for planning effective regional and labor market policies. While the British and French governments were heavily investing in the steel industry in the early 1970s, the German government was assisting rationalization plans among its steel companies, more clearly foreseeing competitive problems ahead. Though the Japanese steel industry is currently the world leader, Japanese officials are already anticipating a decline in its future importance as many developing countries expand steel production.

Regional Policies

Regional policies play a crucial role in assisting transitions of industrial structure in Europe. Germany's regional policy has been perhaps the most successful. The purpose of this policy is to provide incentives for new industrial investments in areas of chronic unemployment or recent job losses. Germany's policy of regional development affects more than half the population. It is financed jointly by the Federal Republic and the 11 states (*Lander*). Special emphasis is placed on three problem areas—the Ruhr, the Eastern Boarder Zone, and West Berlin.

The regional programs are large, with an average annual budget of over $4 billion (1980) over the last decade, representing 15 percent of total German industrial investment. Resources allocated under regional cash grant and federal tax-reduction programs have more than doubled since the mid-1960s in real terms.

Industrial investments are promoted through direct cash grants, tax reductions, subsidized land and infrastructure, low-interest loans, and loan guarantees.[3]

Projects do not automatically qualify for government assistance but are screened to select those that will have a positive impact on the region's industrial structure. Investments that create high-skilled jobs receive a higher subsidy, and the *Lander* do not hesitate to support rationalization investments even if they temporarily reduce employment, since this may be the only way to ensure the long-term viability of the majority of jobs. Because of the high ceiling for subsidies (over $2 million per project), even capital-intensive projects can be supported. Projects are rarely funded solely through the government; typically, the cooperation of local banks and chambers of commerce is also enlisted.

The British government has an active regional program to support industrial development in weaker regions, but these policies are less successful than those in Germany since they are less selective and they have tended to support nonviable projects.

The British government provides an automatic grant of up to 22 percent of fixed assets for investors in various distressed regions of the U.K. Interest-rate subsidies on loans for investors, manpower training grants, and, in some areas, employment premiums for adding workers are also provided. These benefits are open to foreign as well as domestic investors. While these programs have brought investment to distressed areas, they have often been administered indiscriminately, focusing on short-term job creation rather than on the long-term defensibility of the industry. Thus, a considerable number of projects eventually go bankrupt or require continuing subsidy. British regional policy also involves significant inefficiencies; for example, each region competes to attract mobile investment, often bidding up the price paid to a foreign company contemplating investment.

In France, less money is spent directly on regional programs, though the government has recently sought to encourage new investment in distressed regions. DATAR, the French regional development agency, has begun to meet with large companies to discuss their future plans for job creation or layoffs, and to coordinate necessary transition programs.

Labor Market Policies

Labor market policies also play an important role in easing industrial transitions. Labor market programs are an integral part of Germany's policy of accelerating economic modernization. These programs include extensive retraining for displaced workers, substantial severance payments, and payments to communities to offset some of the costs they must bear from plant closings. These programs supplement normal unemployment insurance schemes.

In addition, the government's transitional voucher program provides a subsidy to workers who are unemployed because of a plant shutdown. Under this program, the individual worker negotiates with a new employer for a wage package that roughly approximates prior earnings; the employer receives a subsidy that pays the difference between the audited cost of hiring and retraining the worker and the worker's audited contribution to the firm's profits.

West Germany has directed this voucher program at the long-term unemployed, people who have been out of work for more than a year. Employers who hire such workers are eligible for wage subsidy for two years. Workers' councils have been given legal authority by the Protection Against Dismissal Act to see that subsidized workers are not dismissed without cause once the subsidy period runs out.[4]

This West German voucher program is part of a larger program that provides short-term allowances to workers employed less than full time because of temporary business downturns. To qualify, an applicant's work week must have been decreased by at least 10 percent for four consecutive weeks, and at least one-third of the firm's employees must be affected. The government subsidizes wages for a period of up to six months under this program; during 1975, allowances were paid to 750,000 workers. The government estimated that 170,000 workers were saved from unemployment because of this program.

Japanese labor market policy places responsibility on companies to maintain employment. When factories are closed by large companies, it is common for companies to find employment for affected workers at other existing company facilities or by building new facilities for other company enterprises in the affected region. In cases of total company bankruptcy, the government often assists employment transitions. On occasion, the government also pays companies to maintain employees during recessions.

Industry Rationalization Schemes

A number of countries have programs to help make potentially competitive portions of an industry more efficient and to close down portions that can never be competitive.

Before the 1973 oil crisis, Japanese officials did not concern themselves with specific policies to aid industrial rationalization. With real growth rates in excess of 10 percent per year, labor shortages were more common than surpluses. In recent years, however, a number of industries—including aluminum, shipbuilding, fibers, and foundries—have faced considerable difficulty.

In May 1978, the Japanese Parliament (Diet) passed the Structurally Depressed Industries Law, enabling the Japanese Ministry of International Trade and Industry (MITI) to develop stabilization plans for depressed industries using government funds. Industries become eligible for assistance only if two-thirds of the producers petition MITI, which then decides whether to grant their request. This eligibility condition helps the Ministry to bring about a working agreement among the producers, whose cost positions and proposed solutions usually differ significantly. Major creditors, such as the Industrial Bank of Japan, sit on *ad hoc* committees with MITI to study the problems of a particular industry. The law establishes a government loan guarantee fund to aid producers to scrap or mothball capacity.

The French government has also devised policies to aid industry rationalization. In 1974, the French government formed CIASI an interministerial committee for industrial restructuring to help individual companies in difficulty. Since its formation, CIASI has helped over 500 firms. Coordinated by the Treasury Department, CIASI works closely with the business and banking communities to structure rationalization measures and put together financial packages to support them. Although it can use the low-interest funds of government banks, it tries to leverage its financial support with commerical credit and private equity.

Over the past three years, CIASI activities have been as significant as the regional development schemes, in terms of both expenditures and jobs created. CIASI's methods have involved modest cash outlays and have typically consisted of promoting mergers between healthy and unhealthy companies or of completely restructuring local industries.

CIASI has deliberately avoided large problem industries such as steel and shipbuilding, focusing instead on the more fragmented industries and smaller pockets of unemployment, such as textiles in the Vosges and shoes in Bretagne. In these situations, CIASI's cooperative and flexible mode of operation has enabled it successfully to restructure many local industries. Over the past year, it has been overwhelmed with requests from failing companies. The overall success of its efforts is yet to be determined.

In sum, our major trading partners have used measures to protect uncompetitive companies at the expense of their taxpayers and consumers. However, they also have adopted active policies to ease transitions from uncompetitive industries. In Germany and Japan, government policies have sought to act in advance of events. They have emphasized development of new investment opportunities in affected regions and assistance to affected workers and communities. Japanese policymakers have also assisted industries to rationalize. British policy has been more reactive and has often taken a short-term view. French policy, though traditionally closer to British efforts, has recently shown signs of moving closer to the Japanese and German methods, though the results are as yet unclear.

FOOTNOTES

[1] Franko, Lawrence. *European Industrial Policy Past, Present and Future.* The Conference Board in Europe, February 1980, p. 1.

[2] Other provisions of the agreement included rationalization of the steel companies' corporate structure (mergers and forward integration); capacity reductions at the seven least productive mills; a reduction of 16,000 jobs (10 percent of total employment) before 1980 through early retirement, with 70 percent income guaranteed; formal government control of the use of the agreement funds; and regional subsidies to create new jobs.

[3] The *Länder* can make cash grants based on investment in fixed assets (7.5 to 20 percent). Each region selects its own projects, but the criteria consistently favor viable investments that can secure long-term employment. Guidelines for the North Rhine region, for instance, explicitly state that threatened sectors should not be assisted if such aid would retard necessary industrial restructuring.

The federal government can also give an additional corporate tax reduction amounting to 7.5 percent of the investment cost. Projects are screened for long-term growth potential and are discussed with regional experts in the Ministry of Economics. Funding decisions reflect both the long-term outlook of the industry and the financial situation of the applicant.

Further, the communes can support certain investments by selling land at the lower price, providing free infrastructure, or even granting special tax privileges. It is also possible to obtain low-interest loans with favorable conditions from the Marshall Fund trust and from two state banks, the Kreditanstalt für Wiederaufbau and Lastenausgleichsbank. Lastly, small businesses can get government loan guarantees from the *Lander* or the federal government at a very low interest rate.

[4] Workers' councils are elected by workers in virtually all enterprises. They fulfill many of the functions performed by local union shop committees in U.S. industry plus many other responsibilities mandated by Germany's co-determination laws.

23

Foreign Policies for Growing Businesses

In addition to policies for assisting adjustment in troubled businesses, the major trading partners of the United States have also undertaken elaborate programs to assist growth businesses. These programs have taken the forms of assistance in new product and process development, aid for overseas marketing, and restructuring of firms to pursue growth opportunities.

ASSISTANCE IN RESEARCH AND DEVELOPMENT

Germany

The most direct government efforts to promote new products and processes are found in the Federal Republic of Germany. The German government has funded major research projects in nuclear energy, space, and defense for almost two decades. With the founding of the Ministry of Technology (BMFT) in 1972, Germany became extensively involved in selectively funding projects with specific commercial potential.

Since 1969, the share of total business R&D funded by the federal government has grown from 14 to 20 percent. The BMFT's annual budget for industrial R&D was about $3.2 billion in 1979. The German R&D effort has also become more directed. In 1968, half the government aids for R&D were in the form of general tax incentives; by 1977, this portion had shrunk to 10 percent; today, direct cash grants allocated on a selective basis are the major means of funding new projects.

The BMFT uses a sophisticated decisionmaking process to allocate its resources. Public appropriations by the Parliament (Bundestag) are authorized each year for such general programs as "Securing of Energy" or "Humanization of the Work Place." Although they involve broad policy issues, these programs are convenient "packages" for specific actions at a finer level of detail.

Individual projects proposed by companies are screened by a committee composed of government officials, industry representatives, independent consultants, and, increasingly, labor representatives. The final decision is made by the BMFT, and a project leader is chosen from outside the government to act as a link among the different parties involved.

Projects are evaluated on the basis of technical merit and long-term impact on Germany's business position. BMFT officials work closely with industry and shape policies around the competitive dynamics of the different businesses they plan to support.

Financing is generally given to projects that are too large or too risky for an individual company to fund, but the company must have the resources needed to exploit the innovation. Typically, 50 percent of the project is funded by the BMFT and 50 percent by the company. Because government R&D expenditures are matched by private investment, companies have a strong incentive to ensure the success of the projects.

Mechanical, electrical and electronic engineering businesses have had the greatest emphasis in recent years, receiving 35 percent of total federal R&D funds in 1979, compared to only 8 percent in 1969. About 30 percent of all R&D in these industries (excluding transportation equipment) is now funded by BMFT programs.

For example, in the mechanical engineering area, a traditional center of Germany industrial strength, the BMFT has initiated or supported projects through expenditures that totaled $500 million in 1979 (Exhibit 82).

An electronic components program was established in 1970. Electronic components were viewed as a key feeder industry that would promote the growth of other industries, but one in which German companies could not independently compete effectively with the major U.S. leaders because of U.S. Defense Department and NASA support and purchases. From 1970 to 1978, the Germans attempted to keep pace with the U.S. in integrated circuits, materials development, and production processes for semiconductors.

Germany is now refocusing its efforts away from basic products for which competitors have achieved scale economies not now possible for German companies and into the applications of those products, such as optics and microprocessors for process control and machine tools, areas in which German producers can be more competitive.

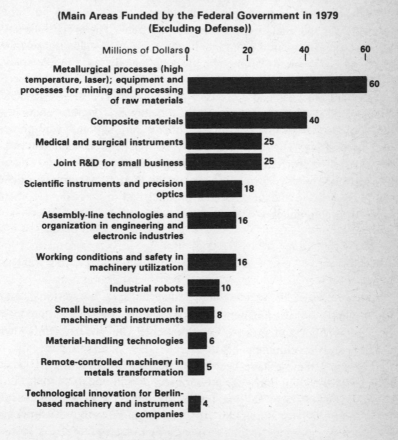

EXHIBIT 82
Public Funding of Mechanical Engineering R&D in Germany, 1979

(Main Areas Funded by the Federal Government in 1979 (Excluding Defense))

Millions of Dollars	
Metallurgical processes (high temperature, laser); equipment and processes for mining and processing of raw materials	60
Composite materials	40
Medical and surgical instruments	25
Joint R&D for small business	25
Scientific instruments and precision optics	18
Assembly-line technologies and organization in engineering and electronic industries	16
Working conditions and safety in machinery utilization	16
Industrial robots	10
Small business innovation in machinery and instruments	8
Material-handling technologies	6
Remote-controlled machinery in metals transformation	5
Technological innovation for Berlin-based machinery and instrument companies	4

Source: Bundesbericht Forschung VI.

The BMFT also has a program to encourage other industries to use these products. Through close cooperation among research institutes, component manufacturers, and labor unions, the BMFT has offered special assistance to those industries that were threatened by the introduction of semiconductors. The aim has been to consolidate these industries and to help such varied businesses as clockmaking, sensors, and weighing machines to restructure around defensible segments in which new technologies can be applied to existing products or processes. The leadership of the BMFT has been vitally important in helping pull together these highly fragmented industries.

During the last decade, German government support of industrial R&D has focused increasingly on building strong business positions in businesses that can support a high wage rate. The BMFT uses its funds to support focused programs that contribute to industrial restructuring. The multiplicity of projects has not created a huge bureaucracy. Rather, the BMFT is using a wide network of independent experts drawn from business and education to act as links with government. For example, although 300 projects are now in progress under the urban transportation program, a staff of five civil servants administers the whole effort. They are assisted by 60 independent technical consultants and 40 project managers drawn from companies and institutes.

While controversy surrounds some of the BMFT's programs, on the whole, they have encouraged new product and process development in German companies.

Japan

The Japanese government also carries out an extensive aid program for new product and process development. The government's own research and development effort is relatively small; in part, this is because the Japanese have been so successful in exploiting the basic research of U.S. and European government and university laboratories. It is also because large national applied-research projects are managed by government laboratories but performed under contract by working groups of corporations. MITI's Agency of Industrial Technology has 16 associated research institutes that organize and manage long-term, large-scale projects to develop system technologies for commercial use. Some current examples are VLSI semiconductors, high-performance jet engines, water desalinization, and natural resource recycling. These projects may run for five to eight years; they can cost hundreds of millions of dollars; and they are typically performed and cofunded by *ad hoc* associations of several large corporate and university laboratories. They are exempt from the Anti-Monopoly Law.

The government also uses a variety of more modest incentives and supporting tools for corporate research and development. These include tax credits,[1] grants,[2] and sponsorship of R&D associations.[3] Some are available to all corporations, while others are tied to particular MITI objectives.

The government has substantially increased its commitment to research and development over the decade, mainly in the form of a few high-priority projects. The assistance given to Japan's industrial machinery sector provides a specific example.

MITI's Agency for Industrial Science and Technology (AIST) gave the industrial machinery sector matching grants of about $15 million annually between 1973 and 1976 and $12 million during 1977 and 1978. These appropriations were primarily directed to the area of machine and whole plant integration.

A seven-year, large-scale research project, combining government and industry funds, has also been developed in the industrial machinery area to develop an ultrahigh performance laser control system. This project will receive a total of about $60 million in government assistance, plus individual contributions from companies.

A third source of research and development funding for the industry has come from the Bicycle Rehabilitation Association (JBRA), a group sponsoring bicycle races. In 1978, the JBRA awarded almost $40 million for research and development in the machinery area. An additional $700 thousand was awarded from a minicar racing fund. MITI undoubtedly influenced these allocations, although it did not officially control them.

Finally, for the benefit of the industrial machinery industry, the AIST maintains permanent research laboratories, including the Mechanical Engineering Laboratory in Tokyo and the Industrial Research Institutes in Osaka (for materials) and Nagoya (for forming processes). In 1978, AIST provided $40 million in financing for these labs.

In addition, there is a complex series of loan programs to stimulate research and development. Primarily carried on by the Japan Development Bank, this lending program has grown steadily over the years and now represents about $40 to $50 million per year in the industrial machinery sector. These project-related loans have played a significant role in the commercialization of new technologies, in the development of prototypes for commercial production, and in the commercialization of new technology for small enterprises. Low-interest loans are available for financing users' purchases of prototype machinery and manufacturers' purchases of equipment to be used in making new types of machines. Loans are also available to finance the actual development of new types of machines themselves.

Tax incentives for research and development in the industry were worth about $70 million in 1978. In addition, the government's special depreciation allowances are thought to have an annual value of roughly $30 million. From 1968 until 1975, a special depreciation program existed for machinery that embodied commercial application of new technologies. Regional property taxes as well as corporate income taxes were shielded by this program, which assisted both users and manufacturers of new machinery. Overall, about $250 million of equipment was covered during the lifespan of this program.

Finally, tax credits are allowed for cooperative research among companies. Over 25 cooperative research associations have been created. The funds paid into them can be substracted from the individual company's income.

When one considers the amount of funds available and the flexibility of instruments with which to assist companies, Japanese programs are probably even more supportive of industry than are the German programs.

Britain and France

British and French efforts to support new product and process development have been more limited than those of the Japanese and German governments. Government R&D expenditure in the U.K. during the 1970s actually declined from $300 million (1980 currency) in 1972 to less than $160 million in 1980. Eighty percent of government R&D has gone to aircraft, space, and nuclear projects, notably for the Concorde and Rolls-Royce.

The U.K. has a complicated network of government agencies that provide R&D assistance. The oldest of these, the National Research and Development Corporation (NRDC), was established in 1949. NRDC supports various national laboratories and research centers that carry out basic and applied research; it also supports research associations that provide technical information and advice to specific industrial sectors. By and large, these groups are not focused on commercial development. The NRDC does make grants (including interest relief) and loans to individual companies, but its budget is relatively small.

Government assistance in the U.K. has focused increasingly on commercial applications. This is a current objective set by the Department of Industry for its research establishments and through its research requirements boards, but as yet this effort is not far advanced.

France has developed a set of aid mechanisms to cover the entire innovation process from basic to applied research, product development, and market introduction. These programs are small when compared with those in Germany or Japan, but larger than programs in the U.K.

The bulk of French R&D expenditures has been in the defense area, under the Directorate of Research and Training (DRME). Most of the civilian R&D expenditure has been in large prestige projects—in nuclear energy, computers, and aircraft. Significant expenditures have also gone through the national center for space research to develop the ARIANE satellite launcher and other related projects (Exhibit 83).

The French government has also developed public institutes to perform industrial research; currently, 11 institutes spend more than $100 million per year. These institutes have played a significant role in the development of the French offshore oil equipment, nuclear, and telecommunications industries. There are also projects to directly fund companies that are doing their own research.

France was the first European country to introduce a scheme of cooperation between government and business on R&D projects. Introduced in 1965, the Aid to Development program subsidizes the development cost of industrial projects. This assistance is to be repaid in cases of commercial success. An analogous program for predevelopment expenditures was also established, initially focusing on heavy electrical equipment and machinery, but funding has been relatively small.

EXHIBIT 83
Public Funding of Industrial R&D in France, 1980

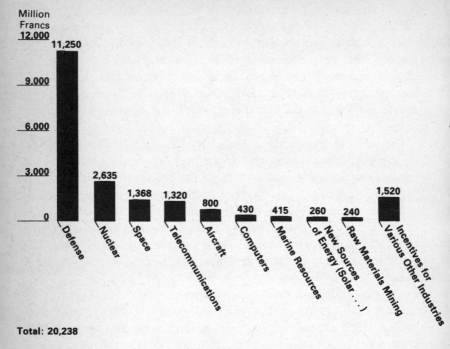

Total: 20,238

Source: Client study.

In 1967, a special agency, ANVAR, was created in the Ministry of Industry to offer support at the market introduction stage of the innovation process. The focus was to be on small firms and investors. Special tax advantages were given to newly created venture capital firms and risk credit was provided to innovative firms through a letter of agreement.

AID FOR OVERSEAS MARKETING

All four of the major trading partners of the United States have programs that are more comprehensive than that of the U.S. to encourage overseas marketing by their companies. These measures take many forms, including financial incentives for overseas marketing investments, low-cost financing of exports, and insurance against various types of risk associated with exporting.

France

French export promotion policies are perhaps the most elaborate. Shortly after the Second World War, two companies were created to promote the financing of French exports. The French Foreign Trade Bank (BFCE) provides a large part of the capital required for exports, especially long-term credit. In addition, the Banque de France refinances medium- and long-term export credits by the commercial banks at a favorable discount rate, usually 1 percent below market.

The Export Guarantee Company (COFACE) provides government guarantees for both regular commercial transactions (short-term guarantees) and special political or economic risks.[4] In addition, the state-owned Foreign Trade Center (CFCE) offers companies information and consulting services on international markets and procedures; the CFCE also organizes trade shows abroad.

Overall, exports to new markets, such as developing countries and the OPEC nations, and system sales of whole plants or complex machinery have been considerably helped by the government. Economic risk guarantees have increased substantially since the 1973 oil crisis, rising from an average of $150 million in the period from 1972 to 1976 to almost $300 million in 1978 and to $550 million in 1979. Interest subsidies for long-term loans distributed by BFCE go mainly to capital goods manufacturers. They have doubled since 1975, amounting to $200 million in 1979.

France uses mixed credits arrangements to finance capital goods exports to developing countries, combining low-interest loans (3 percent under official aid programs) and commercial credit. These mixed credits amounted to about $300 million in the first half of 1977. Finally, about $600 million of capital aid to developing countries was tied to the purchase of French goods in 1976. Since then, this amount has grown considerably.

Direct investments abroad can be financed with the help of a state association. Investments in developing countries receive a favorable tax treatment—a five-year tax defferal based on the cost of the investment. Small companies that wish to invest abroad can get equity from a state-owned financing company.

Japan

Though not as extensive as French programs, Japanese aids for overseas marketing are also substantial. Through the early 1970s, the Japanese government stimulated exports, restricted manufactured imports, and assisted large-scale raw material imports. By means of special reserves and accelerated depreciation, the tax system effectively shielded significant portions of export revenue from taxation. The Bank of Japan discounted short-term export bills at less than market interest rates; and cheap, long-term credit for export-related investment was available from the Japan Development Bank and the Long-Term Credit Bank of Japan. Assistance was given to overseas projects in mining, forestry, and the like with financial guarantees and government-to-government assurances in order to strengthen supply security in basic materials. Tax incentives were also heavily used to promote exports, adding about $100 million to the cash flow of companies in 1976.[5]

The story is different now. Broad export incentives are gone. The tax system retains incentives only for exports by small and medium-size companies and for overseas investment.[6] Although MITI no longer directly assists exports, certain government policies and practices do aid selected knowledge-intensive industries.[7] Loans remain a major factor in export promotion. Both supplier and buyer credits are extended according to rules laid down by international agencies.

However, large national projects that are sold to the governments of other countries can be financed by mechanisms that fall under the broad heading of economic aid. Unlike Export-Import Bank loans, these mechanisms are not regulated by the OECD. In Japan, the agency responsible is the Overseas Economic Cooperation Fund, a public policy company under the direction of the Ministry of Finance, the Ministry of Foreign Affairs, and the Economic Planning Agency. Yen credits are a highly desirable form of financing from the borrower's point of view—very low interest is charged (3 percent and less); amounts can exceed the value of the narrowly defined project; and longer repayment terms than those of Export-Import or private financing can be provided.

It is often difficult to discover an explicit link between a government-to-government or even a central bank-to-central bank financing package and a large machinery or plant order. Yet such connections are there. Though the Japanese feel that the French are the masters at this type of activity, they themselves have devised a number of inventive financing measures, helped by the strength of the yen and Japan's large dollar balances.

Financing of whole plant sales has received special attention recently. Financing is crucial to the purchase of large plants, particularly in developing countries, which now account for about half of the market for machinery. Many of Japan's institutions work effectively together to promote whole plant sales.[8]

Fully 60 percent of Export-Import Bank loans are now directed to plant export. These loans are often supplemented by financing that is arranged through large banks to which the government has close ties. The most significant form of financing assistance, however, is government-to-government credit in yen, often tied directly to machinery sales.

Apart from sales arranged between governments, the trading companies play the most significant role in arranging financing, making three-cornered deals, and putting together packages for a sale. The government may review prices or give guidance on the selection of a particular subcontractor, but most of the work is done by the manufacturers and trading companies involved.

Germany

Germany has also developed an elaborate system of incentives for overseas marketing, particularly for assisting private investments in developing countries. For example, information on investment opportunities and markets is collected by the German Foundation for Developing Countries and the Federal Agency for Foreign Trade.

In addition, the Marshall Plan fund provides loans at very low rates of interest for investments in developing countries made by small and medium-sized German businesses. Further, companies investing in a developing country can obtain a tax deferral equivalent to 40 to 100 percent of the investment cost.

The German Development Bank (DEG), created by the federal government in 1962, acts as a development bank for German businesses. It prospects investment opportunities, provides consulting services and investment data, brings partners together, and typically makes a limited equity investment to help the project to succeed. DEG is owned by the federal government, which has so far invested $350 million in equity. DEG has helped structure investments totaling $1.4 billion, mostly for medium-sized companies in mechanical engineering.

Between 1970 and 1977, these various government aid programs contributed 12 percent of German investment in developing countries.[9] Through a special company, Treuarbeit, the federal government also guarantees investments abroad against political risks.[10]

Export financing in Germany has traditionally been handled by the commercial banking system. Throughout the 1960s, the three major commercial banks (Deutschebank, Commerzbank, and Dresdner Bank) expanded the scope of their services to exporting companies and also extended their branch network world-wide. Starting in the mid-1960s, the smaller banks also became involved in export financing.[11] The very low interest rates prevailing in Germany make it unnecessary for the government central bank (Bundesbank) to refinance export credit at favorable interest rates. In fact, many private banks are able to offer 10-year loans at rates below those specified by the OECD "consensus agreement." Ausfuhr Kredit (AKA), a consortium of 52 German banks established in 1952, provides credit for capital goods exports and long-term agreements. In 1977, more than half of this credit was used to finance sales of whole plants, particularly power plants. The remainder was used for shipbuilding and machinery. Overall, AKA financed 10 percent of capital goods exports in 1977.

Complementing the commercial banking system, the Kredit-Anstalt für Wiederaufbau (KFW) provides special financing for exports of capital goods to developing countries. Financed by the federal government, the Marshall Plan Fund, and financial markets, KFW is a state-owned bank that extends long-term credit (from five to eight years) at fixed interest rates. KFW financing grew from 13 percent of capital goods exports to developing countries in 1973 to 29 percent in 1976.[12]

Over the past five years, the German government has also increased its credit guarantees to German exporters and their customers. These guarantees have grown from 5.2 percent of exports in 1973 to 12.3 percent in 1977. This growth comes mainly from large contracts, particularly whole plant sales, which represented 43.5 percent of all guarantees between 1975 and 1977.

Finally, the government provides insurance through a private company for political, credit, currency, and shipping losses. Since 1975, the *Lander* have also guaranteed export credits given to small and medium-sized companies. Between 1975 and 1978, these guarantees amounted to over $300 million.

Britain

The British government has also conducted an active program to promote exports. The U.K. provides more export insurance than any other country except Japan, and also insures a wider variety of risks, including inflation and performance bond insurance for major overseas projects.

Historically, the greatest proportion of government expenditures was allocated to the refinancing of fixed-rate export credits. Export customers were advanced credits by commercial banks, which then refinanced the loan through the Bank of England. After April 1, 1980, the government no longer refinanced new sterling fixed-rate export credits. A net repayment of refinance is expected in the next few years.

There has been a shift in emphasis to interest support programs and cost escalation schemes. Under the first programs, exporters are compensated by the government, which extends credit at fixed interest rates for "losses" due to changed external conditions. Under the second, exporters are given some protection against certain cost increases of competing export contracts for large capital goods. These programs are all administered by the Export Credit Guarantee Department. Established in 1954, this body has steadily grown in importance and now guarantees a significant proportion of British exports.

The other government body involved in export promotion is the British Overseas Trade Board, which sponsors trade fairs and provides technical information. Expenditures for these programs have been relatively small.

This summary of programs is illustrative of the efforts being consciously undertaken by America's major trading partners to assist industrial development in high-growth industries. These efforts to help companies with product and process development and overseas marketing play a significant role in assisting and accelerating higher-risk investments, particularly important in ensuring the long-term productive health of an economy.

FOOTNOTES

[1] There are three principal corporate tax incentives for technological development. One stipulates that 25 percent of any year-to-year increase in research and development expenditures over the previous year is a tax credit, up to a limit of 10 percent of total corporate tax. In 1978, manufacturing companies realized a benefit of about $10 million through this credit. The second tax incentive is accelerated depreciation on research and development facilities and hardware, which can mean as much as a 60-percent write-off of the original purchase price in the first year. The provisions try to conserve the cash flow of high-technology businesses. As the growth of an industry slows, these incentives become ineffective, and more cash flow is exposed to tax. The third tax incentive is a lower tax rate on income received from technology licenses overseas. In 1978, this tax rate was worth about $50 million dollars to the manufacturing sector.

[2] In cooperation with other institutions, the government also funds research and development directly, most commonly through matching grants. Ministries receive applications in designated research and development areas either from companies or from associations formed for that purpose. Many associations are groups of small companies that could not finance new technologies on their own. Often the technology issue is straightforward—developing a continuous textile operation to replace a vertically fragmented one, for example. For small business, MITI or the trade association sponsors these arrangements.

Motor car and boat racing tax proceeds also benefit research and development. MITI guides the direction of these funds to various industry associations, which then distribute the money to specific projects for rationalization, research, and export promotion. They are separate from the government's official budgets and help to finance sectors and products that are not household words in Japan.

[3] The Japan Development Bank makes loans under various program headings—commercialization of new technology, development of prototypes, and commercialization of new technology for small enterprise. These loans are project related and represent low-cost funds; hence, they are marginal incentives. Loans are provided primarily to manufacturers, and sometimes to users, of the qualifying machinery. These programs have grown throughout the 1970s; in 1976, the government lent a total of $100 million to all Japanese industry.

[4] Coface also administers special schemes to promote exports, including guarantees for amortization of marketing costs in new foreign markets, an exchange risk guarantee, and a guarantee for French investments abroad. There is also an "economic risk" guarantee that covers the difference between a normal rate of inflation (6.5 to 8 percent) and the actual cost inflation incurred on capital goods orders that require more than a year to deliver.

[5] Tax incentives played a very significant role in the 1960s but were less important in the 1970s. Of several measures still technically in effect, only the technology export income deduction is significant today.

[6] Export-related accelerated depreciation—worth $200 million to the manufacturing sector in 1970—was eliminated in 1972. The discount on export bills is now only a quarter of 1 percent off domestic bill rates. This subsidy works primarily to bolster Japan's declining exporters of such products as textiles, plywood, and flatware.

[7] In all of these loan programs, MITI has ultimate authority over individual companies. Any transaction by the Export-Import Bank that is not settled within six months must be submitted to MITI for approval. Similarly, reviews are made of the credit worthiness of all manufacturers and exporters. Thus, while MITI does not actively screen each transaction, it has a means of review whenever it is necessary. In Japan, the controls on foreign transactions have not been dismantled, just relaxed.

[8] MITI has published a 400-page book on whole plant selling and has informally assisted the formation of groups of companies to study particular market opportunities. The industry associations and trading companies also play an important role in coordination. The informal connections among MITI, the banks, the industry associations, and the companies allow a flexible mode of interaction that is very helpful in making the complex arrangements needed for whole plant sales.

[9] In addition, a large proportion of Germany's official capital aid to developing countries, although officially untied, in fact flows back to German companies.

[10] Between 1970 and 1976, these guarantees represented 6 percent of total investments made by German firms. Twenty-five percent of the guarantees were for investments in Brazil.

[11] The union-controlled Bank für Gemeinwirtschaft, for example, plays an important role in export financing to eastern European countries.

[12] In 1976, two nuclear power plants in Brazil were financed at a level of $1 billion.

24

Foreign Restructuring of Firms to Pursue Growth Opportunities

Perhaps the most controversial industrial activities of foreign governments have been the restructuring of industries to take better advantage of growth opportunities. The Japanese and French governments have often enacted such measures, as have the British and German governments on occasion.

JAPAN[1]

The Japanese government has sponsored successful programs that have brought about industry consolidation and greater international competitiveness in many fragmented industries such as automobile parts and sewing machines. In other cases, such as automobiles and computers, MITI's attempts at consolidation have been resisted by companies in the industry.

Perhaps the most significant aspect of Japanese industrial policy is the way in which MITI is able to find the right competitive levers to assist the development of specific industries at specific times and to vary these as the competitive economics of businesses evolve. This makes policy both efficient and effective. MITI's role in the industrial machinery industry illustrates this point well.

In the 1950s and 1960s, the machinery industry consisted of two basic types of businesses. The first involved the production of mechanical components such as gears, bearings, valves, heat exchangers, and springs. Competitive success in these businesses depends primarily on large-scale production and long runs of standard products, together with a sufficient volume of production to be able to dedicate production lines to special products. The second type of business was machine assembly: mechanical components, structural metals, and castings are assembled into paper machines, steel-rolling mills, or metal-working machine tools. Since the capabilities and efficiency of new machine designs have an enormous effect on sales, research and development is crucial in this type of business.

During the 1950s and early 1960s, Japan was far behind major European and U.S. companies in production scale and design capability, partly because of war damage. Between 1956 and 1960, the main goal of policy was to impose basic standards on an industry that was made up of thousands of small producers. The Japan Development Bank provided funds for modernization of equipment; MITI authorized rationalization cartels for purchasing parts and importing materials; specifications were set for the industry; and guidelines were established for production technology improvement. During this period, the government provided almost 400 loans, totaling about $30 million.

Between 1960 and 1965, there was a twofold policy approach. Mergers were encouraged in such areas as car parts and bearings, areas in which large-scale production and long runs are essential to achieve low cost. In other areas—such as the making of special springs, gears, or castings—scale of production is less important; therefore modernization was encouraged within the small companies. Industry associations were formed to facilitate the flow of information, rationalization cartels were authorized, and there was an emphasis on financing through the Small Business Finance Corporation to modernize equipment.

By the mid-1960s, these measures had succeeded in rationalizing the machine industry, and emphasis shifted to making companies internationally competitive. The size, capacity, and level of technology of major overseas enterprises were carefully examined. In order to improve the structure of the Japanese industry, a cartel was formed to allocate product categories among companies or to group enterprises, and to establish joint ventures. In some businesses, such as chemical machinery, individual producers were encouraged to cooperate in the development of new products; in other businesses, such as machine tools, some enterprises were encouraged to drop certain products. In cases such as printing machinery, joint ventures and mergers were sponsored.

Throughout the 1950s and early 1960s, only machinery that could not be made in Japan was allowed to be imported. This restriction guaranteed a market for Japanese producers and encouraged foreign producers to license their technology or to form joint ventures in Japan, since outright exports to Japan were impossible.

In addition, a series of loan programs helped domestic machinery suppliers become more competitive in the home market. Special depreciation laws were enacted both to promote mechanization and to encourage the purchase of Japanese-made machinery.[2] Finally, the government set up two export insurance programs, one covering all industries and the other compensating for losses caused by inadequate consultation on overseas machinery projects.

By 1970, the process of industry rationalization had essentially been completed. The Japanese industry was fully competitive in its home market and had made inroads into world markets for some products, particularly simple machine tools and textile machinery.

Two broad industry trends had a significant impact on industrial machinery businesses in the 1970s. The first was the development of so-called "systems businesses," or the sale of whole plants. This means that various machines and construction materials are assembled into whole plants that are sold and installed as a package by one producer (though parts of the package may be subcontracted). The development of whole plant sale businesses has increased the significance of applications engineering in the overall cost structure of the industry. Because purchases are bigger, the importance of long-term buyer financing and insurance of seller's risk has also increased.

The other major development in the machinery industry in the 1970s was the introduction of new technologies that were integrated into machinery design, particularly miniature electronics, lasers, and ultrasonics. Examples of these new technologies include intelligent control in machines, the use of laser cutting and printing, and ultrasonic testing. As a result, machinery makers have had to undertake massive research and development in unfamiliar fields in order to remain competitive in the industry.

Accordingly, in the early 1970s, government policy turned away from rationalization, home market protection and stimulation, and export assistance measures. Instead, as we have showed in the previous chapters, it focused on research and development and assistance to companies for whole plant sales abroad. The goals are to move Japan into the forefront of machinery technology, to build world market share by attacking the new growth markets in developing countries, and to build upon strong Japanese process industries to emphasize whole plant sales.

These efforts to guide industry development have achieved considerable success. Compared to Germany and the U.S., Japan has only a small export share in ordinary machine tools, but a higher share in more sophisticated numerically controlled machine tools. Its market share is growing rapidly in both product areas.

FRANCE

Japan's success in industrial restructuring stands in marked contrast to several efforts of the French government in the 1960s and early 1970s to build competitive industries. Major projects in aircraft (Concorde) and computers (Plan Calcul) were undertaken, with dubious results. Some of the reasons for these failures can be seen from a closer look at the Plan Calcul.

Government studies of the French computer industry began in 1963-64. A major impetus to action was the U.S. refusal in 1963 to sell France a large computer needed to develop its nuclear capability. As a result, then-President Charles DeGaulle saw the need for an independent French industry in large main-frame computers. The second spur to action was the financial difficulties of the French computer company, Machine Bull, the number-two company in Europe after IBM. In 1964, the government allowed Bull to come under the control of General Electric.

Despite early studies, it was not until 1966 that the first computer plan actually went into effect with the formation of Compagnie Internationale pour l'Informatique (CII). This company was formed by merging a number of small companies that had little export experience and incompatible product lines. Bull, with 25 percent of the French market, 45 percent of its production exported, and an excellent technical staff, was left out of the merger because of its American parent relationship.

The French electronics companies, CGE and Thomson, were enlisted as private shareholders in CII. It was hoped that they would provide both investment capital and management expertise; in fact, the government's hopes were never realized. Either because of a lack of enthusiasm or a lack of resources, CII's private shareholders contributed little capital. Between 1966 and 1976, CGE and Thomson invested $30 million in large computers; the government put up $1 billion. In any case, CGE and Thomson were rivals in the electronics and electrical industry and were not inclined to cooperate with each other.

The Délégation à l'Informatique, a government agency originally intended to coordinate government aid and purchasing with CII, was forced to fill the gap left by the private shareholders.

The companies that formed CII were expected to develop a new product line to compete with IBM's 360-40 and 360-50 models. However, CII had only a fraction of the $5 billion that IBM had spent to develop and market the 360 series. Although CII's IRIS computer was a technological success and competitive with the 360-40 in terms of hardware, it was not introduced until 1971. By then, IBM's series had been available for six years and customers had already made the investment in IBM software.

CII and Honeywell-Bull merged in December 1975. The new company, CII-Honeywell-Bull, is 53 percent French owned, 47 percent Honeywell owned. The government owns 17 percent of the French shares. Although the government no longer has the direct control over decisionmaking that it had over CII, government assistance to computers has increased dramatically. Nevertheless, the competitive situation of France's computer industry has actually declined. IBM-France remains the largest employer in the French computer industry, as well as the largest contributor to a positive trade balance. CII-Honeywell-Bull, the remaining French-controlled company in large-size computers, has a smaller share of the European marker than the top three French companies did in 1966. Moreover, the computer industry continues to need government assistance to compete.

French industrial policymakers have learned from this and other past mistakes. French industrial policy has become more focused, trying through various mechanisms to assist companies in attaining competitive advantage. Policy has moved away from orchestrating large complicated projects, and toward assisting public and private firms through a series of discrete measures, including conditionally reimbursable loans, financing of purchasers of prototype products, and various tax incentives and capital grants. A series of planning agreements have been negotiated with individual companies to target government aid where it can be best used (Exhibit 84).

A number of more recent efforts to promote growing industries have yielded some success. For example, French Dassault Mirage jet fighters, Aerospatiale civilian and military helicopters, SNECMA aircraft engines, and the airbus have all enjoyed competitive successes in the world marketplace. The French offshore oil equipment industry is now second only to the U.S. industry, having grown tenfold in the last decade with active government support. By 1985, the French nuclear industry will supply 55 percent of all France's energy needs. The industry already employs as many people as the whole French steel industry. Both Renault and Peugeot are thus far holding their own in the world automobile consolidation, thanks in part to government assistance.

Even in the data-processing field, French efforts have become more sophisticated. Following the reversal of French policy in large computers, the government embarked on new ambitious goals in other areas of the data-processing and electronic industry. In May 1977, the government decided to spend $35 million dollars per year to develop a domestic integrated circuits capability.[3] As a result of its various initiatives, it is expected that French integrated circuit production will reach a level equal to domestic demand in 1982. In terminals and peripherals, a "growth planning agreement" has been undertaken with Benson to help the French graphic terminal producer acquire an international position. In software services, French industry already has reached a number-two position behind the U.S.

BRITAIN

British attempts at industrial restructuring to promote growth have, on the whole, been less extensive and less successful than either the Japanese or French ventures.

The Industrial Expansion Act of 1967 created the Industrial Reorganization Corporation (IRC) with an annual budget of 150 million pounds. The IRC has a board of business, government, and union representatives. Its mission was to promote advanced technology in-

EXHIBIT 84
French Planning Agreements for Promotion of
Growing Sectors

Industry	Government Funds In Millions of Francs	Companies
Electronic Components	120 5-Year Period	Thomson Radiotechnique CEA
Peripheral Equipment	110 4-Year Period	Logabax Sintra Pyral G35 Intertechnique
Machine Tools	120 3-Year Period	CIT-Alcatel Ernault-Somua plus two others
Medical Instruments	na	CGR Instruments S.A.
Minicomputers	1,210 3-Year Period	Thomson
Food Processing	250 3-Year Period	29 companies or cooperatives
Office Automation*	na	CIT-Alcatel
Consumer Electronics*	na	Videocolor
Industrial Robots*	na	Peugeot
Biochemical Industry*	na	na
Offshore Oil Industry*	na	na
Energy-Saving Equipment*	na	Jeager
Strategic Innovations in Textile & Clothing *	na	na

*future agreements

Sources: CODIS (Orientation Committee for the Development of Strategic Industries), 1980.

dustries. The IRC played a role in a wide variety of industries, from nuclear plants to fisheries. The basic goal of promoting advanced technology was reflected in efforts to rationalize the electric and electronic equipment industry and to create a strong national computer industry.

The authority given to the IRC was considerable; it could make grants and loans, purchase equity, and effect or prevent mergers. Some of its actions—particularly its interventions within specific firms during merger negotiations—were perceived as arbitrary, involving excessive use of government power. Although relatively uncommon, such cases were widely publicized and led to the disbandment of the IRC in 1970.

In 1975, a new agency for industrial development was formed, the National Enterprise Board (NEB). Its purpose was to promote changes in the management and organization of individual companies, as well as to secure the desired restructuring of a sector for long-term viability and to provide financing for companies in key sectors. The Board's main concern was to help develop growth sectors—that is, advanced technology industries—but it was also empowered to assist troubled industries or specific firms if such assistance were necessary to prevent high unemployment. Candidates for this sort of rescue support were to be designated by the Secretary of State for Industry.

The NEB was originally intended to have considerable freedom in choosing particular industries and firms for promotion. In practice, the main resources of the NEB have been absorbed by helping major companies in trouble—British Leyland, Rolls-Royce, Alfred Herbert, and, for a time, Ferranti (Exhibit 85). The NEB is more associated with troubled parts of industry than with the promotion of growth sectors.

Moreover, the notion that the NEB could be a major instrument of industrial reorganization changed in 1979 with the new conservative government. Substantial shareholdings of the NEB have been disposed of. Responsibility for Rolls-Royce and the NEB shareholding has been transferred to the Department of Industry. The government has continued to support the NEB's role as an investor in high-risk, high-technology initiatives. It has interests in underwater engineering, electronics, and computers. A particularly important investment ($115 million committed) has been in INMOS, a greenfield venture to create a new integrated semiconductor development and manufacturing activity. In addition, the NEB is investing in office electronics and software systems companies. Recently, however, the NEB and the NEDC have been merged and the NEB's role in these new ventures may be further constrained.

The British government also provides substantial direct subsidies

EXHIBIT 85
NEB Investments by Sector, 1979

	Millions of Pounds	Percent of Total
British Leyland	1,004.9	69%
Rolls-Royce[1]	296.0	20%
Alfred Herbert (machine tools)	33.4	2%
INMOS (Semiconductors)	8.6[2]	1%
Software and Office Equipment Companies[3]	35.2	2%
Offshore[4]	5.5	1%
Engineering & Instruments	48.9	3%
All Other	17.8	1%

Source: Annual report (National Enterprise Board).

for investments in selected industries, such as electronics and machine tools. Capital grants averaging 131 percent of fixed investments are given to new projects, whether initiated by British or overseas companies. Administered on a case-by-case basis, these grants amounted to over $500 million in 1979.

An example of these programs is the Microelectronics Industry Support Scheme (MISS), which was initiated in 1978 to provide selective support to the U.K. electronic components industry. By the end of 1980, 27 projects had received over $100 million for integrated circuit development and for the creation of businesses serving the microelectronics industry. Under the microprocessor applications project, over $120 million has been spent since 1980 to encourage U.K. British firms to adopt microprocessors in their production processes or products.

Schemes also exist for encouraging product and process development in general access industries and for the specific development of instruments, software, computer, robotics, machine tool, and automated process industries. Grants provided are given on a selective basis to projects that are considered to be in the national interest.

---

[1]Shareholding transferred to Department of Industry.
[2]Investment to date: £50 million planned.
[3]13 companies.
[4]2 companies.

GERMANY

The German government has played a less direct role than other governments in industrial structure. A notable exception is in energy, in which the government has formed public and publicly directed companies. The German government has not generally forced mergers or created new companies to pursue new businesses, though the Ministry of Technology (BMFT) has played a role in fostering industrial cooperation. However, two aspects of Germany's general industrial and financial organization have ensured that questions of industry structure are discussed at centralized levels.

First, the German banking system has played a central role in allocating resources throughout the postwar period. The rate of internal financing in industrial companies (between 30 and 35 percent) is low in comparison to that in other developed countries. The role of both commerical and investment banks in business investment decisions contributes strongly to a coherent allocation of resources. In 1960, the three major banks had 119 chairmanships and 96 deputy chairmanships in German corporations; they also had 45 percent of the voting power in the 500 largest companies.

Second, German industry has agreed to share control with unions in some areas of policy. As a result, cooperation between workers and management is greater than in many European countries. Since most unions are highly centralized, informal industrial policy discussions often occur at a national level among industry, union, banking, and government officials.

FOOTNOTES

[1] A more thorough discussion of the Japanese government's industrial restructuring efforts can be found in Magaziner, I.C. and Hout, T., *Japanese Industrial Policy*, PSI, London, 1980.

[2] A recent survey by the Japanese taxation agency reports that the government forfeited over $5.2 billion of tax revenue to these special depreciation programs between 1963 and 1976.

[3] To this end, it created the Telecommunications Research Center (CNET), an integrated circuit corporation, in 1979. In 1977, Thomson-Brandt and CEA started a Very Large Scale Integrated Circuit (VLSI) program. In

addition, the CEA and the CNRS (a fundamental research group) have created a special research group for ICs. Finally, the government has supported five new joint ventures with international firms—Thomson and Thomson-CEA, (each with Motorola); RTC (with Philips); Saint Gobain (with National); and MATRA (with Harris).

25

Organization of Industrial Policy Abroad

Foreign industrial policies, both for structurally depressed industries and for industries with growth potential, are more consciously applied and, in many cases, more extensive and sophisticated than policies in the U.S. The organizations that formulate and implement these policies vary significantly among countries. The most successful organizations are relatively small, have clear lines of authority, maintain significant links with both business management and unions, and are relatively free from the effects of political changes in government.

JAPAN

Perhaps the most efficient structure for forming and implementing industrial policy can be found in Japan. MITI, the Ministry of International Trade and Industry, is the most important institution in Japan's industrial policymaking process.[1]

MITI has responsibility for business development as well as for regulating business excesses. Difficult trade-offs are made and various policies are integrated informally within one ministry culture. Thus, MITI considers the whole range of potential government measures—tax, antitrust, special lending, price and capacity controls, export and import measures, environmental regulations, raw materials price setting and procurement, technology subsidy, dislocation subsidy, regional policy—that influence a business's performance and its effect on other businesses.[2]

MITI does not employ all these tools in every industry, nor does it act independently of other agencies. In fact, the treatment of various businesses differs enormously. Many businesses experience little or no special policy intervention for long periods of time, while a few, such as petroleum refining and computers, are highly coordinated or subsidized. Moreover, MITI is neither autonomous in determining policy nor can it directly finance its own programs. The Fair Trade Commission limits MITI's structural initiatives, the Diet and prime minister's office circumscribe it politically, and the Ministry of Finance passes judgment on its budget.[3]

The staff of MITI is remarkably small, with fewer than 2,500 professionals. The small ministry size and its broad range of responsibilities give its professionals great breadth of experience and close relations with one another. Thus, MITI officials can negotiate solutions to a problem intramurally, with give and take on both sides. An example is MITI's adjustment in the metal flatware business, hit hard by yen revaluation in the late 1970s. Steel is a major cost element to this business, but flatware is a small customer to steel producers. MITI was able to negotiate raw material price relief for the flatware business and make up the loss to the steel companies elsewhere.

MITI is the center of a web of organizations that influence industrial policy; many of these are not part of government but include large trade associations and large commercial banks.

Japan has four major business federations that lobby for business interests in general. In addition, there are industry associations that are concerned with policy toward individual sectors; they maintain a working relationship with MITI's industry bureaus and divisions. These organizations are far more than data-collecting and lobbying groups. They put forward proposals for MITI consideration and implement the policies that are adopted.[4] Japan's antimonopoly law, for instance, permits MITI to authorize and supervise cartels that operate through these associations. These cartels are limited in duration and must serve specific purposes.[5]

The large private banks also play a considerable role in industrial policy. The 13 large commercial banks extend one-quarter of all loans and discounts made by public and private financial institutions. Their principal borrowers are large corporations. The ministries and the banks discuss the issues together closely, often setting up *ad hoc* committees to examine specific problems.[6]

Thus, a number of common interests, as well as more direct financial or political ties, link these private and quasipublic institutions to the government policymaking bodies. Considerable tensions, of course, exist between the government agencies whose concern is Japan's overall international competitiveness and business associations organized to protect their own interests. But there is a process to resolve them.

In sectors of policy interest, MITI collects a good deal of market and competitive data, gives administrative guidance to firms, and issues reports in support of a policy. Communication between MITI and individual firms takes place frequently and at several levels. Some observers of this process have mistakenly concluded that MITI is dictating investment rates in the industry. This is not MITI's intention. Market prospects and not ministries stimulate investment in growth businesses and ultimately discourage investment in declining ones. MITI understands that it would be counterproductive to force wary producers to invest. Instead, MITI tries to develop a shared perception of a businesses's future and then designs incentives and subsidies to accelerate the desired course.

MITI does not normally have the power to dictate investment choices to businesses. Indeed, the autonomy of the individual firm sharply limits the government's ability to change industrial structure. For example, in the 1960s, Japan's motor car companies welcomed the government's import protection, low-cost lending, and tax deferrals, but rejected MITI's attempts to merge producers and keep minority foreign capital investment out of the industry. In the 1970s, the key mainframe computer producers—Hitachi, Fujitsu, and Nippon Electric—remained independent competitors despite MITI attempts to consolidate the industry. In electronic calculators, Sharp and others successfully deflected MITI's attempt to shut off U.S. integrated circuit imports, which threatened Japan's fledgling high-cost production. While serving MITI's longer-term structural aims, this import ban would have seriously damaged the calculator producer's cost position. More recently, aluminum producers have resisted MITI's allocation plan for permanent capacity retirement. The producers want short-term relief only in order to preserve long-term strategy flexibility.

The process of discussion and debate between MITI and the companies in response to developments in the marketplace creates a dynamic decisionmaking process. MITI aptly refers to Japan as a "plan-oriented market economy."

The actions of Japan's ministries are generally free from short-term political pressures. There is a strong tradition of skilled bureaucrats overseeing industrial affairs. The Diet's acts enunciate only essential policy and give broad charter to the ministries. The ministries are staffed by a competent core of career officials, many of whom enter politics when they retire from the ministry. The pattern has provided good working relations between the Diet and the ministries.

Diet members do have considerable influence, particularly in the appointment of staff to ministries and in tax and expenditure policies. To the ministries, however, belongs the responsibility for developing coherent programs, drafting legislation, and carrying it out with broad discretion. Changes in the Diet's composition and mood do not greatly move the boundaries of the ministries' authority and effectiveness in industrial policy matters.

FRANCE

As in Japan, government administration in France is centralized and extremely influencial in all areas of the economy. Responsibility for industrial policy, however, is fragmented among dozens of different agencies representing many different philosophies. A particular industrial problem may be handled by a number of these agencies before resolution is achieved.

In theory, the French Ministry of Industry has responsibility for formulating and implementing industrial policy. It is organized by industry and has direct relationships with the major French corporations.[7] In practice, however, the Ministry of Industry has to work within the constraints imposed by the Ministry of Economy and the other government departments that are responsible for key industries such as the Ministry of Transportation for shipbuilding, Post and Telephone for telecommunications, Defense for military production and the entire aircraft industry, and Agriculture for food industries.

In addition, government research policy is made by a number of different agencies. The Defense Department finances three-quarters of the R&D grants provided to companies. The remaining quarter is divided among the Ministry of Industry, Post and Telephone (for telecommunications), the Crédit National (a state-owned bank), and the Research Agency, a semiautonomous policy body currently reporting to a Secretary of State for Research.

Regional policies are shared between the Regional Development Agency (DATAR) and the Ministry of Economy, which supervises grants and tax agreements for major projects. Grants for investments of less than $2 million are authorized at the local level by the prefect, who reports to the Minister of the Interior.

Many of the most important policy decisions are still made by the Ministry of Economy and Finance, now divided into two separate agencies, Economy and Budget, that oversee the commercial banking system and the financial markets. The three major commercial banks are nationalized, and the medium- and long-term commercial banking function is carried out almost exclusively by state-owned institutions. In addition, the central bank (Banque de France) can direct commercial credit selectively by credit rationing or can refinance certain loans at favored discount rates, through export credit, for example.

The Direction du Trésor, a subdivision of the Ministry of Economy, determines the timing of every important public issue, bond or equity. It coordinates the Fund for Economic and Social Development, which makes loans to industry totaling about $400 million a year. This gives it virtual control over a number of investment decisions.

The Ministry of the Budget prepares the budget, controls the use of funds, and has responsibility for the tax administration. It also controls export aids and decides on such measures as interest subsidies and tax credits.

Since 1975, the government has created three new funds to respond to increasing structural problems in industry: These include CIASI (1975), to rescue small and medium-sized companies that can be made viable; CIDISE (1978), to help growing businesses with special "subordinated" loans; and FSAI (1978), whose temporary mission is to restructure northern and eastern French industry away from steel and coal.

In 1979, on the recommendation of the Minister of Industry, the prime minister created a mechanism for coordinating industrial policy. This group, CODIS, comprises the Ministers of Economy, Industry, Budget, and Foreign Trade under the overall authority of the prime minister, but the day-to-day work is done by a task force headed by the Director of Industry and involving all the agencies concerned with industrial policy.

This fragmentation in organization often hinders the flexibility and efficiency of French policymaking. Decisions can be slow to emerge on key issues. The reason for this slowness is often political in-fighting among agencies rather than a careful consensus-forming process. As a result, policies are often altered and inconsistently implemented.

The new and powerful CODIS group is designed to overcome this fragmentation and bring together at a high level the policymaking functions of all key departments. While it is a positive step in theory, in fact, its implementation is not viewed as particularly successful.

GERMANY

Germany's industrial policy structure, in existence for only a decade, is less comprehensive than those in France and Japan. Since 1972, responsibility for industrial policy has been divided between the Ministry of Economics and the Ministry for Technology. The task of managing the transition away from sectors in structural decline, such as coal mines, steel, shipbuilding, and textiles, falls to the Ministry of Economics. It is responsible for regional development policy, which is crucial to positive restructuring efforts.

Support for growing knowledge-intensive industries is the responsibility of the Ministry of Technology, whose efforts support new product and process development. In addition, the various export insurance and overseas investments are coordinated individually by separate financial institutions. Germany's extensive labor market policies are coordinated by the labor department.

Besides the programs run by the federal government, the individual provinces *(Lander)* run their own development projects, which can be quite extensive. These projects are not usually reflected in intercountry comparisons of aid levels. Exhibit 86 shows an enumeration of some of these policies. The exact amounts of these subsidies are hard to determine; however, in at least one *Land,* Lower Saxony, the funds selectively spent or guaranteed for industrial development are actually greater than those allocated to the region in the federal budget.

The key to the success of Germany's industrial policy is probably the widespread agreement among government, banks, management, and unions that the economy must be restructured away from sectors that cannot support Germany's high incomes. By its consistent em-

EXHIBIT 86
German Industrial Programs Run by the *Länder*, 1978.

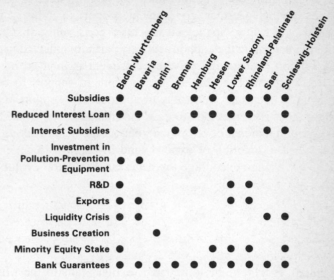

	Baden-Wurttemberg	Bavaria	Berlin¹	Bremen	Hamburg	Hessen	Lower Saxony	Rhineland-Palatinate	Saar	Schleswig-Holstein
Subsidies	●				●	●	●	●	●	●
Reduced Interest Loan	●	●			●	●	●		●	
Interest Subsidies					●	●	●		●	●
Investment in Pollution-Prevention Equipment	●	●								
R&D	●						●	●		
Exports	●	●					●	●		
Liquidity Crisis	●	●							●	●
Business Creation				●						
Minority Equity Stake	●					●	●			●
Bank Guarantees	●	●	●	●	●	●	●	●	●	●

Source: Zeitschrift Für gesamte Kreditwesen, Sonderaufgabe, 1978.

phasis on improving the competitiveness of German industry, yet minimizing human disruptions, the government has played an important role in developing this consensus.

The revaluation of the Deutschemark has forced the banks to review their loan and equity investment decisions in view of the apparently inevitable restructuring. Aided by codetermination, the unions have increasingly focused their efforts on recovering employment that is defensible in the long term. Government selective aids have gone primarily to growing industries.

Good communication among the different interest groups helps ensure that resources are allocated appropriately. Business investment plans are made in the light of government policy. The dialogue among the banks, government, labor, and businesses promotes rationalization. To be sure, disagreements on specific issues often arise; it is common to hear business leaders complain about BMFT "meddling" or for trade

---

¹ Does not include specific federal programs for Berlin.

unions to contend that business leaders are not aggressive enough in their investments. Nevertheless, these frequent disagreements are usually part of a healthy dialogue that does not inhibit effective action.

In sum, although German government support to industry is not coordinated by a central agency, it reflects a consistent policy. Government involvement in the economy is only partially reflected in direct financial support. Substantial private investment is induced by a selective R&D policy. The absence of government support to certain areas is equally important. A variety of approaches—support of high-technology industries, methods to ease the transition out of declining industries, aid in regional development, encouragement of active labor market policies, promotion of exports, and investment in developing countries—are used to encourage the necessary structural evolution of the economy.

GREAT BRITAIN

British industrial policy undergoes major upheavals every few years as successive governments change both the policies and the institutions designed to formulate and implement the policies.

In the early 1960s, when Great Britain's relatively poor industrial performance began to arouse concern, the Conservative government then in power created the National Economic Development Council (NEDC) and 21 Economic Development Councils for specific industries. Made up of representatives from management, labor, and government, the Councils were to offer industry information and advisory services on a wide variety of subjects, such as supply and demand forecasts, export performance, manpower trends, and R&D. The NEDC and the specific councils have survived many institutional changes and still exist today (albeit with changes in their functions) as an important forum for discussion.

The Labor administration, which came to power in 1964, had greater ambitions for industrial policy. A National Plan was developed to increase the underlying growth rate of the economy. The Department of Trade and Industry coordinated the activities of other agencies involved in industrial policy; great emphasis was given to promoting high-technology sectors, such as aircraft, electronics, and nuclear plants. The Industrial Re-organization Corporation (IRC) was created as a government holding company with discretionary investment and intervention powers.

In the early 1970s, when the Conservatives returned to power, the IRC was disbanded in favor of regional and sectional grants administered by the Department of Trade and Industry.

During the mid-1970s, with the return of the Labor government to power, an attempt was initiated to formulate a more integrated industrial strategy. First, it was recognized that the economic rewards from high-prestige R&D projects such as Concorde were limited; expenditures of this sort were substantially reduced as the last of these projects were phased out. Second, the 1975 Industry Act established a framework for new sectoral assistance programs and created the National Enterprise Board (NEB), a more focused successor to the IRC. Third, the government tried to promote planning agreements in each industry sector. The intention was for representatives of business, unions, and government to jointly develop sectoral strategies, and for major companies to sign planning agreements based on these discussions. These agreements have never really been implemented.

While these industrial policy plans were being debated and attempted, an implicit policy was being conducted by the Department of Industry (now separated from the Department of Trade) in the form of a long string of company bail-outs—nationalizations and subsequent subsidizing of losses, and straight grant, loan, guarantee, or tax subsidies.

In 1979 and 1980, with the change back to a Conservative administration, the emphasis in industrial policy switched to a "hands-off" approach by government. Economic and industrial policies have focused on three aims: (1) to concentrate on creating a favorable macroeconomic environment for business expansion and investment, abandoning selective interventions and sectoral planning; (2) to reduce support to companies in trouble; and (3) to reduce government ownership of industry by sale or return of government holdings to private ownership.

In practice, many of the instruments and agencies of previous governments have remained intact, but their use has been greatly curtailed and given a very different emphasis. An exception to the general curb on selective policies has been in the electronics sector, but even there activity has been reduced from the levels previously envisaged. The government has allowed the steel and auto industries to contract with significant plant closures but has still committed substantial funds. The government has taken action toward the privatization of the public sector and the breaking up of public monopolies, such as the sale of some of the government holdings in British Petroleum, the sale of the NEB's holdings in the British computer company (ICL) and Ferranti, and the Transport Act of 1980, which allows private competition in national coach and rail services. This privatization has not, however, proceeded at the pace and scale originally intended. For instance, denationalization of the shipbuilding industry and of British Airways has been delayed.

Amidst these major policy shifts over the past 15 to 20 years, the fundamental problems of industrial development in the U.K. remain unchanged and largely unaddressed. There is little consensus on the aims or practices of industrial policy; there is no agreement about the causes of or remedies for industrial decline; and there is persistent mistrust and misunderstanding among the different groups involved in policy-making. The continuing changes of policy direction as each new administration has taken office have effectively undermined the formulation of coherent policy.

FOOTNOTES

[1] MITI has been assigned responsibility for shaping the structure of industry and adjusting dislocations that arise in transition; guiding the healthy development of industries, especially their production and distribution activities; and managing Japan's foreign trade and its commercial relations. MITI is also responsible for ensuring adequate raw materials and energy flows to industry and for managing particular areas, such as small business, patents, and industrial technology. The breadth of its charter, in both function and spirit, gives MITI a comprehensive panorama of industries and policy areas.

[2] MITI's structure is well suited to its broad policy role. The Minister's Secretariat and four bureaus—Industrial Policy, International Trade Policy, International Trade Administration, and Industrial Location and Environmental Protection—develop and coordinate policy across industries. The three bureaus of Basic Industries (steel, chemicals, fertilizer, etc.), Ma-

chinery and Information Industries, and Consumer Products Industries develop programs, implement general policy, and solve problems at the individual industry level. Finally, there are nine regional bureaus that reconcile policy to local issues and develop MITI's extraordinary data base on industries. The acuteness and soundness of MITI policy are attributable to the interplay between these horizontal policy bureaus and the vertical industry bureaus with their broad powers, comprehensive data base, and first-rate career staff. Japan has thus far avoided the proliferation of layered agencies that single-issue politics has brought to America's industrial policy.

The Industrial Policy Bureau has played the major role in guiding overall industrial development. Within the Bureau, general divisions work out actual policy details: the Industrial Structure Division projects the desired future structure of industrial output and designs broad measures toward achieving it; the Business Behaviour Division studies tax measures and labor issues; the Price Policy Division is responsible for seeing that appropriate industries are adequately financed. This last division recommends which businesses and projects should gain access to low-interest funds through the Ministry of Finance's Fiscal Investment and Loan Plan.

³ Other ministries play roles similar to MITI's in some major industries. Telecommunications producers and Nippon Telephone and Telegraph Corporation are supervised by the Ministry of Posts and Telecommunications. The Ministry of Transport oversees railway equipment producers and operting companies. The pharmaceuticals industry responds to the Ministry of Health and Welfare.

The Ministry of Finance (MOF) plays a key role in concert with MITI by using its control of the Bank of Japan and the commercial banking system. The MOF manages the Fiscal Investment and Local Plan (FILP), which channels government trust funds into industrial sectors via public corporations that offer loans and grants. These public corporations include the Japan Development Bank, Japan Highway Corporation, and the Export-Import Bank; together they equal one-half the government's general account budget. The FILP is a major government lever on cash flow in the economy. Nevertheless, MITI remains the focal point of industrial policy in Japan.

⁴ The tradition of strong trade associations dates from the prewar period, when government ran industry through this mechanism. The structure remains much the same today, but the functioning is less one-sided. Officers of the associations sit on formal MITI advisory councils attached to the industry bureaus. Considerable data are passed to MITI through informal contact in Tokyo and in regional offices. It is because MITI is exceptionally well informed at the working level that the government-business communication works so well. The government prefers to deal with organizations that can focus constituents' interests, speak conclusively for them, and implement

policy once it is reached. Splinter interest groups fighting for support through the media are anathema to MITI.

[5] Specific purposes for cartels include long-term rationalization of production (used effectively in bearings and car parts industries); orderly reduction of excess capacity (currently being tried in some heavy process industries such as aluminum); and promotion of vertical integration (currently being tried in small downstream textile companies). The requirements of the cartels include short-term production allocation (used frequently during recessions in the heavy process sector such as chemicals and steel) and setting export price floors during trade crises.

[6] These large banks are also linked to the government through the Bank of Japan. Supervised by MOF, the Bank lends money to the 13 city banks that in turn lend to major Japanese industries. MOF can exert considerable leverage over the banks; on occasion, it will suggest which projects to support. Although privately owned, the banks rarely resist. Such a relationship helps both parties: The ministries occasionally need the assurance of funds for their client industries, and the Bank's portfolio sometimes needs government assistance to remain sound.

[7] The Ministry supervises the activities of the Nuclear Energy Agency (CEA), the Space Agency (CNES), most of the nationalized companies in the manufacturing sector (including Renault, two chemical companies, the tobacco monopoly, and the computer company) and those in the energy field (petroleum, coal mines, Électricité de France, and Gaz de France).

26

Summary: Lessons from Abroad

Notwithstanding important differences among major foreign countries and the sharp differences that separate them from the United States, their experiences with industrial policy suggest some useful lessons for managing industrial decline, promoting growth, and organizing economic development.

MANAGING INDUSTRIAL DECLINE

Societies vary significantly in their ability to address problems of "crisis industries." Great Britain, for example, has spent billions to keep bankrupt companies above water, deluding itself for years about the possibilities of revival. Other countries, such as Germany and Japan, have been more successful in holding down the absolute level of expenditures and in gaining better results from funds utilized. A number of principles can be distilled from these examples.

Mechanisms to Anticipate Problem Areas

First, whenever possible, it is crucial to act in anticipation of events. Structural declines of industries can often be seen a number of years in advance, at least before serious bankruptcies develop. Thus, when the need to rationalize the German steel and coal industries was seen in the late 1960s, the government began a major program for industrial reconversion in the Ruhr area of North Rhine-Westphalia. Over $1 billion was spent between 1969 and 1976 to build new industry in the area and to rationalize existing coal and steel operations.

Similarly, in 1975, MITI began urging limitations on Japanese investments, in steel and shipbuilding, despite the fact that these industries were then world leaders and still in expansion phases. Many companies did not share MITI's view and had optimistically planned for the future. Nevertheless, a dialogue began then that assisted reconversion developments in the late 1970s. When the steel crisis came in the late 1970s, the dislocations were far less severe in Germany and Japan than they were in France and Great Britain. France had been adding steel capacity at Fos and Dunkirk and not retiring old mills in Lorraine; Great Britain had embarked on a major expansion program in 1973 with no plant retirements.

Realistic Rationalization Plans

A corollary to this principle of anticipation is that governments must be capable of distinguishing between major structural declines and temporary problems that can be overcome with adequate funding. The tragedy of much government intervention—particularly in steel, shipbuilding, coal, and iron ore in Europe—is that the government often provides huge subsidies from the public treasury, after which more funds are added, and still more a few years after that. Meanwhile, workers are still laid off, and communities and regions suffer the consequences of gradual economic decline. By contrast, in successful cases, the government helps industry to devise a rationalization plan. This is accompanied by labor market and regional policies designed to ease the adjustment. These policies ensure that government funds will be spent in a way that salvages potentially competitive parts of the industry and minimizes hardships to workers and communities.

Consultative Mechanisms

A third lesson involves decisionmaking mechanisms for industrial policy. A number of countries have established various forms of tripartite bodies representing management, labor, and the public for the purpose of considering the problems involved in an industry. When these bodies have been formed after an industry is already experiencing competitive problems and when they exist primarily at a centralized level, they have generally been unsuccessful. As is the case in France or Britain, they often become mechanisms by which government and management try to convince unions to accept lay-offs and wage declines, or by which management and unions try to receive more government assistance. Tripartite consultation is most successful when it is part of an ongoing process within subsections of industry and when it is open to participation by broad cross sections of affected communities. Under these circumstances, such bodies can be forums in which rationalization plans are created.

Creation of New Businesses

A final lesson, which Japanese and German policymakers have long understood and which the French have embraced more recently, is that the only long-term solution to competitively declining businesses is the creation of new businesses to replace them. In Japan, the primary responsibility for identifying new competitive opportunities rests with the companies themselves. The companies often comprise a mix of businesses, some of which are growing, while others are declining. When whole companies fail, other companies in the region often provide assistance. The Japanese government provides funds to assist these new growth opportunities. The German government likewise provides incentives to expanding firms for new plants in regions where declines in traditional industry are anticipated. In both cases, funds are distributed to growing companies and businesses, rather than to declining companies and businesses.

The worst policy allows companies to fail, but does not encourage companies with growth opportunities to fill the gap. Jobs are lost but no attempts are made to create new ones. This has been the British policy for the last two years, and thus far it has had dire consequences. As a political reaction against seemingly limitless subsidies of uncompetitive companies, this policy initially gained short-term popularity. In the long run, however, it is proving to be painfully unproductive.

Industrial decline is necessary and inevitable in a vital economy. Successful industrial policies minimize the hardships associated with decline by accelerating the generation of new businesses to replace the old. In this way, they promote market changes rather than resist them.

PROMOTING GROWTH

Programs designed to simulate industrial research and development have existed since the early 1950s. In the early years, they focused on universities and research institutes that were undertaking basic research. Since 1970, both the level and mode of operation of many of these programs have changed. Governments have significantly increased their R&D funding, and more funds have been directly allocated to industry for applied research. This change derives from the realization that development and commercialization of new technology is often more expensive and risky than basic research, and that better coordination between industry and universities provides a quicker diffusion of innovations.

Increasingly, in Germany, Japan, and France, projects are funded at the initiation of companies that put up a share of the total budget. Consideration is given to the international competitive environment for the products that might be generated from research efforts. Funds are often divided among companies so that each can pursue a different technological solution to a common problem and then share the information with the others. Commercialization of the innovation, however, is competitive.

In addition to R&D funding for industry, foreign governments have supported industrywide programs designed expressly to overcome specific technological gaps with the U.S. Some of these programs—British and French Concorde and French and German computers—have been failures. On the other hand, programs involving French offshore industries, the German-French airbus, the German, French, and Swedish power generation programs, and French helicopters have helped develop competitive industries. Even in cases where commercial success has been achieved, however, the efficiency of such programs is the subject of much debate. Supporters of these programs claim that some failures will inevitably occur; failures also occur in totally private ventures, and these programs are even riskier than normal private-sector investments. Detractors claim that even the successes are too costly.

Increasingly, it is recognized that such industrywide programs are too broad, and that the key to success lies in specialization and dominance of specific businesses. In most countries, industrywide programs are giving way to more specific business-based projects, in which governments provide targeted assistance for marketing, foreign investment, or consumer financing. Mechanisms for promoting new industry in Germany and France are coming to resemble those that have been used in Japan, that is, a combination of incentives administered according to the competitive economics of particular businesses.

There is a corresponding trend toward projects that are initiated by business rather than by government. Government agencies selectively respond to the requests of companies rather than dictate proposed new areas of investment.

There is also a trend toward greater encouragement of marketing investment in foreign countries, particularly in developing countries. Governments are providing the type of financing and investment that reduces risks associated with these programs. These initiatives are helping these countries overcome trade imbalances caused by the rise in oil prices.

Finally, Germany, France, and Japan are placing greater emphasis on measures to assist the growth of competitive productivity, rather than merely to subsidize production or export. Rather than subsidizing existing export sales or products, they are focusing their expenditures on research and development for specific company projects, risky investments in new product areas, and the penetration of new markets. All these measures improve long term competitive position.

ORGANIZING ECONOMIC DEVELOPMENT

The most effective organizations for industrial policy appear to be those in which policy explicitly emanates from only one or two places in the government and in which jurisdictions are clearly defined. In Japan, MITI has clear authority over industrial affairs. Although its budget must be approved by the Ministry of Finance and it must work through certain other institutions to implement policy, it is clearly in charge. In Germany, the Ministries of Economy and Technology have clearly defined spheres of responsibility, as do the agencies responsible for export and overseas investment assistance. On the other hand, the

French structure is a virtual alphabet soup of agencies, ministries, boards, and *ad hoc* groups. As a result, policymaking is often diffused among groups and is subject to political infighting. This has been a source of weakness for French industrial policy.

A second principle for effective organization of industrial policy is that a competent group of civil servants must be responsible for designing and implementing it. Business leaders in all countries are naturally wary of government intervention. Nevertheless, this resistance has been overcome in Japan, Germany and France, where the caliber of government officials responsible for industrial policy is extremely high.

A third principle is that policymaking must be transparent. Public knowledge of government programs helps ensure public confidence in industrial policy. In Germany, for example, the amount, type, and destination of government aid to companies is made public. In Japan, such information is also available to the public, although great persistence is required to uncover details.

A fourth principle, related to transparency, is that the public must support the broad goals of industrial policy. At its most basic level, effective industrial policy rests on social consensus, a collective commitment to productivity on the part of the public-at-large. In Great Britain, for example, industrial policy falls prey to divisiveness because different groups fundamentally disagree about how the economy should be organized and how the fruits of new productivity should be distributed. Social consensus can be facilitated through decisionmaking processes in which many segments of the public are consulted and informed.

Finally, industrial policy should not depend on a large bureaucracy, which only complicates effective administration. It renders internal transactions less efficient and confronts business leaders with bewildering red tape. MITI has only 2,500 officials in its Tokyo office; the relevant German ministries are also relatively small.

GENERAL PRINCIPLES OF INDUSTRIAL POLICY

The lessons in industrial policy that the U.S. can learn from the experience of its trading partners relate more to the discipline and conduct of analysis and to the process by which industrial policy is undertaken than to the content of specific programs. Below are some general principles that are emerging in France, Germany, Japan, and Great Britain.

● The key goals of industrial policy are economic restructuring and improvement of competitive productivity.

● Success in many projects results from having well-established labor market and regional policies that are administered with long-standing and well-defined participation from management, labor, financial institutions, and government.

● To ensure success and cost efficiency, industrial policy instruments must be matched to the needs of a given competitive situation. No general policy can succeed in all competitive situations. Mechanisms such as across-the-board export subsidies or employment subsidies that do not foster industrial restructuring are being discouraged. Particularly in France and the U.K., such policies have generally been unsuccessful and wasteful of national resources. In Japan, matching specific actions to the key competitive levers in a business has been a major factor in the success of the industrial policy. European governments also are becoming increasingly sophisticated in their use of policy tools.

● Investment decisions should not be dictated by government but should be initiated by businesses that are close to the marketplace. The role of government has been most effective when it has involved intelligent response and dialogue with businesses rather than heavy-handed direction.

The experiences of the major trading partners of the United States provide examples of both effective industrial policy and misallocated resources and bureaucratic bumbling. And yet, with the exception of Great Britain,* these countries continue to develop industrial policies that are becoming more sophisticated in design and application. Since the most effective of these industrial policies are often the most subtle, it is very difficult to evaluate precisely their extent and effects. With some notable exceptions, however, these policies are playing a positive role in the countries' economic development.

---

* Even in Great Britain, momentum is rapidly building to introduce a more active industrial policy as the current policies of the conservative government continue to flounder.

FOREIGN VS. U.S. INDUSTRIAL POLICIES

Direct comparisons between U.S. and foreign industrial policies are difficult to draw. Different political traditions and economic experiences lead to substantial differences in industrial policy. For example, the U.S. economy is larger and more complex than those of Western Europe or Japan; the U.S. system of politics and government is more decentralized; U.S. culture is less homogeneous. Nor has the U.S. had a tradition of a strong and independent civil service, as have many of its trading partners. Moreover, none of these other countries spend as great a proportion of their GNP on defense as does the United States. This overwhelming fact alone must alter the frame of reference through which comparative industrial development is viewed. Nevertheless, a few broad comparisons do suggest themselves.

• Foreign industrial policies explicitly seek to improve the competitive position of their home-based industries; U.S. policy has seldom, if ever, been based on this justification.

• Foreign industrial policies seek to assist the restructuring of their industries toward industries that provide higher real wages; U.S. policy has not been aimed at augmenting worker income.

• Foreign industrial policies seek to assist workers and communities that are hard hit by industry restructuring by providing them with new jobs in new industries; U.S. policy provides short-term income maintenance to some workers in troubled industries, but these programs are limited.

• Foreign industrial policies seek to promote the growth of high-technology industries through the funding of research and development, high-risk investment, and initial market development; the U.S. has no such policy, although spin-offs from defense and space programs have inadvertently had this effect.

• Foreign industrial policies sometimes seek industrial restructuring, including mergers and joint ventures, to improve international competitiveness; U.S. policy has focused only on preventing inordinate industrial concentration.

• Foreign industrial policies seek to help their companies become successful exporters; U.S. trade policy has sought to protect companies from imports, while providing relatively small and unfocused export promotion.

● The Japanese, French, and Germans have developed sophisticated tools for industrial policymaking. They are employed by highly respected bureaucrats who have an intimate understanding of business issues; U.S. policies are often imprecise, tending toward broad regulations or industrywide subsidies. They are often administered by bureaucrats with little business experience or knowledge.

● Foreign industrial policies provide mechanisms through which management, labor, financial institutions, and the public can seek a consensus on key issues of economic development; the U.S. has no such formal consensus-forming machinery.

● Foreign industrial policies are administered by government departments that are explicitly responsible for industrial development. These departments form strategy and coordinate various general and selective policies; the U.S. has no such departments.

Despite significant differences in the U.S. economy, the U.S. now faces an economic challenge similar to that faced by its major trading partners—how to facilitate the adjustment of its economy to rapid changes in the world economy. A rational industrial policy, carefully tailored to the unique economic and political institutions of the U.S., is necessary if the nation is to maintain its competitiveness.

IV

TOWARD A RATIONAL INDUSTRIAL POLICY

An avid reader of company annual reports might quickly form the conclusion that booming sales and profits result from good management, while poor performance, on the other hand, is caused by extraneous factors in the economic environment that are beyond management's control. Recently, it has been fashionable to blame government policies for poor U.S. competitive performance. Companies are underinvesting, it is said, because government environmental, safety, and consumer regulations stifle business initiatives. Further, social welfare-related government deficits, poor management of the money supply, and an excessive tax burden on wealthy savers supposedly make funds for investment scarce or expensive. Everyone seems to have a favorite example to illustrate the ineptitude of government bureaucracy and the inefficiencies of social welfare programs.

There is little doubt that economic policymakers have made mistakes and that greater efficiencies can and should be introduced into the conduct of regulatory and social welfare agencies. It may also be appropriate to lower government deficits and taxes. However, even when all of these measures have been accomplished, we doubt that the competitive position of U.S. industry will have been enhanced.

America's competitive decline has more to do with the strategic failures of U.S. business and of U.S. industrial policy than with excessive government deficits or overzealous environmental regulations. Today's policymakers are no doubt correct when they focus on the supply side of the economic ledger and ask what conditions would generate growth, productivity, and increased competitiveness. It is their answer that is wrong, not their question.

A truly "supply side" series of policies must address the pattern of investment, the mechanisms for industrial transitions, and the development of human resources, and not just entrepreneurial incentives and aggregate levels of savings and investment.

In Part II, we briefly touched on some of the systems and attitudes in the business community that must change to improve U.S. competitive performance. In the following section, we discuss general directions that must be taken by government and business together if U.S. competitiveness and living standards are to improve substantially over the coming decade.

27

Why Have an Industrial Policy?

Today, many people argue that the economic problems of the United States stem from too much government interference in the market, and that the proper economic course is one that requires less government intrusion rather than more. They contend that the decentralized market decisions of countless consumers and investors are preferable to government decisionmaking for determining which goods and services should be produced in the economy and how investment should be allocated. A decentralized market provides a richer source of information about the competitive potential of various industries than does government; it also spreads the risk of mistakes and poor decisions among all the actors in the market instead of aggregating that risk in one place. The contention is that private investors respond to market signals while government decisionmakers too often respond to political pressures of the moment.

Why, then, do we recommend an industrial policy? Why not simply rely on the market to allocate capital, labor, and other resources? Why not limit government to setting broad rules to limit inflation, unemployment, and excessive industrial concentration?

Such a minimalist role for government might be appropriate in an economy that was sheltered from international competition. It might also be appropriate in an economy that was growing so quickly that structural adjustments were relatively easy—so that, for example new jobs and investment opportunities were readily available to replace old ones. But such is not the case. A laissez-faire approach is both naive and dangerous for a national economy with slow growth and for a nation within an interdependent world economy that is prone to sharp and often sudden changes in supply, demand, technology, and politics. Active government policies are necessary to enable the economy to respond quickly and efficiently to worldwide structural changes.

An active government role does not, however, imply that a large, intrusive government bureaucracy is necessary. Nor does it suggest that government direction should be substituted for market signals. On the contrary, if an industrial policy is to enhance the economy's international competitiveness, it must do so with a scalpel rather than with a sledgehammer—through careful, discrete interventions that impose minimal dislocations. Industrial policy must pay careful attention to international market signals, noting pending structural shifts and helping the domestic economy adjust to them. Properly conceived and executed, industrial policy should ease and accelerate the adjustment process. Industrial policy should be an agent of global market forces in seeking to improve the responsiveness of labor and capital to new circumstances, such as technological changes, changes in relative productivity, the opening of new markets, and the migration of certain businesses to low-wage countries.

An active industrial policy to improve American living standards is necessary to supplement and circumscribe private business decisions. The following sections describe the reasons why an active government role is required.

SOCIAL DISLOCATIONS

Real social costs are generated when industries suffer competitive decline. As large industries begin to lose competitive advantage in world markets, many thousands of workers may lose their jobs. In order to obtain other jobs, they may have to relocate or gain new skills—both of which are costly ventures, particularly for the newly unemployed. Because the movement of capital is relatively swift, while the movement of workers is often slow and painful, such unemployment can have lasting effects on a local or regional economy.

In the U.S., job dislocations are often severe for several related reasons. First, U.S. firms do not provide their employees with the same degree of job security as is provided by many Japanese and European firms. The notion that a worker may earn a vested right to employment with a particular firm is common in Japan and Scandanavia, but is seen in the U.S. mainly as a Utopian ideal. Partly as a result of this relative lack of job security, job mobility is markedly higher in the U.S. than in other advanced industrial economies.

Unemployment is a constant threat to American workers. In good years and bad, labor in the United States tends to be a commodity in absolute surplus, which makes having a job and retaining it a matter of considerable importance for those whose primary source of income is the sale of their labor. In the 50 years since the onset of the Great Depression, the United States has experienced only 13 "normal" years—that is, years in which the country was neither at war nor in a major economic slump. During each of those normal years, official unemployment rates were in the range of 4 to 5 percent. Recent rates have been much higher.

Many labor economists think that in any normal year there is an overhang of potential employables equal to twice the official number of unemployed. This group is made up of people who have removed themselves from the labor market but who would come in if jobs were available—retirees, students, housewives, welfare recipients. Indeed, they do start to come into the labor market in large numbers whenever unemployment rates fall below a certain point, providing a major explanation of why it is so much harder to bring unemployment down from 4 to 3 percent than from 8 to 7 percent.[1]

In addition to this reserve of potential employables, the economy harbors a significant number of underemployed persons—people working for a low wage that puts them below the official poverty line, workers employed involuntarily on a part-time basis, and those working at jobs below their capabilities. Many members of this group are dependent on government subsidies, including food stamps. The public thereby makes up the difference between what the private market will pay for such labor and their subsistence needs. These people form a large pool of accessible labor, particularly at the lower end of the skill spectrum. Since their labor is available at or close to a minimum wage rate, many unskilled and semiskilled workers feel considerable concern at being pushed out of their jobs. A large number of unemployed people are young and willing to accept low wages, and they may not present the same problems of pensions and seniority rights.

Training costs for many firms have been substantially reduced because of the low skill levels required in the fastest growing segments of the economy. The availability of a large pool of relatively inexpensive, easily trained, and un- and under-employed labor has led to the substitution of low-wage labor for increased capital investment in a number of industries. Other situations may further encourage the substitution of low-wage labor for capital—for example, proposals to "reindustrialize" the country by suppressing wage demands, by exempting certain categories of labor from minimum wage, or by reducing Social Security protection. Labor spokesmen are naturally concerned about such "reindustrialization" policies, which assume increased job mobility and lower wages. Recently, they have been understandably alarmed by the increase in the velocity of capital movements, coupled with a growth in employment in low- to moderate-paying service jobs.

The loss of a job is also feared because it may mean loss of seniority and status. U.S. employers typically use career ladders as the primary means of assigning rewards and penalties within the work place. This is partly due to a tradition of craft and guild organizations in certain industries. But it is also due to the employers' desire both to retard job mobility among skilled workers during labor shortages and to render bargaining over wages and work conditions more flexible. The status of most workers is based on achieved rank within a specialty, within a firm, and often within an individual plant. Whether such status is earned by skill or seniority is of little importance; status and seniority are often nontransferable. A foreman in one specialty shop may be on a wholly different ladder than a foreman in another shop in the same plant. Therefore, the possession of a particular job with a particular firm may be of much more importance than simply having "work."

Finally, in many people's work lives, there is a large, legitimate element of conservatism and inertia, factors that are sometimes described as company and community loyalty. Many workers are willing to make substantial sacrifices in terms of physical comfort, life style, and economic rewards to stay with the same firm rather than move to another job.[2] Fellow workers, familiar surroundings, and known work patterns and status all help to create a comfortable atmosphere. Work places are, at bottom, communities. People generally do not like to sever community ties,[3] particularly when they have developed friendships, status relationships, patterns of recreation and shopping, financial ties, and family and social responsibilities in the region.

These personal and social costs are often magnified within communities and regions affected by economic decline. Ripple effects are felt across the whole economy as people stop making purchases, fail to pay their bills, or dump their homes onto the market. Local governments lose revenue precisely at the time when demands for social services increase. Public facilities such as schools and playgrounds are in less demand as the population declines. A substantial number of the newly unemployed have health and social problems that are aggravated by the tensions and insecurities connected with a loss of role and a fear that the community is collapsing. Crime often increases as some workers let off their tensions; health problems increase as others bottle up their anxieties and fears. An increased death rate is also associated with unemployment; most suicides in the U.S. are by out-of-work males in their middle to later years.

Lack of job security and high levels of general unemployment, career patterns that involve a sizable element of nontransferable rights, the trauma inherent in any major disruption of work and living patterns, and the effects of unemployment on community life—all these factors reinforce a collective desire on the part of many workers within declining industries to retard economic change.[4] The result is often a coalition of workers and employers petitioning the government for assistance in preserving the economic base of the region or community.

The U.S. has not coped with these adjustment problems nearly as well as have many other countries. It has responded to economic change largely by protecting its industries against foreign imports and by providing them with bail-outs and subsidies. But these policies have cost consumers and taxpayers billions of dollars, without improving long-term competitiveness. Meanwhile, the country maintains high levels of unemployment and provides only meager assistance to workers for retraining or to regions for developing new industry. In addition, wide differentials have developed between wages paid for similar work in different industries.

In short, the U.S. has merely reacted to the problems of adjustment, spending large sums of money but not solving the underlying problems. The first and most basic rationale for an industrial policy is the economic, social, and political necessity of programs to encourage adjustment in anticipation of industry decline.

PUBLIC VERSUS PRIVATE INVESTMENT CRITERIA

The benefits of an investment are often different for private investors and for society as a whole. The investments of individuals and companies sometimes have negative side effects, as when a company builds a factory that discharges pollutants into the air or water. But often the side effects are positive, such as public benefits in the form of new products and jobs and a higher overall standard of living. In either case, public benefits will be different from individual benefits—that is, the public as a whole would be better off with a higher level or a different type of investment than individual investors are willing to make. Under these circumstances, government intervention may be in order.

Research and Development

Many benefits from an investment in research and development are enjoyed by people other than the initial investors. Innovations may make life safer, cleaner, or more pleasant for generations of citizens. Innovations may find their way into unrelated products or may breed further innovations in the same product area.

A small but growing body of economic analysis has attempted to measure the social and private rates of return from investments in new industrial technology. One detailed study looked at 17 industrial innovations in the fields of primary metals, machine tools, industrial controls, construction, drilling, paper, thread, heating equipment, electronics, chemicals, and household cleaners. The study found that the social rate of return on these investments averaged about 56 percent; the average before-tax private rate of return was only about 25 percent. This evidence suggests that, from society's point of view, private investors may be committing too few resources to research and development.[5]

The gap between private and social rates of return from innovation arises because the innovator cannot recoup the full social return from an investment. This may occur because the innovation cannot be patented or because patent protection is weak. It may also be because commercial application by the investor is so remote that there is no ready market for the invention.

This gap may also occur when the social return comes in the form of job experience and training which lead to new innovations and businesses. New industries often develop in geographic areas where a "critical mass" of new skills has been created. Defense and aerospace research have had this synergistic effect both in California's "Silicon Valley" and in and around Cambridge, Massachusetts. Several state governments are now actively trying to establish other high-technology research centers in the hopes of replicating the successes of California and Massachusetts. Unfortunately, because these state efforts have not been integrated into an overall U.S. industrial policy, they are more apt to compete against one another for resources and personnel than to build strategically upon each other's strengths.

Linkage Industries

Another situation in which the private return on an investment may not take full account of the public return is in circumstances where a particular business is critically linked to the cost competitiveness of many other businesses. For example, steel comprises a significant part of the cost of ships, autos, many appliances, and various machine components. Foreign domination of the steel business could therefore jeopardize the competitiveness of many sectors of our domestic economy. If Japanese steel producers are able to manufacture steel 25 percent more cheaply than U.S. steel producers, Japanese makers of steel-using products can gain a total production cost advantage over their U.S. competitors. Some cost advantage would exist even if the U.S. competitors imported Japanese steel, since U.S. customers would have to pay the cost of transporting the steel. Moreover, the Japanese steel producers might give home-based customers preferential treatment in price or in delivery during times of shortage. Similarly, U.S. competitors might be disadvantaged because of increased difficulties in coordinating quality control, precise product requirements, inventory control, and payment terms with their Japanese suppliers.

The U.S. company that opts for cheaper Japanese steel for a particular project does not generally worry about these problems. But the combined choices of all the U.S. producers of steel-using products to purchase Japanese steel further erodes the competitiveness of the U.S. steel industry. By the same token, individual investors eschew U.S. steel producers because their future appears gloomy. Robbed of the funds it needs for new investment, the U.S. steel industry falls further behind the Japanese. As the price differential between U.S. and Japanese steel widens further, the international competitive position of all

U.S. producers dependent on steel grows correspondingly more vulnerable.

In this instance, the decisions of individual economic actors do not take full account of the costs and benefits of their decisions to the economy as a whole. They underinvest in key "linkage" industries because they do not recoup the full social return on their investment, nor do they bear the full cost of their failure to invest more fully. A rational industrial policy would seek to identify such linkage industries—semiconductors and fiber optics, for example—and try to facilitate a level and type of investment necessary to ensure their continued competitive success.

Infant Industries

A third instance in which public benefits from a given investment may substantially exceed private returns occurs where a domestic industry is still too small and fragmented to compete internationally. This may be so even if the industry as a whole holds great promise of international success. In these circumstances, individual investors in particular firms may face far higher levels of risk and lower potential returns than they would if the industry were to be rationalized for international competition. This could be accomplished for example, by dividing the industry into fewer firms of larger scale, with specialized foreign marketing and distributing capabilities. Yet precisely because of investor reluctance, no single firm may have the resources to undertake such a rationalization. Indeed, individual investors may find it more profitable to invest their funds in foreign firms that are already more developed as strong international competitors. At the present time, for example, a private investor might prefer to place funds in leading Japanese consumer electronics firms rather than U.S. ones.

Since the national economy suffers as a result of these individual calculations, governments often seek to develop infant domestic industries that have the potential for becoming strong international competitors. During the 1950s and 1960s, for example, the governments of Japan and France provided seed money, coordinated overseas marketing and domestic technology, and promoted mergers in a number of industries in order to enhance their international competitive position sufficiently to attract continuing private investment. Through its defense procurement and tariff policies, the U.S. government has also promoted certain infant industries, although this promotion has been largely inadvertent.

Low-Wage Labor

Finally, private firms may underinvest in productivity improvements if they can readily substitute low-wage labor for added productivity. By reducing the real relative wages of workers, firms may be able to reduce their competitive costs and thereby improve their profitability. But this strategy does not increase the wealth of the nation as a whole nearly so much as an investment in increased productivity. By definition, a reduction in real relative wages reduces relative living standards. While firms that reduce real wages may become more competitive internationally, their workers are likely to become poorer relative to workers in other countries. As a national strategy, the substitution of lower real relative wages for productivity improvements would eventually make America a relatively poor country, albeit one with a healthy balance of payments. Accordingly, a rational industrial policy should encourage firms to invest in productivity improvements and increased output rather than reduce real relative wages.

SLOW MARKET MECHANISMS

A third justification for an industrial policy occurs in circumstances where market forces could be relied on to stimulate growth and productivity, but the pace of these effects would be too slow to improve the nation's international competitive position.

In the current climate of slow world economic growth, high inflation, and energy uncertainty, many firms and private investors have understandably adopted conservative investment strategies. Ironically, this conservatism comes just at a time when large investments are necessary to keep up with technological change, increased process scale, and shorter product generations. In many businesses, international competition has become a race in which the first producer to achieve high volume and gain experience can underprice and maintain leadership relative to potential international rivals. Because of this disparity between the conservatism of capital markets and the need for speed in international competition, governments in many advanced industrial countries have devised selective schemes to encourage greater risk-taking and to assist with particularly large projects. Unless the U.S. adopts similar measures, U.S. firms and private investors may continue to opt for safer investments that do not build long-term competitiveness—investments such as distributing foreign-manufactured products in the U.S., developing real estate, or acquiring already well-established firms.

Just as capital markets can be slow to respond to competitive opportunities, labor markets also can be slow to adjust to the need for new skills. Thus toolmakers and engineers remain in short supply in many industrialized countries that simultaneously suffer from unemployment. This lag in labor markets has prompted many governments to establish generous retraining programs that are focused on growing segments of their economies.

Finally, without adequate knowledge and resources, small and medium-sized firms may not adjust quickly enough to international opportunities. Foreign governments have accelerated the movement of such businesses into international markets by providing them with the capital and know-how they need. Unless the U.S. institutes similar measures, small foreign companies that are assisted by their governments may preempt smaller U.S. firms by aggressively moving into the U.S. market.

In all these cases, the competitive success of the United States is at stake. While our capital or labor markets may eventually respond to growth opportunities, other countries will gain a competitive edge if they respond more quickly.

IMPLICATIONS OF OTHER GOVERNMENT PROGRAMS

Various government programs, such as defense procurement and defense-related research and development, are designed to accomplish goals other than the improvement of our international competitiveness; however, they often have a substantial effect on the growth of specific industries, many of which constitute a large part of U.S. foreign trade.

Defense programs have greatly affected the development of civilian aircraft, communications equipment, engineering and scientific instruments, and semiconductors.

U.S. defense-related procurement and research and development programs constitute a much larger proportion of the GNP than defense-related programs in other industrial countries. Indeed, total government procurement as a percent of the GNP is twice as high in the U.S. as it is in Japan. For this reason, major U.S. trading partners have long regarded U.S. procurement and R&D programs as industrial policies that have spurred the international competitiveness of many U.S. industries.

Unless the U.S. considers the implications of these programs for international competitiveness and regards them as aspects of a coherent industrial policy, they may instead have the effect of distorting domestic market incentives and retarding commercial development. In cases where the military's needs are substantially different from civilian needs, a large procurement or R&D program may drain off skilled engineers and research and productive capacity from commercial development, thereby enabling foreign manufacturers to gain a competitive edge.

In sum, the justifications for an active and coherent industrial policy are fourfold: to ease social disruptions caused by necessary decline in certain industries; to overcome substantial disparities between public and private returns on investment; to accelerate sluggish market forces; and to ensure that other government activities, notably defense, are undertaken with due regard to international competitiveness. In addition, without a coherent strategy for industrial policy, individual industrial policy measures will inevitably be introduced in response to the political pressures of the moment. A coherent strategy for pursuing the goal of international competitiveness is surely preferable to *ad hoc* policies that are developed in response to the politically powerful but often less competitive businesses within various industries.

FOOTNOTES

[1] Testimony of Honorable Eli Ginzberg, Chairman, National Commission for Manpower Policy, before the Joint Economic Committee, 95th Congress, 2d session, June 15, 1978, Part 2, Washington, D.C.: U.S. Government

Printing Office, 1978, p. 774; Ginzberg, Eli. "The Job Problem," *Scientific American,* November 1977, p. 43; Sweezy, Paul and Magdoff, Harry. "Economic Stagnation and Stagnation of Economics," *Monthly Review,* April 1971, p. 1; Braverman, Harvey. *Labor and Monopoly Capital,* New York: Monthly Review Press, 1974, p. 390.

[2] See "More Employees Accept Cuts in Pay to Help Their Companies Survive," *Wall Street Journal,* October 22, 1980, p. 25, col. 4.

[3] Samuelson, Robert. "On Mobility," *National Journal,* August 16, 1980, p. 1366, notes that the change in the nation's age profile may make it even more difficult for political planners to appear passive in the face of massive uprooting of populations due to sectoral shifts. As the "baby boom" matures, it is likely to become progressively more settled. Of 500,000 workers receiving trade adjustment assistance between 1974 and 1979, only 2,700 took available out-of-town job search money, and only 1,700 actually relocated. Too much can be made of such statistics (since most of these workers ultimately appear to have been rehired by their former employers), but they are suggestive nonetheless.

[4] See Chapter 17.

[5] Mansfield, Edwin, *et al.* "Social and Private Rates of Return for Industrial Innovations," *Quarterly Journal of Economics,* 91, No. 2, May 1977, 221–249; Mansfield, Edwin *et al. The Production and Application of New Industrial Technology,* New York: Norton, 1977.

28

The Substance of a Rational Industrial Policy

A rational industrial policy must accomplish two interrelated objectives. First, it must strive to integrate the full range of targeted government policies—procurement, research and development, trade, antitrust, tax credits, and subsidies—into a coherent strategy for encouraging the development of internationally competitive businesses. Second, it must seek to facilitate the movement of capital and labor into businesses that permit higher value added per employee. In these ways, industrial policy should complement the strategic decisions of U.S. firms.

Basically, a rational policy would include four types of measures. It should encompass measures to assist workers and regions facing industrial displacement, so that they do not have to assume a disproportionate share of the disruption caused by industrial restructuring. It should also include measures to correct market imperfections in situations where the public return on investment is likely to be substantially greater than the sum of private returns. Third, such a policy should include measures to encourage the productive investment of capital in circumstances of high-risk, large-scale, or long-projected payback and corresponding measures to ensure development of manpower needs to fit such growth opportunities. Finally, in order to ensure productive growth, it should include measures to coordinate government policies that have selective effects on industry.

MEASURES TO EASE LABOR ADJUSTMENT

For reasons both of social justice and sound economic policy, the U.S.

must develop comprehensive programs to assist workers displaced involuntarily by industrial restructuring. Programs must also be developed to assist regions that are disproportionately affected by plant layoffs and closures. The U.S. is the only major industrialized country without such programs.

The transition of declining businesses can be eased if the government seeks to develop the most productive segments of such businesses and tries to provide the means for generating new, competitive businesses within the same regions. Strategies should be designed to assist the private sector in preserving existing regional employment and in creating healthy new regional employment, thereby diffusing the effectiveness of political demands for protection of dying industries. Such strategies need to be put into effect early, in anticipation of economic decline.

Industrial adjustment policies must do more than provide workers with unemployment insurance while they find something else to do with themselves. Government therefore should expand its current efforts to assist workers in finding new jobs and training for them.

There are several approaches for addressing the adjustment problems of workers and communities. Among them are the use of transitional vouchers, advance notification of major shutdowns, and regional assistance programs.

Transitional Vouchers

A number of West European countries use transitional vouchers to provide a partial wage subsidy for experienced workers who are forced to seek new employment as a result of major shutdowns. The individual worker negotiates with a new employer for a wage package that roughly approximates prior earnings; the employer receives a subsidy that pays the difference between the audited cost of hiring and retraining the worker and the worker's audited contribution to the firm's profits. The worker has a measure of discretion as to which firm will receive the subsidy, and training is on the job rather than in an artificial schoolroom situation. Coupled with relocation allowances that permit workers to move from one region to another, voucher programs have proved particularly attractive. They offer a useful supplement to a policy of unemployment insurance and severance payments.

West Germany has directed such a voucher program at workers who have been out of work for a year or longer. Under a similar program, Sweden pays an hourly subsidy to firms that provide training for workers. The program is essentially a job-maintenance measure that seeks to keep unemployment levels low during periods of recession; it also offers protection to workers in industries that are being restructured. Most types of training can be subsidized under the program, thus enabling workers to increase their present skills, learn new skills that result from technological change, or learn the jobs of other workers in order to increase production flexibility. The program is relatively expensive, but it has been popular among both business and labor.

Such programs do, of course, have drawbacks. They can prove expensive. They may also give rise to social tensions if employers prefer workers with vouchers over job-market entrants without them. Such a situation in an American context if not administered correctly could easily lead to outcries that the program was perpetuating existing patterns of job discrimination against minorities and women.

Even with vouchers, special categories of workers could still prove difficult to reemploy. It is doubtful, for example, that a voucher program alone would be of much service to a severely handicapped worker trained to do very specific tasks. Special training programs, or "exceptional case" vouchers, might be needed, and with them a bureaucracy for determining eligibility. Some workers might prove to be relatively immobile—because of familial obligations, home ownership, and so forth—and view their job opportunities as geographically limited. Other workers might be too old or too close to retirement to be attractive to new employers. To such workers, resisting change in the employment patterns of a declining industry by actively attempting to block or retard such changes might seem a more rational course than attempting to peddle a voucher in a situation where total job opportunities are few.

Finally, of course, there is a host of other issues to resolve—for example: Should vouchers be available only in "extraordinary" situations, and how should "extraordinary" be defined? Would the program apply only to closings that result from competitive shifts or from technological changes within the industry, or will it also cover situations that arise merely because the firm's directors decide to move to a warmer climate? Would vouchers be available for intrafirm transfers from one plant to another, and under what circumstances? Would vouchers be linked to some guarantee from new employers regarding seniority or pension rights?

In spite of various drawbacks, a program of vouchers for subsidizing on-the-job training would probably smooth the transition of labor and make economic change easier to bear. At the same time, the program would not discourage the mobility of capital out of declining lines of business.

Advance Notification of Shutdowns

Adjustment problems of workers and communities could also be eased if private employers were to give their employees advance notice before any major shutdown of a plant or facility took place. This system would apply both to sudden terminations of operations and to major employment cutbacks that a company intended to carry out over time. Advance notification is close in nature to the requirement that businesses inform local governments of projected expansions so that the community can better plan for future sewage, police, transportation, fire protection, and social service needs.

Alone among modern industrial democracies, the United States fails to require major employers to give advance notice before closing a facility and throwing large numbers of people out of work. Arguments against an early warning system have been based primarily on the view that such notice would interfere with the free, though sometimes punitive movement of industry, thereby rendering markets less efficient. Business strategy arguments have also been invoked; secrecy is justified because it keeps competitors off balance if they cannot learn of a shutdown until it has taken place. It is also said that advance notice might limit the flexibility of the owners, either in terms of a last-minute reprieve or in negotiations with potential buyers. Anticipation of losing employment might also sap the morale and lower the performance of workers during the last few months of a facility's operation. Finally, of course, many owners do not plan shutdowns or permanent layoffs until the last moment, when sudden shifts in circumstances make such events inevitable. In other cases, plans may be highly contingent; giving advance notice might lock a firm into a course of action that it would rather not take.

There is some validity to each of these arguments, but a lot less than meets the eye. The decision to close a major operation or shift it elsewhere is rarely a last-minute decision for any large enterprise. Sudden closures arise most commonly for firms with limited facilities, in limited numbers of business lines, and in an industry that is patently in trouble. The desire to keep competitors guessing no doubt has some competitive value, but it hardly offers adequate justification for permitting substantial injury to local governments, communities, and workers. From medieval statutes on nuisance abatement to modern zoning restrictions, governments have traditionally limited the commercial use of private property when it inflicts harms on third parties.

Requiring advance notice would be far less intrusive than mechanisms that are currently imposed by other advanced industrial countries. A number of Western nations, including France, require government authorization to open or close any major economic facility. Other countries, including Great Britain, France, Belgium, Sweden, and West Germany, require that closings be accompanied by substantial severance payments and retraining allowances.[1] Often, private payments are required to local governments to help defray the costs connected with the disruption that closings create. The underlying reasoning is that if the firm must factor the costs that third parties would otherwise have to bear into its own decision, it might think twice about taking such decisions.[2]

If government is to respond to problems created by plant closings, it needs information about the specific situations that are created by the closing of individual facilities and the patterns of closings. Either prior to or immediately after any major planned shutdown, businesses contemplating a shutdown should be obliged to provide public authorities with information on such matters as total employment and payroll; the demographic characteristics of the work force; job categories and skills of the work force; total sales and a listing of principal customers; the volume and nature of the goods and services purchased locally; plans for disposing of the facility, land and equipment; and the company's future plans for the community and the present work force.[3]

Regional Assistance Programs

Unless we want to gradually depopulate our older industrial regions—and endure the social costs such a strategy would entail—we must develop new industries in these areas. While a number of federal programs already provide assistance for regional development, many of these are multipurpose and diffuse, and promote neither balanced growth nor the smooth transition from declining sectors to burgeoning ones.

Many states have programs of subvention for new industry, including low-cost loans and tax exemptions. In most cases, however, these programs simply seek to lure into the state any firm that can be persuaded to come. For large enterprises, such financial assistance is seldom the determining factor in deciding where to locate a facility.[4]

The federal government should target its procurement and R&D funds to support regional enterprises that show the most promise in technological and product innovation. Such enterprises might well turn into seedbeds for a region's development. The skillful use of government procurement and choice of location for particular development facilities could meet immediate employment needs and put local economies on a new footing. Other incentives could be used to induce private industry to locate in depressed regions. Most Western European countries assist depressed regions in attracting industry through tax benefits, direct grants for a percent of capital invested for machinery, the provision of factories that are leased at favorable rates, interest rate subsidies on debt, and training grants.

Other Restructuring Programs

Currently, far too little is known about the value and utility of the many other programs that have been suggested for easing labor adjustment. Income maintenance payments, for example, have been criticized by certain economists on the ground that they lessen the incentive of unemployed workers to vigorously seek new jobs. Few empirical studies, however, find a simple relationship between income support and attempts to find work.[5] Similarly, moving allowances should encourage workers to leave areas of high unemployment for burgeoning areas; in practice, however, they have been unpopular, and many workers seem to make their decisions without regard to the expense of moving.[6] For certain groups and in particular situations, these allowances might prove quite valuable—if, for example, large numbers of people were all moving to the same new community. At a minimum, workers' benefits should be fully portable as well as practical.

More comprehensive government efforts should also be made to retrain skilled and older workers. Firms that are closing certain facilities but that have others already operating or about to open, should be required to absorb and retrain a portion of the redundant work force. Intrafirm retraining and reassignment is common in Japan, where a worker's utility is defined primarily in terms of ability to learn new skills rather than in terms of present job skills.

In Europe and Japan, programs to ease the problems of labor adjustment are far superior in their variety and breadth to the meager efforts in the United States. Programs vary from country to country, but common elements stand out. West Germany, France, Britain, Sweden, Belgium, the Netherlands, and Italy typically all provide some form of income maintenance; retraining allowances; liberal severance pay requirements; and subsidies for maintaining payments of health and social welfare insurance. In addition, there are job location assistance; subsidies for relocation and job-related travel expenditures; early retirement pensioning of older or handicapped workers; and government support of noncompetitive workers. Other programs include transfer rights for redundant employees; special development programs for depressed areas; the establishment of reserve funds to capitalize facility conversion; and subventions to maintain employment in periods of downturn by stockpiling excess inventory. Finally, there are provisions for funding regional economic impact statements before major openings or closings; restricting the location of new facilities to areas of high unemployment; and subsidizing area redevelopment planning.

The U.S. has no comparable approaches. The customary government response is to treat most factory closings as natural events to be expected in a market economy. Since unemployment levels are generally high, workers are pitied more because they *suddenly* find themselves unemployed than because they are unemployed. At best, federal, state, and local governments react by scrambling to assemble an *ad hoc* program to meet immediate community and worker needs. The U.S. must develop an overall strategy for labor adjustment. The only alternative to such a strategy is for workers, communities, and the broader public to endure the substantial social costs of unemployment and regional decline and the substantial economic costs of protectionism.

MEASURES TO CORRECT MARKET IMPERFECTIONS

A rational industrial policy should enable the government to employ discrete measures in situations where private calculations of investment return are substantially below the long-term rate of return for the economy as a whole.

Research and Development Policy

The U.S. government funds a significant portion of the nation's R&D, but most of the funds that go to industry are intended for defense and energy development.

By contrast, the major U.S. trading partners have developed large R&D programs specifically targeted to new technologies in well-defined business segments, which can lead directly to an improved competitive position. German and French agencies provide significant R&D funds; the Japanese government has devoted substantial funds to a range of development efforts in computers, semiconductors, robotics, and other new technology areas.

While defense R&D will continue to provide some spin-offs for commercial application, much of it is not well suited to commercial development because military requirements are often unique. Moreover, the vast bulk of defense R&D grants goes to very large businesses that are equipped to undertake large-scale defense projects, rather than to small innovative businesses. Accordingly, defense R&D is a relatively inefficient means by which to fund industrial development.

Several principles should guide an industrial research and development policy. For example, funds should be allocated to small businesses as well as large. The German Ministry of Technology makes thousands of R&D grants each year; half of these go to large German companies, while the rest are allocated to a myriad of small and medium-sized companies.

In addition, matching funds should be allocated to proposals that originate within the companies. Sharing R&D costs creates an incentive for companies to propose worthwhile projects. Moreover, if the companies rather than the government have primary responsibility for proposing new projects, it is more likely that the ideas will be directly applicable to competitive development.

Furthermore, decisions about which proposals to fund should be undertaken by teams of officials from government, industry, and universities or research institutes, thereby ensuring that a range of experiences and insights can be brought to bear. Successful research efforts in Germany, France, and Japan are organized by broad industry groupings, with specialized committees overseeing each segment.

Another guiding principle should be that research results are made public in such a way that the companies who have shared their costs have some confidential lead time in using the results. In addition, joint research ventures among companies should be encouraged. It is common, particularly in Japan, for research ventures to be undertaken among domestic competitors that develop the innovations separately and then bring them to market competitively. This arrangement combines the advantages of cooperation in research with the advantages of competition in the marketplace.

Finally, the government should share the funding only of projects that are not likely to have commercial application in the short term. Projects with direct commercial application are normally fully funded by individual companies and have little value to any other companies.

Policies for Key Linkage Industries

It is no accident that most of the trading partners of the U.S. have developed specific industrial policies for their steel, automobile, energy, computer, machine tool, and semiconductor industries. They have long recognized the key linkages that these industries have with the rest of their economies. By contrast, the U.S. has no overall policies, expertise, or institutional mechanisms to deal with the competitive problems of its auto and steel industries. Nor does the U.S. have the capability to assess the persistent and aggressive attempts now being made by other countries to catch up in linkage industries, such as machine tools, semiconductors, and computers, in which the United States is still the world leader.

The U.S. response to the competitive problems facing its steel industry, for example, has been to provide protection and indirect income maintenance, but no strategy to regain competitive productivity. The income maintenance has impaired the competitiveness of other industries dependent on steel; it has also been expensive for the American consumer. Similarly, the U.S. response to the problems of its automobile industry has been to provide a direct subsidy to Chrysler and temporary subsidies to affected workers; however, there has been no clear agreement on long-term objectives. Should Chrysler be preserved? Should foreign producers be encouraged to establish assembly operations in the U.S., even though basic engineering and components come from the foreign country? Is temporary protection needed? What measures can be taken to ensure that such protection does not become permanent? These are questions that U.S. public-policy mechanisms have failed to address.

At the most fundamental level, the government must develop strategies that consider the competitive structures of businesses dependent on the key linkage industries, as well as the costs of such strategies to consumers and the general public. This sophisticated form of cost-benefit analysis is also relevant to trade negotiations with other countries, since linkage industries increasingly receive direct or indirect subsidies from most advanced industrial countries. U.S. linkage industries may be jeopardized if the U.S. government and industry are not sufficiently versed in industrial policy to be able to negotiate international trading agreements for these industries.

Explicit policies for linkage industries do not require intrusive government regulations or controls over their development. Rather, their development requires a dynamic interaction between government and industry, in which the government is able to play a supportive role to ensure the industries' competitive success.

MEASURES TO ENCOURAGE PRODUCTIVE INVESTMENT IN LONG-TERM PROJECTS

As has been noted, U.S. firms may underinvest in new products both because of the slowing down of world growth and because of long-term economic and political uncertainties. This problem is exacerbated because the scale of necessary investment in many industries has increased, capital cost inflation has exceeded average inflation, and international competition is fiercer than it was a decade ago. Foreign competitors have grown and overcome technological and productivity gaps that existed until the late 1960s or early 1970s between them and their U.S. counterparts. A rational industrial policy for the U.S. would therefore include several programs to stimulate market adjustment to long-term opportunities.

High-Risk Lending

To fund high-risk investments, several U.S. trading partners have established special loans that are repaid only if the project is successful. In other cases, governments have provided assistance for marketing investments in developing countries to encourage exports to these fast-growing but risky markets. In order to stimulate new product development in certain capital goods areas, some governments have provided incentives to companies to purchase new prototype capital goods. Government agencies have also served as direct sources of venture capital to stimulate high-risk investments. Finally, for very large projects, governments have encouraged the creation of consortia of companies and banks through subsidized loans or grants. In all of these cases, government incentives are carefully focused on the particular risk that must be overcome in order to stimulate productive investment.

Outside the defense and energy areas, the U.S. has no such programs to stimulate investment in high-risk ventures. A government-subsidized lending institution should be established to fill this need for high-risk capital. The charter of such a U.S. development fund should allow loans for "expense investments" as well as for capital investments. Moreover, this institution should be able to fund the purchasers of new capital goods as well as the manufacturers. Loans made by a development fund should be at subsidized interest rates, to be repaid only when some minimal level of success is achieved. Finally, loans should be made only if companies themselves provide partial funding. In addition to development fund loans for high-risk projects of large size, the government should provide investment tax credits if success is achieved.

The development fund and tax credits should be reserved for projects that show substantial promise of international competitive success, but whose long-term risks and high capital requirements have prevented companies from undertaking investments on their own. In these cases, government-supplied funds can reduce the risk sufficiently to tip the balance.

Overseas Market Stimulation

Along with other industrialized nations, the U.S. has established programs to finance exports and to provide insurance for various risks associated with exports. Although the effectiveness of these programs is difficult to evaluate and comparisons are hazardous, the U.S. seems to have lagged behind other nations.

France and Japan, like the U.S., have established government-owned banks that lend directly to exporters and that refinance commercial banks. In Germany, a government bank provides special rates of financing for developing-country exports. In Germany, the U.K., Belgium, and the Netherlands, central banks refinance commercial bank consortia for certain types of credits. Unlike the U.S., these countries subsidize interest rates on these credits. Although fixed through international agreement, these subsidies in fact vary considerably. Many countries, including France, Japan, and Germany, provide "mixed credit" for selected large export sales—general government-to-government loans combined with traditional financing. The absolute rates of interest on such loans are often less important than the spread between domestic market rates and government-supported rates. In a world of free capital flows and flexible exchange rates, market interest rate disparities are offset by different expectations of currency fluctuation. Thus, the interest rate offered in a Deutschmark loan may create vastly different incentives than the same interest rate offered in a U.S. dollar loan.

Perhaps more important than offering direct export financing is providing export insurance. Most countries now offer similar coverage for commercial and political risks. In some countries, this coverage is administered through government-owned insurance companies; in other countries, the government reinsures a private company for all its risks. Governments may also provide additional insurance coverage for foreign exchange losses and foreign inflation. These forms of coverage provide significant competitive benefits that allow greater aggressiveness in overseas sales, particularly in Eastern Europe or developing countries. In the U.S., as we have seen, OPIC plays a limited role, mainly for exports to developing countries. Overall, the U.S. insures a lower percentage of total exports (Exhibit 87) and covers fewer categories of risk than do other countries (Exhibit 88).

EXHIBIT 87
Government Insurance as a Percent of Total Exports, 1977

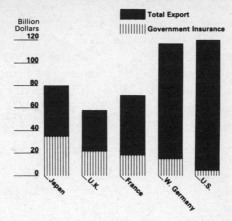

Source: U.S. Export-Import Bank, Export Credit Guarantee Department.

EXHIBIT 88
Types of Risks Insured, 1977

	U.K.	Japan	France	W. Germany	U.S.
Commercial Percent of Cover usually Guaranteed	● 90–95%	● 60–90%	● 90–95%	● 90%	● 70–90%
Political Percent of Cover usually Guaranteed	● 90–95%	● 90%	● 90–95%	● 90%	● 70–95%
Currency Inconvertibility	●	●	●	●	
Shipping	●	●	●	●	●
Exchange Loss		●	●	●	
Inflation	●		●		
Performance Bond	●	●			

Sources: U.S. Export-Import Bank; client study.

The U.S. does offer income tax deferral on all direct export sales through the DISC program. The U.S. is the only country that offers such an across-the-board incentive; other countries use tax incentives far more selectively. France, for example, provides tax incentives only for goods that are purchased abroad and sold in a third country; Germany offers them only for capital goods exports in which direct equity is involved. Japan and Belgium offer tax-free reserve provisions for overseas marketing costs; Germany, Japan, and France also provide accelerated depreciation or tax deferral for selective foreign investments. As we have seen, largely because of its lack of discrimination, the U.S. program is wasteful and may not necessarily encourage investment.

A final form of export market stimulation is direct marketing assistance, provided by all countries to assist exporters in finding customers and promoting products. The Commerce Department currently funds such programs for U.S. firms. In other countries, particularly in Germany, Japan, Great Britain, and France, additional programs are designed explicitly to assist small companies to export. Although the U.S. Small Business Administration has recently expanded its activities in this direction, its programs are as yet quite small.

Exhibit 89 summarizes export assistance programs provided by various governments. In general, measures such as the DISC program, which does not discriminate among investments, do little to promote productivity levels or to encourage risk. Moreover, they are expensive to maintain. While they may stimulate some specific sales in the short run, they are likely to be wasteful in the long run. Because of their breadth, they also may lead to unproductive trade wars. On the other hand, selective measures that encourage risk-taking in the development of new markets, that provide small companies with an initial impetus for overseas marketing, or that promote greater productivity in distribution can benefit the national economy that institutes them and the world economy that enjoys the fruits of such greater productivity.

The U.S. should reduce its indiscriminate export subsidies and provide more funds for selective programs of insurance coverage, assistance for small business exports and marketing abroad, and assistance for overseas distribution.

Programs for Small and Medium-Sized Businesses

A final means of government support for growth industries involves assistance to small or medium-sized firms. Small business development is crucial to a country as a source of dynamic innovation and regional employment. In most industrialized countries, the largest number of small businesses are sheltered from international trade. These include distribution businesses, construction, many service businesses (such as medical care, real estate agencies, or insurance agencies), and some manufacturing businesses (such as simple plastic mouldings and steel structurals).

A second group of small businesses typically succeeds in carving out a niche in a mature industry where they achieve a stable position either because larger companies do not find it worthwhile to tool up for such a small market or because there are no particular economies of scale. Significant portions of the German economy consist of small and medium-sized firms within this category; often subsuppliers to larger exporting firms, they dominate special branches of the machinery, machine tools, and mechanical components industries.

A third category of small business consists of new, innovative companies that are pioneering new products. These companies are on their way to becoming large businesses.

U.S. programs to promote small business (mostly through the Small Business Administration) have focused almost entirely on sheltered small businesses. By contrast, most foreign governments—particularly Germany, Japan, and France—have focused their small business programs on the latter two categories. They provide small businesses in mature industries with loans or grants to modernize equipment or to promote switching of product lines to prevent obsolescence; they give incentives for mergers, joint factories and warehouses, joint computer and accounting services, and joint marketing agreements with other companies in similar product lines or regions. Finally, most foreign governments provide assistance for establishing joint offices in foreign countries for initial market penetration.

For small innovative companies that could become strong international competitors, most foreign countries also provide special research and development subsidies. In addition, Japan and Germany have established programs that explicitly encourage the manufacturing and

EXHIBIT 89
Export Assistant Programs

Financing	France	W.Germany	U.K.	Belgium
1 Government Loans for Exports to Developed Countries	Non XX[1]	Refinancing Only	Non Refinancing Only	Refinancing Only
2 Government Loans for Exports to Developing Countries	XX	XX	Refinancing Only	Refinancing Only
3 Interest Subsidies to Developed Countries	Non EEC	X	Non EEC	Limited
4 Interest Subsidies to Developing Countries	XX	X	X	Limited
Insurance				
5 Credit Insurance Guarantees (Commercial and Political	XX	XX	XX	XX
6 Foreign Exchange Loss Guarantee	X	X	X	X
7 Inflation Coverage	XX		X	
8 Performance Bond Coverage			X	
9 Income Tax Deferral or Direct Import Sales	Limited Cases	Limited Cases		
10 Tax Free Reserve for Marketing Costs Overseas				X
11 Accelerated Depreciation on Investments Abroad		X		
12 Tax Deferral on Investments in Developing Countries	X	XX		
Marketing Assistance				
13 Information and Promotion	X	X	XX	X
14 Incentives for Small Businesses	X	XX	XX	

Sources: OECD, U.S. Export-Import Bank, interviews.

[1] XX:Important financial incentive (more than $100 million U.S.)
[2] X:Small financial incentive (less than $100 million U.S.)

—exhibit continued—

Financing	Netherlands	Sweden	Japan	U.S.
1 Government Loans for Exports to Developed Countries	Refinancing Only	X^2	XX	Exim XX
2 Government Loans for Exports to Developing Countries	Refinancing Only	X	XX	Exim XX
3 Interest Subsidies to Developed Countries	For Exports of Ships Only	Limited	X	
4 Interest Subsidies to Developing Countries	Ships Only	Limited	XX	
Insurance				
5 Credit Insurance Guarantees (Commercial and Political	XX	XX	XX	CPIC XX
6 Foreign Exchange Loss Guarantee		X	X	
7 Inflation Coverage				
8 Performance Bond Coverage			X	
9 Income Tax Deferral or Direct Import Sales				Disc XX
10 Tax Free Reserve for Marketing Costs Overseas			X	
11 Accelerated Depreciation on Investments Abroad			X	
12 Tax Deferral on Investments in Developing Countries			X	
Marketing Assistance				
13 Information and Promotion	X	X	X	Commerce Department Programs X
14 Incentives for Small Businesses			X	

marketing of innovations developed by small firms, since innovation alone is not adequate to ensure profitability. In order to build commercial success, a firm must be internationally competitive in cost, distribution, and technical service within a few years after invention— otherwise, large international competitors will copy or develop substitutes for the new invention and use superior manufacturing, distribution, or financial resources to gain competitive advantage.

By virtually ignoring the competitive potential of many small businesses, the U.S. is missing a major growth opportunity. Given the proper boost, a large number of small to medium-sized companies, particularly in engineering industries, could be successful internationally. To be sure, it would be necessary to sustain losses during initial market penetration abroad, and significant "expense investments" would be required, but competitive successes could be achieved. The U.S. government should provide incentives for these businesses either through loans or tax credits. The government should also have sufficient knowledge of foreign markets and business structures to advise small businesses about appropriate competitive strategies.

MEASURES TO COORDINATE GOVERNMENT POLICIES

The U.S. government will continue to have many programs that inadvertently affect the international competitiveness of various industries. R&D procurement will be required for defense, energy, and other policies; tax and credit policies will be undertaken; some form of environmental, consumer protection, worker safety, and antitrust programs will be necessary; and a whole range of special tariffs, quotas, loans, and guarantees inevitably will be administered.

It is vitally important that the government undertake these functions with full consideration of their effects on the competitive position of U.S. industries.

Government R&D and Procurement

These programs should be undertaken with due regard for their effects on the future competitiveness of civilian markets. Policymakers should assess, for example, whether a large proposed procurement program for a particular product or technology would allow domestic manufacturers to exploit scale economies and gain substantial experience that could be used in commercial production. On the other hand, perhaps the government's needs are so different from civilian needs that the program would be likely to have the opposite effect—draining off skilled engineers and research and productive capacity from commercial development, thereby enabling foreign manufacturers to gain a competitive edge.

Government Management of Capital Markets

Programs in this area should come under similar scrutiny. Federal loan guarantees, insurance subsidies, tax and credit subsidies for homeowners, farmers, and certain other industries should be assessed according to their effects on the price and availability of capital elsewhere in the economy, particularly with regard to emerging industries that promise to be highly competitive in world markets.

Trade Regulations

Antitrust, trade policy, and price-entry regulations constitute another subset of industrial policy. Some businesses are so vulnerable to import competition that there is little reason to be concerned about the growth or merger of firms within the business. In these circumstances, a policy of reducing tariff and nontariff barriers is likely to be superior to conventional antitrust regulations as a means of achieving the benefits of large-scale efficiency while avoiding the distortions brought on by monopoly or excessive market power. Some firms show so much promise of becoming strong international competitors that the government should allow and encourage them to engage in horizontal or vertical mergers and to expand capacity readily—notwithstanding that these strategies may lessen competition in domestic markets in the short run.

In general, it is important to recognize that different types of businesses, with different cost structures and at different stages of their life cycles, require different antitrust enforcement. Conduct that might be anticompetitive in a mature industry that is sheltered from international trade might be procompetitive in an emerging industry that is subject to international trade.

Protection Regulations

Environmental, consumer protection, and worker safety regulations should also be tailored to different competitive situations and different stages of industry growth. For example, for emerging industries that are subject to international trade, consumer protection and environmental regulations should be harmonized as far as possible with the needs and requirements of other nations. In this way, U.S. producers can exploit scale efficiencies in meeting these standards and can also use the standards as a marketing tool abroad. By the same token, declining industries should only be required to meet standards that are appropriate to the remaining useful life of the industry. It would make little sense, for example, to require that a factory that is to be reconverted to new use within two years be retrofitted with expensive pollution-control technology that is designed to last for ten years. In general, the government must develop the capability to assess when such regulations seriously hinder competitiveness and when they do not. The government should also be capable of coordinating discrete regulatory programs that affect the growth and competitiveness of particular industries.

In sum, the substance of a rational industrial policy consists of labor market and regional policies that are designed to facilitate the movement of labor and capital out of uncompetitive businesses with a minimum of social disruptions. It also includes measures to reap the public return on investment when it substantially exceeds the sum total of private returns; and measures to promote rapid, positive adjustment of the economy toward new high-growth opportunities. A rational industrial policy also consists of measures to tailor and coordinate the broad range of government programs in order to ensure that they facilitate growth in competitive productivity. The U.S. is sorely lacking an industrial policy that meets any of these criteria.

FOOTNOTES

[1] Sweet, Morris L. "Industrial Location Policy: Western European Precedents for Aiding U.S.-Impacted Regions," *Urbanism Past and Present,* Winter 1978–79, p. 1.

[2] C. and R. Assoc., "Plant Location Legislation, Community Costs of Plant Closings: Bibliography and Survey of the Literature," Report to the F.T.C., November 1978; C. and R. Assoc., "Legislation in Western Europe on Mass Dismissals and Plant Closings: A Review of Studies and Commentaries, with Policy Implications for the U.S.," Report prepared for the F.T.C., Washington, D.C., February 1979; Labor Union Study Tour Participants, "Economic Dislocation: Plant Closings, Plant Relocations and Plant Conversions," UAW-USA-IAM, Washington, D.C., May 1979.

[3] C. and R. Assoc., "Measuring the Community Costs of Plant Closings: Overview of Methods and Data Sources," Report submitted to the F.T.C., Washington, D.C., December 1978, p. 71.

[4] Jacobs, Jerry. "Corporate Subsidies from the 50 States," *Business and Society Review* Spring 1980, pp. 49–50; Schmeiner, Roger W. "How Corporations Select Communities for New Manufacturing Plants," Harvard-MIT Joint Center for Urban Studies, Cambridge, September 1979.

[5] Feldstein, Martin. "The Economics of the New Unemployment," *Public Interest,* Fall 1973, pp. 3–42.

[6] MacKay, D.I. and Reid, G.L. "Redundancy, Unemployment and Manpower Policy," *Economic Journal,* V. 82, December 1972, p. 1256; Dorsey, J.W. "The Mack Case: A Study in Unemployment," in *Studies in the Economics of Income Maintenance,* Brookings Institution, Washington, D.C., 1967; Marstom, Steven. "The Impact of Unemployment Insurance on Job Search," Brookings Papers on Economic Activity Vol. 1, 1975.

29

Industrial Policymaking

Because industrial policy is selective in nature, the substance is inextricably linked to the means used to carry it out. By what mechanisms—tax credits, subsidies, tariffs, licenses, insurance, or loan guarantees—should industrial policy be undertaken, and how should it be focused? The choice depends to a great extent on four interrelated factors: the clarity of the policy goals, the stage of the business in the international economy, the competitive cost structure of the business, and any specific cost problems to be remedied.

CLARITY OF POLICY GOALS

To be effective, industrial policy must be undertaken in a manner that conforms to the competitive positions of individual businesses. Policies should be selective, but they should be sufficiently flexible to allow individual businesses to adapt them to their own unique strategies.

Government can apply its tools across-the-board to all industries in a nondiscriminatory fashion—for example, by extending the life of all new patents or by granting accelerated depreciation to all new investments. Or government can apply its tools selectively—for example, by extending the patent life of new drugs or by granting accelerated depreciation for farm machinery. The advantage of general as opposed to selective policies is that the former allows innumerable market transactions to determine the pattern of investment rather than having it influenced by the government. This, in turn, helps ensure that investment will be allocated to where it can be of greatest productive value.

But selective application may be more efficient, particularly when investment priorities are relatively clear. For example, if there is a critical need to develop energy sources, it makes little sense to provide general subsidies or tax credits for any industrial research and development. Unless there is a clear notion of what type of energy source promises the most savings, however, it might be preferable to grant the subsidy or tax credit to a broad range of energy projects—biomass, coal conversion, gasohol, and nuclear fusion—rather than to any one particular type.

Similarly, some policy instruments are more flexible than others—that is, they are likely to mimic, with fewer side effects, what the market would do were the market functioning efficiently. For example, tax credits, accelerated depreciation, and subsidies are likely to be more flexible than government contracts, tariffs, quotas, or licenses. This is because the former group creates economic incentives for industry rather than imposing specific commands. It allows firms to devise their own means of achieving desired results; this, in turn, encourages innovation. Tax credits, accelerated depreciation, and subsidies can also be designed to approximate the amount of public benefit at stake, bringing industry decisionmaking into line with the public interest. By contrast, contracts, tariffs, quotas, and licenses give firms no choice in their response. Different firms, facing different competitive situations, are treated the same. There are occasions, therefore, when these more rigid policies are highly inefficient, wasting valuable resources and inhibiting innovation.

Even between tariffs and quotas, there is a difference in the degree of flexibility. Unlike quotas, tariffs do not set an absolute limit on the amount of a good to be imported but merely increase its price. In cases where actual demand exceeds predicted demand, therefore, quotas may exacerbate shortages; tariffs allow the goods to continue to be imported, though at a higher price.

When the desired outcome is clear, however, flexible tools may be *less* efficient than more specialized tools. For example, if we want to ensure the supply of a certain quantity of a particular technology for defense preparedness, it may be more efficient for government to contract directly for the technology rather than to encourage its manufacture indirectly by means of tax credits or subsidies.

Many areas of industrial development fall between the two poles of clear and less clear goals. That is, overall investment priorities are relatively clear, but we have no precise idea about which technologies should be emphasized nor how development should proceed. For example, over the next decade, there is good reason to believe that intense international competition will occur in high-technology industries such as lasers, fiber-optics, semi-conductors, and biotechnology. Since these knowledge-intensive industries are likely to form a critical part of the cost structures of a wide variety of other industries, a competitive lead in these high-technology industries will help ensure competitiveness within the rest of the economy. Policies aimed broadly at accelerating development in these industries will therefore be advantageous.

At the same time, there is no way of predicting exactly how development will proceed in any of these industries. Flexible policy instruments such as tax credits and subsidies may therefore be more appropriate for stimulating innovation than specific contracts or licenses.

How should government determine the appropriate degree of selectivity and flexibility of industrial policy for a given business? Appropriate policy mechanisms will depend upon at least three variables: the stage of the business in the international economy, the competitive cost structure of the business, and the particular cost problem that the policies are designed to remedy.

THE STAGE OF THE BUSINESS

At any given time, the industrial structure of a country is comprised of three types of businesses. First, there are businesses that are losing competitive advantage as raw materials become depleted or uncompetitive, or as low-wage countries enter the business. Second, there are complex-factor cost businesses that are enjoying a competitive advantage internationally, or sheltered businesses that are not threatened by international trade. Third, there are complex-factor cost businesses that are in their infancy but are soon to be in competitive battle in the international economy, or businesses that are temporarily uncompetitive but that can be revived.

For businesses in the first group, industrial policy mechanisms must efficiently achieve capital disinvestment, consolidation, and labor market adjustment. Industry declines must be treated as problems of reorganization, in which labor and capital should be reallocated to their most productive uses. The government should seek to sustain only competitive businesses in the industry and otherwise minimize the hardships on workers and regional economies. Careful planning is required to anticipate these events and implement solutions gradually. Planning is also necessary to distinguish these long-term cases from temporary situations.

For businesses in the second group, government should provide only general incentives to increase productivity, stimulate demand, and moderate inflation. Businesses in these situations require less selective policies.

For businesses in the third category, government must selectively apply policies that encourage long-term growth by sharing risk, encouraging R&D, and promoting rapid investment. While targeted subsidies are often necessary to prompt restructuring of declining industries, targeted tax credits, reimbursable loans, and insurance schemes are often more efficient vehicles for stimulating growing businesses.

THE COMPETITIVE COST STRUCTURE

The competitiveness of different businesses depends on different elements in their cost structures. While manufacturing is the key for some businesses, in others it may be applications engineering or marketing and distribution. Industrial policies that are designed to encourage businesses to become strong international competitors should target key areas of cost leverage precisely.

For example, in businesses for which applications engineering is critical, tax benefits for capital investment or grants for R&D assistance are likely to be irrelevant. Policies to assist in the bidding process for particular orders, or in preintroduction marketing and software development would be far more useful. Similarly, in businesses for which large distribution scale on a country-by-country basis is critical, export financing, R&D assistance, or capital investment incentives are only marginally useful. Selectively targeted measures to assist overseas distribution investments would be much more important.

Blanket assertions—that the U.S. government should provide more funding for R&D or better incentives for capital investment or more export financing—miss the crucial point: Key competitive levers differ from business to business. To be efficient, policy mechanisms must be carefully tailored to the particular needs of each type of business.

COST PROBLEMS TO BE REMEDIED

Competitive success may also require the reduction of certain excessive costs that affect other elements of the business's cost structure. Effective industrial policy, therefore, must be aimed at alleviating these cost problems. For example, when the Japanese government sought to assist its troubled steel industry, it aimed policies at three specific cost problems—the lack of indigenous raw materials, the need for large investments, and the havoc created by sudden changes in the demand for steel. The Japanese government coordinated overseas investments to secure raw materials, provided guarantees and interest rate subsidies to modernize equipment, and established recession cartels to maintain prices and profitability in market downturns. Similarly, the cost problems of different parts of the evolving mechanical engineering industry required different solutions. Large-scale manufacturing was essential for the production of many auto parts and components, and Japanese firms were too small to be competitive. Policy therefore focused on encouraging small business cooperation, joint ventures, and mergers. Later, government-subsidized export insurance and loans provided the means of overcoming Japan's lack of experience and cost disadvantage in the area of systems financing.

THE APPROPRIATE MIX OF POLICY MECHANISMS

It should be clear from these examples that effective industrial policy requires a variety of policy mechanisms, intelligently applied. The appropriate mix of policy mechanisms depends on the economic structure of the business, its place in the international economy, and the particular cost problems to be remedied. Because of the diversity of business situations, across-the-board economic incentives are often very wasteful. Indiscriminate incentives may subsidize businesses in ways that do not help them gain competitive strength—for example, giving capital investment incentives to an applications-engineering-based firm; or they may be wasted on businesses without growth opportunities—providing export tax allowances for uncompetitive, low-wage, manufacturing-based assemblers, for instance.

Selective measures can also be costly and inefficient, unless they are undertaken intelligently, with adequate data and analysis about competitive conditions.

PREREQUISITES OF INDUSTRIAL POLICYMAKING

Debates about appropriate decisionmaking processes for industrial policy are often overgeneralized and ideological, haunted by the specter of centralized bureaucrats in capital cities who engage in picking winners and losers from among various industries, or oligarchies of industrial barons who systematically exchange campaign contributions for selective government largesse. These caricatures, although simplistic, do point up a central challenge of industrial policymaking—to ensure that it is both analytically sound and democratically responsive.

The U.S. needs to institutionalize four prerequisites for sound industrial policymaking: coherence, foresight, accountability, and competence.

Coherence

Most of the programs that comprise U.S. industrial policy have been initiated in isolation. Industrial policy is currently the product of fragmented and uncoordinated decisions made by executive agencies, the Congress, and independent regulatory agencies. More importantly, there is no integrated strategy to use these programs to improve the competitive productivity of the U.S. economy within the world economy as a whole.

Since the U.S. lacks a centralized government agency that is responsible for devising a rational industrial policy, the country has allowed that responsibility to fall primarily to the federal courts. Each year, a growing number of lawsuits inundates the 94 federal district courts and the 10 appellate courts that are called upon to reconcile the diverse and sometimes inconsistent industrial policies that emanate from different parts of the government. Although these lawsuits concern individual grievances, there are also broad, underlying questions of industrial policy at issue. What did Congress intend to accomplish with this program? How can it be reconciled with other programs? What is underlying the public interest in the program? What is its effect on efficiency and productivity?

A good deal of industrial policymaking also occurs under the aegis of special masters appointed in bankruptcy proceedings. There the questions are more pointed: How can this business best survive? What can be salvaged?

Unfortunately, neither the federal courts nor bankruptcy proceedings are ideal forums for devising industrial policy. Federal judges are ill-equipped to understand or respond to the dynamics of international competition. Bankruptcy masters are generally dealing with unique instances of competitive failure, at a point very late in the game.

Efforts to revitalize various industries have sometimes been entrusted to tripartite boards of government, business, and labor representatives. But such boards are inadequate to formulate industrial policy. Generally, they are called into existence to meet a crisis, and they operate at a level that is too remote from individual businesses to be effective. Typically, industries are composed of diverse businesses, each of which employs a different competitive strategy and experiences different competitive problems. These businesses are therefore likely to have quite different views on appropriate government policy. National tripartite boards do not accomodate well to this diversity of views. Too often in the past, these boards have enabled the least competitive but most entrenched businesses to consolidate their political bases and form powerful coalitions against structural change.

Foresight

There is currently no agency in the U.S. that has the responsibility for sophisticated analytic or predictive work on a business or industry level. For example, when Congress received the proposal to guarantee loans to the Chrysler Corporation, it was forced to turn to a private firm for an eleventh-hour study of the industry, even though the increasing difficulties of the automotive industry were well known to business strategists, Wall Street, and academic analysts.

The government has access to a considerable amount of information on industrial trends. Unfortunately, this information is spread throughout the government. Individual agencies that work with particular industries often have information that they refuse to share with other agencies because of internal government politics or their so-called "good relations" with the industry.

Business firms and trade associations have generally been reluctant to permit the government to have the data necessary for any cooperative effort at anticipating structural changes. Industry reaction to requests for raw information generally tends to be adversarial, even when the requests are in pursuit of a larger national interest. In part, this is because industrialists face a mountain of time-consuming, often poorly formulated requests from a plethora of agencies.

Moreover, it can be politically difficult to identify declining businesses. Managers rarely want to admit to investors, the public, their workers, their creditors, or even to themselves, that their businesses are declining. Understandably, their tendency is to blame some extraneous factor or to put the best possible face on matters, expressing hope and expectation that performance will improve. Because there may be occasional periods when things do perk up, hopeful utterances can seem reasonable. In addition, if some businesses in a troubled industry are doing well, there is often a deliberate failure to focus on other businesses that are doomed.

Government bureaucrats and politicians do not want to bear nor confirm bad tidings, lest they be accused of bringing to pass the very thing that has been predicted. Therefore, government policy usually amounts to waiting until even the most hopeful industry spokesman begins to panic. Even when the crisis is at hand, choices are limited because of the lack of any serious advance analysis or planning. While trying to hide the fact that indifference is the option actually chosen, the government often chooses to remain indifferent to the social consequences of a wave of facility closings, massive layoffs, and widespread dislocations. Or the government hurriedly stitches together a program that offers various grants to local governments, provides whatever income support it can find funds for, and perhaps adds a few government contracts, loan guarantees, and tariffs.

Accountability

Largely because of its incoherence and lack of foresight, U.S. industrial policy has been undertaken with little or no public knowledge or approval. No one is accountable for the aggregate effects of the disparate programs that have been implemented in relative obscurity.

There must be an accountable system for designing, implementing, and reviewing the various programs. The President should establish an agency to evaluate the international competitive consequences of government programs and policies. In order to oversee programs that assist industry, Congress should also develop a capacity to analyze market developments.

Unfortunately, the political problem of designing effective industrial policies will grow even more acute in the years ahead. An important shift in political mood has taken place. Slow economic growth and high rates of inflation have transformed public perceptions of the future. Thoughts of affluence and a better life have been replaced by concerns over scarcity and losing ground. As a consequence, politics in general have become more adversarial. The politics of industrial policy in particular are likely to grow more factious as individuals and groups guard their economic interests more closely.

Competence

One of the major prerequisites of effective industrial policy is a sufficient level of competence and business experience among the officials participating in the effort. Government officials must have a vision of the overall structural development of the international economy, and a thorough knowledge of the products, markets, and competitive dynamics of individual businesses.

Such competence is necessary not only to develop a domestic industrial policy but also to adequately represent U.S. interests in international negotiations. Just as the U.S. takes a strategic view of its defense and foreign policies, it must also be prepared to take a strategic view of industrial policies.

Industrial policymaking is a complex effort, requiring competence on the part of government officials and cooperation in the national interest from managers and workers in industry. This complexity makes successful implementation difficult but does not lessen its necessity if the U.S. economy is to advance in the next decade.

30

The Challenge

The U.S. economy is in crisis. A poor record of productivity improvement, coupled with high unemployment, now threaten the U.S. standard of living. This book has described past failures and present misconceptions that have contributed to the current problems. In the absence of new strategic directions, the crisis can only deepen.

The buoyant economy of the 1950s and 1960s was founded in a benign international competitive environment. While the U.S. was pioneering new industries—plastics and fibers, semiconductors and computers, electronic instruments, jet aircraft, and industrial machinery—other industrialized countries were recovering from the devastation of war and rebuilding their basic industries and infrastructures. Thus, the U.S. had the benefit of a relatively non-competitive international marketplace. A large home market stimulated the growth of autos and the construction businesses and capital goods industries that serve them. Further, many U.S. industries in their early stages received a significant boost through national defense programs.

The international industrial arena of the 1980s and 1990s will be very different from that of the 1950s and 1960s. The U.S. will be confronted with a highly competitive international environment that will threaten many existing businesses and make it far more difficult to develop successful new ones.

An increasing number of businesses that comprised our traditional U.S. industrial base, such as steel, fibers, shoes, clothing, metal parts, ships, and small appliances, will be subject to low-wage competition. Korea, Brazil, Singapore, and other rapidly developing countries will increase the sophistication of their production. Other developing countries with lower wages—such as the Philippines, Malaysia, and Sri Lanka—will move into industries in which these more developed low-wage economies are now dominant.

Meanwhile, in certain high-growth industries where the U.S. currently has a leading position—such as computers, semiconductors, aircraft, industrial machinery, pharmaceuticals, scientific instruments, and offshore technology—foreign companies, assisted by their governments, are actively seeking to close the gap and move ahead. While the strongest U.S. companies in these industries appear unassailable, one must remember how impregnable General Motors and U.S. Steel seemed 10 or 15 years ago.

The past examples of the U.S. decline in steel and televisions are being replicated in other industries today. In 1976, the U.S. had a positive trade balance of $200 million in machine tools, long a leading American industry. By 1979, the U.S. was importing $400 million more in machine tools than it exported. Perhaps even more ominous for the future, the U.S. position in high-technology numerically controlled machine tools has deteriorated substantially. For example, between 1976 and 1980, Japanese production of numerically controlled lathes increased by 350 percent and German production increased by 310 percent. French production meanwhile increased by 340 percent and British production increased by 300 percent. U.S. production increased by only 160 percent. In 1980, Japanese producers captured 53 percent of the U.S. market in numerically controlled lathes, up from less than 10 percent only five years ago. As in consumer electronics, the Japanese are using product and process technology at both the component and final product levels to achieve cost and quality advantages vis-à-vis U.S. producers.

The industrialized trading partners of the U.S. also are seeking to attain competitive leadership in other future growth industries. Foreign companies and their governments are undertaking programs to encourage new development in lasers, biotechnology, composite materials, robotics, and various microelectronic applications areas. For example, the Japanese government is cosponsoring research in robotics. Through the Japan Development Bank, it has provided 60 percent of the operating funds for a special company formed to lease industrial robots. Through its small business finance corporation, it has also authorized $30 million in low-interest loans to small and medium-sized companies that are installing Japanese robots, and it has mandated a special 12.5 percent depreciation provision over and above regular depreciation for robot installation. The French government has active programs to support research and development of new offshore technologies. This effort is accompanied by attractive user financing. Government-supported data-processing and semiconductor efforts continue among all of our major trading partners.

The current direction of U.S. policy is not reassuring. It calls for significant sacrifices in living standard, particularly at the lower end of the income scale, without any clear indication of how these sacrifices will improve long-run living standards. Reductions in government regulations, spending, and taxes for the wealthy have only the remotest connection with productivity improvements and enhanced competitiveness. Similarly, while high-interest rates and restrictions on the money supply can reduce inflation in the short run, they will not remedy the long-term underlying causes of inflation—low productivity and low growth. Perhaps the U.S. must take cuts in its living standard because of past losses in productivity and competitiveness, but such cuts will not prevent future losses. Reducing the government's role in the economy will not necessarily lead to greater savings; greater savings will not necessarily lead to greater overall investment; greater overall investment will not necessarily lead to improvements in competitive productivity.

A rational industrial policy of the sort introduced in this book will not be a panacea for all that ails the U.S. economy. But, properly conceived and executed, it can lead to a better utilization of economic resources, thereby improving U.S. productivity. This can be accomplished without jeopardizing clean air, safe work places, and social welfare programs, all of which constitute a necessary part of improved living standards for all Americans.

The difficulties that stand in the way of creating a coherent U.S. industrial policy should not be underestimated. Unlike Japan and many West European countries, the U.S. lacks the tradition of an expert and independent civil service that could provide the business community and the general public with a high level of advice and analysis.

For similar reasons, it will be difficult for the U.S. to achieve the sort of consensus upon which industrial policy must rest. Such a consensus is necessary primarily to ensure that the sacrifices implied by positive institutional change in the economy are willingly endured. It must also ensure that no group is forced to bear a disproportionate part of the burden of any such change. But consensus-forming institutions in U.S. society have deteriorated over the last two decades. Political parties, civic organizations, religious organizations, charities, and other broad groups have been replaced in recent years by special-interest organizations that seek narrow legislative goals. Increasingly, the U.S. has turned to legislation, regulation, and adjudication as its primary means of resolving social and economic disputes. As the economy slows down, groups in the U.S. battle one another for short-term advantage—Frost Belt against Sun Belt, business against government, federal government against state government, big business against small business.

It is also difficult to fashion a coherent industrial policy in a non-parliamentary system in which power is divided between Congress and the President, and shared with an array of commissions, agencies, boards, administrations, Congressional committees and subcommittees, and departments. Within such a system, coalitions are fleeting. Attention spans are short. Issues rise and fall with a rapidity and specificity that render comprehensive policymaking all but impossible. Indeed, there is so much "noise" in the system—in the form of immediate problems to be remedied and deals to be struck—that issues must be at or near a point of crisis, and already distilled into relatively clear choices, before a large enough coalition can be mustered to get action.

In short, the U.S. is not a nation of planners. The hurly-burly of its democratic system mirrors the untidy competitive marketplace about which we learn in economic texts. But the fact of the matter is that economic success now depends to a high degree on coordination, collaboration, and careful strategic choice. As this book has pointed out, successful competitive strategy depends upon careful analysis and long-term frames of reference. The U.S. has been losing the competitive race in large part because its businesses have failed to plan properly, and its government has failed to facilitate such planning.

Industrial policy is as much a challenge for American business as it is for government. Ultimately, the U.S. standard of living will depend on the wisdom of decisions made by both. Government can create opportunities for an improved competitive position, or it can discourage such strategies. In the end, government and the private sector must work in tandem. There will, of course, be tensions between the public and private sectors, and government would not be doing its job if it did not maintain firm vigilance against business excesses that might harm the public. But the lesson of industrial policy is that the international competitive position of the U.S., and the U.S. standard of living, require careful coordination between public and private sectors.

Finally, and perhaps most importantly, industrial policy requires the sort of international perspective that the large and well-endowed domestic U.S. economy has long avoided.

As the U.S. seeks to rationalize its implicit industrial policy, and as other nations simultaneously seek to improve their own competitive positions, the U.S. can expect strains and tensions in international economic relations. It should not assume that the subsidies and nontariff barriers of its trading partners are motivated by simple protectionism or mercantilism. More often than not, they reflect aspects of national industrial policies.

Some argue against explicit industrial policies, claiming that they will lead to trade wars as each country tries to outsubsidize the other. In fact, the risk of trade wars is greater in the absence of explicit industrial policies and international conventions to regulate them.

Government industrial policies will exist, explicitly or implicitly. The challenge for agencies that are responsible for fostering international cooperation is to establish ground rules that enhance the creation of wealth in all countries—rules that encourage national policies aimed at accelerating market forces by improving productivity, pioneering new products, and easing adjustment to industrial decline; and rules that discourage national policies which retard market forces, or inhibit these forces through artificial protection of hopelessly troubled industries. Where national industrial policies are premised on the promotion of productivity and new industry growth, rather than on retarding structural change, the world economy will benefit.

The challenge for the U.S. is to be more strategic, to explicitly acknowledge that the nation is dependent on a dynamic world economy that must be better understood, and to focus decisionmaking within business and government on the goal of competitive productivity. The U.S. cannot and should not create an "America, Inc." in which allocative decisions are centralized and determined by a loose oligarchy of business and government officials. On the contrary, a rational industrial policy for America must be discrete and precise, affecting particular businesses in very limited ways. A rational industrial policy must also be publicly accountable and rest on a strong public consensus about overall goals.

Such a consensus cannot be merely contrived in the United States. Its melting-pot culture will inevitably suffer from conflicts and tensions that smaller and more homogeneous nations can avoid. But a collective commitment to competitive productivity is possible if it is premised on an economic organization in which the fruits of such productivity are equitably shared. That, after all, has been and continues to be the most fundamental challenge.

Index

About the Authors

Ira C. Magaziner is president of Telesis, Inc., an international consulting firm specializing in long-term economic and industrial policy for governments and unions, and international business strategy for corporations. He has coauthored several books in conjunction with his consulting work, including *Japanese Industrial Policy, A Framework for Swedish Industrial Policy,* and *A Review of Irish Industrial Policy.* He was educated at Brown University and now serves on its Board of Trustees, and was a Rhodes Scholar at Oxford University. He resides in Bristol, Rhode Island.

Robert B. Reich is a member of the faculty of the John F. Kennedy School of Government at Harvard University, where he teaches courses on business strategy, public policy, and public management. He also is a consultant on these subjects for corporations and government agencies. He has been director of policy planning at the Federal Trade Commission (1976–1981) and assistant to the U.S. Solicitor General (1974–1976). He has a law degree from Yale Law School, a masters degree in economics from Oxford University, where he was a Rhodes Scholar, and a B.A. from Dartmouth College. He resides in Cambridge, Massachusetts.